Forest Law and Sustainable Development

Addressing Contemporary Challenges Through Legal Reform

Law, Justice, and Development

The Law, Justice, and Development series is offered by the Legal Vice Presidency of the World Bank to provide insights into aspects of law and justice that are relevant to the development process. Works in the series present new legal and judicial reform activities related to the World Bank's work, as well as analyses of domestic and international law. The series is intended to be accessible to a broad audience as well as to legal practitioners.

Series Editor: Salman M. A. Salman
Editorial Board: Hassane Cisse, Alberto Ninio, Sophie Smyth, and Kishor Uprety

Forest Law and Sustainable Development

Addressing Contemporary Challenges Through Legal Reform

Lawrence C. Christy
Former Chief
Development Law Service
Food and Agriculture Organization of the United Nations (FAO)

Charles E. Di Leva
Chief Counsel
Legal Vice-Presidency
The World Bank

Jonathan M. Lindsay
Senior Counsel
Legal Vice-Presidency
The World Bank

Patrice Talla Takoukam
Counsel
Legal Vice-Presidency
The World Bank

THE WORLD BANK
Washington, D.C.

ISBN-10: 0-8213-7038-3   eISBN: 0-8213-7039-1
ISBN-13: 978-0-8213-7038-4   DOI: 10.1596/978-0-8213-7038-4

Library of Congress Cataloging-in-Publication Data

Forest law and sustainable development : addressing contemporary challenges
through legal reform / Lawrence C. Christy . . . [et al.].
    p. cm.
    Includes bibliographical references and index.
    ISBN 978-0-8213-7038-4
    ISBN 978-0-8213-7039-1
    1. Forestry law and legislation. I. Christy, Lawrence C.

K3884.F67 2007
346.04'675—dc22

Cover design by Drew Fasick.

Contents

List of Boxes

Foreword

The world's forests are today under unprecedented strain, with deforestation and forest degradation both widespread and accelerating in most parts of the world. These phenomena are driven by a wide variety of factors, from rapidly expanding consumer demand and the growth of urban areas, to rural poverty and the hunger for land. Their consequences are similarly diverse—forest destruction poses dire threats not only to the existence of remaining forest areas themselves, but to the ecological benefits that forests provide, and the economies and human livelihoods that depend on them. As a result of these threats, it has been widely agreed since the 1990s that international forest problems are not only an environmental challenge, but a development concern, as reflected in the Statement of Forests Principles issued by the United Nations Conference on Environment and Development (UNCED) in 1992. Indeed, how to achieve sustainable management of the world's remaining forests poses one of the critical governance challenges of our times.

From a legal perspective, one can observe a wide array of approaches, sometimes conflicting, toward the subject of forests. At the global level, in the absence of an internationally binding legal instrument on forests, sustainable forest management issues are touched upon in many multilateral and bilateral environmental agreements. States and international and regional organizations are putting a lot of effort into bringing coherence to the field through a number of mechanisms, including the United Nations Forum on Forests, and the Collaborative Partnership on Forests, or through programs such as the Program on Forests (PROFOR) housed at the World Bank. At the national level, countries are striving to develop effective legal frameworks addressing the increasing pressures on forests, and at the same time reflecting the growing realization of the critical roles that forests play environmentally, socially, and economically.

Forest law is highly complex because of its immense cross-cutting characteristics and the difficulties of balancing multiple interests. Unlike some environmental laws, such as those dealing with protected areas, forest law must blend environmental protection with resource extraction. It must also take into account international obligations pertaining to environment and trade. These obligations are growing and diversifying and now include concerns related to climate change, intellectual property rights, genetically modified organisms, timber certification and labeling, and the rights of Indigenous Peoples. Hence, the array of decisions policy makers must make in conceiving sound forest law is daunting to law and policy makers in any country.

The purpose of this publication is to assist in the development and implementation of sound forest law. It is intended to help those involved in the preparation of new forest laws, or revising existing ones, as well as those who are interested in assessing the adequacy of existing or proposed laws for meeting forest policy objectives. Providing support to the formulation of sound natural resource legislation has been a major area of attention for the FAO Development Law Service and the World Bank's Environmentally and Socially Sustainable Development and International Law Group. Indeed, the World Bank's new Forests Strategy and Policy, which set forth a revised vision of the Bank's engagement in forests issues, both underscore the importance of sound legal frameworks for sustainable forest management. Thus, after many years of collaboration on forest law issues between the World Bank and FAO Legal Offices, we are pleased to offer this publication and hope that it will serve as a useful reference for lawyers, foresters, policy makers, development specialists, civil society organizations, and all others concerned with forest policy and legislation.

Ana Palacio
Senior Vice President and
World Bank Group General Counsel

Abstract

This study is intended to be a systematic and practical guide to the basic features of modern forestry legislation. It identifies a range of issues that should be considered in assessing the adequacy of forest laws and presents options for addressing those issues in ways that may improve the effectiveness of law as a foundation for sustainable forest management.

Part One locates forestry law within the wider legal framework, exploring its complex interrelations with other sectoral and general laws. Land issues are given special treatment because the relationship between forest access and use and land tenure is so important. Part Two explores in detail the legal treatment of core forest management issues, such as forest classification, planning, concessions, licensing, and private forest management. Part Three focuses on the role of national and subnational institutions in the sustainable management of forest resources. As decentralization of forestry responsibilities and devolution of powers are growing, local actors are given more prominent roles in forest planning, use, and management, through such means as community-based arrangements. Part Four explores a range of environmental and trade issues. Part Five examines financial and enforcement measures, emphasizing that compliance and enforcement of forest law should be reinforced by financial and administrative sanctions. The study concludes with some reflections on how the effectiveness of forest law can be enhanced by attention to the principles that guide the process of drafting.

Acknowledgments

This publication would not have been possible without the support of a number of people who are dedicated to the conservation and sustainable management of forests. We received excellent comments from the Forests Team at the World Bank—Gerhard Dieterle, Nalin Kishor, Edgardo Maravi, Tapani Oksanen, Christian Albert Peter, Professor Martin Walter (University of Applied Science, Weihenstephan, Germany)—and from former Bank Foresters James Douglas and David Cassells. The publication has also benefited from the extensive field experience and insights of professionals in the Forestry Department of the Food and Agriculture Organization (FAO) into the role of law in sustainable forest management. We would like to extend special thanks to Eva Muller, Chief, Forest Policy Service, and her predecessor, Manual Paveri; their colleagues Dominique Reeb, Eduardo Mansur, and Patrick Durst; and in particular Thomas Enters, who provided extremely useful comments on earlier drafts. We would also like to thank Ken Rosenbaum, who gave us excellent comments and undertook an extensive review and revision of the entire manuscript, and Mohammed Bekhechi, for his advice on forest law. Close collaboration between the legal departments of FAO and the Bank has been a particularly gratifying feature of this work and was crucial to its success from conceptualization to completion. In this respect, special thanks are due to Ali Mekouar, former Chief of the FAO Development Law Service, who both as scholar and practitioner has been highly influential in promoting advances in comparative forestry law over many years and whose close review of earlier drafts was invaluable.

We are especially grateful to David Freestone, the Deputy General Counsel for Advisory Services at the World Bank Legal Department, who helped us secure the initial funding for preparation of this manuscript. We would also like to thank Laura Ivers, Communications Officer of the Program on Forests (PROFOR) of the World Bank, for her tremendous support and that of PROFOR in enabling the publication to become reality. This publication could not have taken place without these efforts. Our sincere thanks are also due to Salman Salman and Alberto Ninio for their continuous advice and Shéhan de Sayrah for his advice and editorial assistance.

Acronyms and Abbreviations

Aarhus Convention	Convention on Access to Information, Public Participation in Decision-Making and Access to Justice in Environmental Matters
ASEAN	Association of Southeast Asian Nations
Bonn Convention	Convention on the Conservation of Migratory Species of Wild Animals
CAS	Country Assistance Strategies
CBD	Convention on Biological Diversity
CIS	Commonwealth of Independent States
CITES	Convention on International Trade in Endangered Species of Wild Flora and Fauna
COP	Conference of parties
DRC	Democratic Republic of Congo
FOB	Free on board
EC	European Commission
EU	European Union
ECOSOC	Economic and Social Council of the United Nations
EIA	Environmental Impact Assessment
FAO	Food and Agriculture Organization of the United Nations
FLEGT	Forest Law Enforcement, Governance, and Trade
FSC	Forest Stewardship Council
GATT	General Agreement of Tariffs and Trade
GEF	Global Environment Facility
IP	Indigenous Peoples
ILO	International Labor Organization
ITTO	International Tropical Timber Organization

JFM	Joint Forest Management
Kyoto Protocol	Kyoto Protocol to the United Nations Framework Convention on Climate Change
Lao PDR	Lao People's Democratic Republic
MFN	Most favored nation
NAFTA	North American Free Trade Agreement
NGO	Nongovernmental organization
OAS	Organization of American States
SADC	South African Development Community
SCM	Subsidies and countervailing measures
SPS	Sanitary and phytosanitary measures
TBT Agreement	Technical Barriers to Trade Agreement
TRIPS	Trade-Related Aspects of Intellectual Property Rights
UN	United Nations
UNCCD	United Nations Convention to Combat Desertification
UNCED	United Nations Conference on Environment and Development
UNECE	United Nations Economic Commission for Europe
UNFCCC	United Nations Framework Convention on Climate Change
UNFF	United Nations Forum on Forests
WB	World Bank
WCD	World Commission on Dams
WTO	World Trade Organization

CHAPTER 1

Introduction and General Overview

This study is designed to help not just lawyers but also foresters, economists, and other development professionals to identify legal issues that impinge on forests. Originally conceived as a tool for those working with the World Bank, the Food and Agriculture Organization (FAO), and other international development organizations, it has evolved into a study that should be useful to a wide range of experts and institutions dealing with forestry reform.

The ways in which people use and value forests are changing. Growing populations are increasing the demand for forest resources. Changing cultures, technology, and science are altering our notions of the resources forests have to offer.

In recent years forest laws around the world have been significantly revised in response to these changes. The international community has articulated new visions of the forest in, among other documents, the Rio Forest Principles, Agenda 21, the Biodiversity Convention, and the 2003 World Bank Forest Strategy and Policy. These visions have led many nations to move away from regulatory approaches focused primarily on government management and policing of forests as economic resources. National forest policies increasingly recognize the multiple interests that are affected by forest management. They give greater attention to environmental and social values and to sustainable use, and they encourage greater public participation. These policy changes have required a major reorientation of the law in such areas as local and private forest management, the environmental functions of forests, forest management planning, forest utilization contracts, and trade.

In drafting new forest laws or improving old ones, countries often look to the experience of other countries. However, finding systematic guidance on international lessons learned is difficult. There are immense variations between countries not only in the nature, importance, and role of their forest resources but also in their legal and institutional settings. As a result, unlike some other areas of law forest law does not lend itself to model legislation that can be easily adapted from country to country. While there have been important comparative studies of recent trends of forest legislation, they seldom provide direct practical guidance on how to assess the law related to forestry and begin to improve it.

To help fill this gap in the literature, this book identifies a range of issues that should be considered in assessing the adequacy of the law related to forests and presents options for addressing them. It is not intended to be prescriptive; rather, it is a methodological tool to help the reader understand how best to think through a particular problem and assess legal options in a given context.

This study thus proposes a systematic approach to assessment and improvement of forest law. The approach requires at the outset an appreciation of the role forest law plays within the wider legal system and how other areas of law are likely to affect its shape and operation. As chapter 1 illustrates, numerous legal regimes—from international and constitutional law to land law, criminal law, and the law of public administration—have implications for forest law.

Though forest laws have never existed in legal isolation, their connections with other areas of law have become more complex as they have grown in ambition and scope and as other types of laws increasingly impinge, directly or indirectly, on how forests are managed or used. Thus, for example, as the environmental dimensions of forest legislation increase in complexity, the links between a country's forest laws and its general environmental laws become more important. It is often a significant challenge to coordinate and differentiate between these two areas so that they can be coherently harmonized rather than duplicating or even contradicting each other.

Modern drafters must also refer to international law, where provisions on trade, environment, biodiversity, indigenous peoples, and climate change now influence the options that are available. The policies of international development organizations are also increasingly significant sources of influence and inspiration. They give prominence to the law on sustainable forest management and can often stimulate new thinking about the role and scope of forest law. A case in point is the new World Bank Forests Policy, described in detail in chapter 2.

An important issue apparent at the intersection of forest legislation and other areas of law and policy is forest tenure. Clear and secure tenure is increasingly seen as key to sustainable forest management. Yet property rights in forests are often complex and contested. As chapter 3 explores, forests may be owned by the state or private individuals or held as common property by local communities or other groups. There may also be a discrepancy between what formal law prescribes and what is seen as legitimate on the ground; customary law often has a strong de facto role even where a state formally asserts ownership. Policymakers concerned with forest, land, and governance issues are increasingly confronted by the need to define a balance between tenure rights and the interests of different claimants. Recent years have seen particular attention paid to modifying heavily state-centric forest laws to accommodate, to the degree possible, customary tenure regimes or to enhance the rights of access, control, and management of local communities. (This subject is explored further in chapter 7.)

In chapters 4 and 5 the discussion turns to regulation of forest management. While this is a traditional core subject of forest law, here too new trends have emerged with which drafters need to be familiar. For example, forestry laws now pay more detailed attention to planning and to a broader array of objectives than they did in the past. Increasingly, laws require planners to consider a wide range of ecological and social issues that might previously have been outside their purview. Planning procedures also provide an important point for the public to intervene in the design of forest management. Many recent laws require public notice at various stages, opportunities to comment, public meetings, and access to preliminary plans. New legal techniques have also begun to emerge for the more transparent and responsible allocation, pricing, and monitoring of forest concessions and licenses. Finally, drafters have sought ways to use incentives to promote private forestry and to roll back the over-regulation of private forests that characterized many older forestry laws.

The middle chapters of the study focus on the treatment of institutional issues in forest legislation. As chapter 6 discusses, in recent years forest laws have devoted more detailed attention than previously was the case to the role of state forest institutions. Unlike earlier legislation—where state forest administrations are often presented as stand-alone entities answerable only, for example, to a minister—it is now common for laws to create roles for multiple institutions with links beyond the forest sector. These are intended to ensure better coordination on issues that overlap sectors, to promote greater public oversight and monitoring of forest decision-making, to institutionalize public participation, and to encourage greater private sector involvement. That is why intersectoral forest commissions, public forest forums, and the like have become common features of forest laws.

One of the most profound preoccupations of forest law in recent years has been with downward institutional innovation. This is part of a general decentralization trend in government and of a parallel trend to devolve rights and responsibilities to community-based groups. Chapter 7 explores these trends. Decentralization poses challenges in terms of defining what aspects of forest management can effectively be delegated to local governments and how supervision and fiscal authority should be allocated between central and decentralized forest administrations. Devolution of rights and responsibilities to local groups in many recent forest laws has taken a wide variety of forms, ranging from quite modest protection and benefit-sharing arrangements between government and village committees to more ambitious comanagement arrangements and even to the turning over of virtually all indicia of ownership of forests to indigenous communities. The first generation of laws that incorporated community-based management have revealed difficulties with which drafters must grapple, including how best to secure the rights of the local group; how to provide local forest managers meaningful powers while retaining an appropriate oversight role for government; and how to balance local interests with broader public interests in forest management.

Running through all institutional arrangements are general considerations about improving governance in the forest sector. Chapter 8 therefore looks at a number of cross-cutting themes, emphasizing how laws can promote transparency, participation, and accountability in all facets of forest governances. The confluence of these factors in the fight against corruption and illegal activities is examined in depth in the last section of the chapter.

Chapters 9 and 10 explore the closely related issues of environment and trade in forest products. Increasingly, forest laws reflect concerns about biodiversity. The role of forests as carbon sinks is less often featured but can be expected to become more prominent in the future. Forest and other laws in a number of countries provide incentives for forest conservation through the payment of compensation for environmental services. And while there are many dimensions to trade in forest goods, the most prominent considerations in recent times concern the extent to which trade laws, domestic or international, or voluntary trade-related mechanisms like certification can influence sustainable management of forests and help combat illegal harvesting and processing.

Finally, the study returns in chapters 11 and 12 to a traditional focus of forest law: how to deal with and punish violations of the law. Amid all the innovations in forest governance and management reflected in recent laws, the policing role remains central, and the difficulties of apprehending and successfully punishing those who commit forest offenses are immense. Legislation can help by providing incentives for encouraging disclosure of information and by shifting the weight of evidentiary presumptions in favor of forest protections and policy. Where there are large-scale illegal forest activities, new techniques related to antimoney-laundering efforts may be promising. But ultimately, to be effective law enforcement requires a combination of political will and strong financial and human institutional capacity. To build this capacity, training on legal issues and procedures is needed at all levels, starting with foresters, prosecutors, judges, civil society monitors, and community patrols. However sound it is, no law is self-enforcing. The main challenge in the years ahead will be to find ways to narrow the gap between the aspirations of well-drafted forest laws and the continuing degradation of the world's forests.

PART ONE

Forest Law in Context

CHAPTER 2

The Legal and Policy Basis for Forest Law

Forest legislation can address a very broad range of subjects beyond core forestry concerns, from public finance and taxation to land use planning. However, a guide will not be practical if it includes everything that might bear on a subject. General legislation dealing with economic structures, development planning, public institutions, and public finance would be a large topic even for a specialist in development law. While policy and action in sectors that affect forests are highly relevant, they are not the subject of this guide. The present study will therefore focus primarily on forest legislation as it has traditionally been understood— the law that governs forests, whether public or private.

The term "forest" has no universal definition. An ecologist may define it in terms of vegetative structure, an economic planner in terms of potential resource outputs, and a land records clerk in terms of boundaries published in a government survey. Still, a forest is generally understood to be an ecosystem dominated by woody vegetation, potentially subject to the management or oversight of foresters. A lot of forest in this sense is not very forested; it is grazing land, mountains, desert, and water. But it is relevant that the people to whom it is given in charge have been trained as foresters and traditionally have taken the lead in shaping what we know as forest legislation.

Foresters and forest legislation have evolved over time, and forest legislation now includes many precepts that go far beyond the growing and cutting of trees. In particular, legislation generally recognizes the role of forests as habitat for wildlife, resource for grazing and agriculture, and contributor to water and soil conservation. More recently the general principles of environmental law and the more specific values of biological diversity have become a very visible part of forest law.

This study will treat these issues as they relate directly to forests but it will not concentrate on them, principally because wildlife, soil and water conservation, grazing, and biological diversity have become areas of law in their own right. Environmental law is a highly developed specialty that in a sense encompasses all other natural resources law, though not always with the emphasis on resource management that characterizes the others.

Yet even with a relatively narrow focus on forests, any curious person will have to investigate a number of laws other than forest law proper. The most basic is the law governing land tenure, which absent other laws will determine who can claim

7

forest land and how the claimant can profit from the claim. Moving even beyond that, like every other law, land and forest laws will be interpreted in accordance with constitutional and other basic legal principles. When a country is a party to international treaties, they too may need to be taken into account. Depending on the legal system, international law may directly override national law, or at the very least it may oblige the country to make national law comply with international obligations. Other aspects of the legal system may provide for matters that otherwise could be part of the forest law and establish procedures and institutions that the forest sector will have to work with.

The remainder of this chapter will describe areas of the law beyond forest law proper that typically have great influence on forest governance and management.

2.1 Land

While much of the world follows one of two European land law traditions, common law and civil law, there are still many places where customary law holds sway. Moreover, many socialist or formerly socialist countries have systems of land tenure that either do not recognize private ownership or do so in ways that differ from the common and civil law systems.

The basic definition of ownership as the exclusive right to enjoy and dispose of property is common to both civil and common law traditions. In general, the ownership of land includes the ownership of buildings, trees, and other objects fixed to the land, but they still may be divided and sold separately. For example, the Empire State Building and the land under it are separately owned. The ability to divide the rights of ownership also allows contracts for land leases and mortgages and for the sale of standing timber, mining, and water rights where these are private, rights of way, and other attributes of the land without sale of the land itself. As an idea transferred to forestry, this "right of division" supports the concept of "tree tenure" as distinct from land tenure.

Individual land ownership, of course, is subject to limitations in all countries. Planning and environmental restrictions will apply; for instance, land cannot be used to create a nuisance to neighboring land and the natural support and flow of water cannot be interfered with. In all countries governments retain a right to acquire land compulsorily (though almost always adequate compensation must be paid) in order to implement a public purpose or to allow activities in the public interest—though how this power is defined and limited in national law varies extensively around the world.

The general trend over the last two decades has been to strengthen private rights in land, especially since the collapse of communism in Eastern Europe and the former Soviet Union. While a significant number of countries around the world prohibit private land ownership either altogether or with respect to certain categories of land,[1] the State's retention of ultimate ownership of land has not precluded the emergence in a number of such instances of private rights through leasehold or use rights that have many of the attributes of ownership (they may be long-term or perpetual, transferable through inheritance or sale, and mortgageable). Yet in other countries private rights are less secure. In those places the solid discretionary power of the state to terminate or reallocate rights affects incentives, for instance, to grow or preserve trees on the property.

The complex influence of land laws on forestry often cannot be appreciated by reference to formal law alone. In many parts of the world, customary land law—which arises from tradition, is governed by local rules, and is usually unwritten—still has a very important role in how land rights are allocated and defended. In countries where customary laws of land ownership, inheritance, and domestic relations have been incorporated into the formal legal system, there is a good understanding of which rules apply. However, in much of the world, despite the de facto importance of customary rules in defining local property relations, the rules are recognized only ambiguously, if at all, by formal land law. Often holders of customary rights and holders of formal land titles are in conflict over the same land. Needless to say, this competition has effects on agriculture and forestry—as well as on local livelihoods.

Of particular importance to forestry is that, even where governments or colonial powers have been willing to recognize individual claims, based on custom or usage, to land used for agriculture or housing, they have generally ignored traditional-group rights to areas used in common, such as forest or pasture. By treating such land as "empty" during the process of settling rights, governments around the world have vested in the state ownership of vast expanses of forest land.[2] Many standard land laws lack legal mechanisms through which groups or communities can own land they use in common, even assuming they could win recognition in principle of their rights.

In the last decade or so a number of countries have given significant attention to this issue, particularly in Africa and in parts of Latin America and Asia where local communities have asserted land rights based on historical claims.[3]

The Mozambique Land Law (1997), for example, retains the principle that land itself is owned by the state but recognizes within that context a "right of use and benefit" over land. This is a private property right that is not subject to the discretionary will of the state as owner. One of the most interesting innovations

---

[1] *See,* for example, the Land Laws of Mozambique (1997) and Vietnam (2003).

[2] *See infra* § 3.2.

[3] Indigenous land rights are also addressed in the international law context—*see infra* § 2.3.3.

of the Mozambique law is its recognition of "local communities" as entities capable of holding rights to land and obtaining title to land in their name. In effect local systems of land-holding and resource access, within which individual holdings are nested, may be legally recognized. Within a community area demarcated by the law, customary rules (or perhaps more accurately rules generated by and deemed legitimate by the community, whether or not based on long-standing custom) would govern the allocation of land. This device allows communities for the first time to gain legal rights over areas used in common, including forest areas, that are integral to their livelihood strategies and farming systems.

In Africa land law reforms addressing similar issues can be found in Niger, Tanzania, Uganda, and elsewhere. In South Africa an attempt to give clearer legal status to group ownership is the Communal Property Associations Act (1996), which provides that associations can be formed and registered for the purpose of holding title to land, in particular land given in restitution for seizures by the apartheid regime. In the analogous case of recognizing indigenous land rights, landmark laws have been passed in Australia, the Philippines, and a number of Latin American countries, such as Brazil. But while these legislative trends are promising, their limited implementation so far makes it difficult to assess their impact, real and potential.

2.2 Constitution

Constitutions have different values in different legal systems. In formulating development projects, it should be apparent that unconstitutional proposals are likely to be vulnerable eventually even if they are not immediately struck down. The same may be said for ordinary illegal arrangements: Even if they constitute the normal way of doing things, they are not a reliable basis for long-term investment.

Most constitutions specify the basic structure of government, of which the most significant will usually be the legislative power. While this is usually obvious, it is not so in those countries that have suffered unconstitutional changes of government or long periods of emergency rule. It is not being too legalistic to check that the laws and regulations said to be in force were legitimately made. A common error is to draw up a regulation without legal authority to do so. Another is to use a lower-ranking provision to modify or repeal a higher-ranking one. Neither is legally effective.

Some constitutions divide powers between national and subnational governments. Others give the national government plenary power, including the power to delegate authority to subnational units through ordinary legislation or executive acts. Any division of power may limit possible legislation.

Many constitutions have provisions on customary law, the rights of indigenous people, and related matters. The Constitution of Peru (1993) is a good example, since it was followed up in the Forestry and Wildlife Law (2001). The Constitution provides that peasant and native communities are legal persons and that their lands are not subject to adverse possession.[4] Even less direct provisions will alert the researcher to the constitutional importance of these issues.[5]

Constitutions typically have attached a bill of rights that provides for freedom from arbitrary arrest and searches, the right to trial on alleged offenses, compensation for the seizure of property, and similar matters. There is often a rich history of constitutional litigation that gives the bill of rights greater meaning. This can be a serious limitation on the powers that might be recommended for enforcement of forest and other legislation. It also may set boundaries on the substance and procedures for regulating private land use.

Finally, apart from the general constitutional considerations mentioned so far that apply to both forest and nonforest issues, constitutions may also contain provisions that deal specifically with forests, arguably giving them an importance within the legal system that they might not be accorded otherwise. The constitution's treatment of forests may be no more than a passing mention, as in the case of Brazil, or it may be quite detailed, as in the case of Turkey, where it is one of the main sources of substantive forestry law (see Box 2–1).

---

[4] *See* art. 89 of the Political Constitution of the Republic of Peru, 1993.

[5] *See* arts. 231–32 of the Constitution of the Federative Republic of Brazil, 1988; *cf* arts. 184–91. *See also* art. 25(6)–(7) of the Constitution of the Republic of South Africa, 1996.

Box 2–1: Treatment of Forests in the Turkish Constitution

The Constitution of Turkey is noteworthy from a forest law perspective because two detailed articles are devoted entirely to protection and development of forests and protection of forest villagers.

Article 169: Protection and Development of Forests

The state shall enact the necessary legislation and take the necessary measures for the protection of forests and the extension of their areas. Forest areas destroyed by fire shall be reforested; other agricultural and stock-breeding activities shall not be allowed in such areas. All forest shall be under the care and supervision of the state.

The ownership of state forests shall not be transferred to others. State forests shall be managed and exploited by the state in accordance with the law. Ownership of these forests cannot be acquired through prescription; nor shall servitude other than that in the public interest be imposed in respect of such forests.

Acts and actions which might damage forests shall not be permitted. No political propaganda which might lead to the destruction of forests shall be made; no amnesties or pardons specifically granted for offences against forests shall be legislated. Offences committed with the intention of burning or destroying forests or reducing forest areas shall not be included within the scope of amnesties or pardons on other occasions.

The limiting of forest boundaries shall be prohibited except in respect of areas whose preservation as forests is considered technically and scientifically useless but whose conversion into agricultural land has been found definitely advantageous; and in respect of fields, vineyards, orchards, olive groves, or similar areas which technically and scientifically ceased to be forest before 31 December 1981 and whose use for agriculture or stock-breeding purposes has been found advantageous; and in respect of built-up areas in the vicinity of cities, towns, or villages.

Article 170: Protection of the Inhabitants of Forest Villages

Measures shall be introduced by law to secure cooperation between the state and the inhabitants of villages located in or near forests in the supervision and exploitation of forests for the purpose of ensuring their conservation and improving the living conditions of their inhabitants; the law shall also regulate the development of areas which technically and scientifically ceased to be forests before 31 December 1981, the identification of areas whose preservation as forest is considered technically and scientifically useless, their exclusion from forest boundaries, their improvement by the State for the purpose of settling all or some of the inhabitants of forest villages in them, and their allocation to these villages.

The State shall take measures to facilitate the acquisition, by these inhabitants, of farming equipment and other inputs.

The land owned by villagers resettled outside a forest shall immediately be reforested as a state forest.

Source: Constitution of the Republic of Turkey, http://www.tbmm.gov.tr/english/constitution.htm

2.3   International Law and Policy

Though there is little international law that directly governs forestry—in particular there is no world forestry convention—a number of international instruments do affect the forestry options of a country that is a party to them.

The UN Forum on Forests, an intergovernmental policy forum created in 2000,[6] has adopted resolutions on the sustainable development of forests, especially those on Social and Cultural Aspects of Forest and Traditional Forest-Related Knowledge.[7] At the Fifth Session of the Forum May 16–27, 2005, legal issues were one of the priorities. Referring to paragraph 2(e) of ECOSOC Resolution 2000/35, it discussed recommending to the Economic and Social Council of the United Nations and through it the General Assembly a mandate for drawing up law for all types of forests.

2.3.1   Multilateral Treaties

The Convention on Biological Diversity (CBD)[8] has perhaps the most direct effect on forestry. It requires each of its 188 parties to manage its biological resources so as to conserve biological diversity. The CBD also requires member states to establish a system of protected areas, many of which will probably be forested. Even if no new areas are protected, it is evident that managing biological resources for diversity will require reorientation toward sound forest management.

Article 8(j) of the CBD requires parties to "respect, preserve and maintain knowledge, innovations and practices of indigenous and local communities embodying traditional lifestyles relevant for the conservation and sustainable use of biological diversity." The article adds two more objectives: (i) to promote and encourage the application and increased use of traditional knowledge, innovations, and practices, with the approval and participation of indigenous and local communities; and (ii) to ensure that the benefits derived from the use of traditional knowledge, innovations, and practices are fairly shared with those communities. In stating that traditional knowledge may only be used with the approval of communities, the CBD highlights the importance of effective participatory mechanisms to decision-making, policy planning, and implementation. A related provision, article 10(c), requires that each party "protect and encourage customary use of biological resources in accordance with traditional cultural practices that are compatible with conservation or sustainable use requirements."

---

[6] Created by ECOSOC Resolution 2000/35, 46th Plenary Meeting, 18 October 2000.

[7] *See* Report of the Secretary-General: Social and Cultural Aspects of Forests, U.N. Doc. E/CN.18/2004/8; Report of the Secretary-General: Traditional Forest-Related Knowledge, U.N. Doc. E/CN.18/2004/7.

[8] Convention on Biological Diversity, 1760 U.N.T.S. 79.

At the national level, Australia and Panama among others have passed laws to involve indigenous and local communities in decision-making about traditional knowledge. Australia's Environment Protection and Biodiversity Conservation Act (1999) established a Biological Diversity Advisory Committee with indigenous representatives and an Indigenous Advisory Committee to advise the Minister on its implementation.[9] Panama's legislature has passed a Special Intellectual Property Rule on the Collective Rights of Indigenous Peoples to protect and defend the cultural identities and traditional knowledge of Panama's indigenous people.[10]

A number of other international environmental and wildlife conventions significantly affect forestry, especially forests as habitats of protected resources. As its name implies, the Convention on International Trade in Endangered Species of Wild Flora and Fauna (CITES)[11] regulates trade. Relatively few trees are among the species it covers, but some have commercial importance, among them *Swietenia macrophylla,* which is a neotropical mahogany, and a number of species from Indonesia and nearby countries marketed as ramin. Many other listed species are forest dwellers whose status is very much affected by forest development.

Similarly, the Convention on the Conservation of Migratory Species of Wild Animals (the Bonn Convention)[12] and the Ramsar Convention on Wetlands[13] have implications for forests and forest law. The Bonn Convention requires parties to "endeavour" to restore the habitats of endangered species and compensate for the adverse effects of activities that "seriously impede or prevent the migration" of those species.[14] Parties to the Ramsar Convention must promote the "wise use" of wetlands, defined as "sustainable utilization for the benefit of humankind in a way compatible with the maintenance of the natural properties of the ecosystem."[15]

The UN Framework Convention on Climate Change and its Kyoto Protocol may also have important implications for forests.[16] The Kyoto Protocol contains

---

[9] Environment Protection and Biodiversity Conservation Act (1999), §§504 and 505A.

[10] Law No. 20 by Decree No. 12 (June 2000).

[11] Convention on International Trade in Endangered Species of Wild Flora and Fauna, 993 U.N.T.S. 243; 119, 125, 127, 140.

[12] Convention on the Conservation of Migratory Species of Wild Animals, 19 I.L.M. 15 (1980).

[13] Ramsar Convention on Wetlands, 996 U.N.T.S. 245.

[14] *Supra* n. 12, art. 111(4).

[15] *See* Guidelines for the Implementation of the Wise Use Concept, Adopted as an Annex to Recommendation 4.10 (1990), http://www.ramsar.org/key_wiseuse.htm; *see also* Recommendation 3.3: Wise Use of Wetlands (June 5, 1987), http://www.ramsar.org/key_rec_3.3.htm.

[16] UN Framework Convention on Climate Change, 1771 U.N.T.S. 107; UN Doc A/AC.237/18 (Part II)/Add.1; 31 I.L.M. 849 (1992). Kyoto Protocol to the United Nations Framework Convention on Climate Change, UN Doc FCCC/CP/1997/7/Add.1, Dec. 10,

specific commitments by each developed-country party to limit or reduce its net emissions (emissions by sources less removals by sinks) of greenhouse gases to a percentage of 1990 net emissions by the "commitment period" of 2008–2012.[17] Forests are both a source of greenhouse gases when they are harvested and cleared and a valuable sink for carbon dioxide when they are standing. Article 3(3) explicitly recognizes that: "net changes in . . . removals . . . resulting from . . . afforestation, reforestation and deforestation since 1990 . . . shall be used to meet the commitments under this Article." Further forestry activities may be approved for future periods by the conference of parties and may be taken into account during the first period.[18] A draft decision[19] from COP 7 of the Framework Convention includes "forest management" among such activities. Even without the decision, if forestry is a net source of emissions, parties will be obliged either to change their forest management or make even greater reductions in other emissions.

Parties may also use tradable emission rights and clean development credits to fulfill their commitments; these create new opportunities for forestry. The trading of emission rights is relatively straightforward: the emission reduction and enhanced removal undertaken to meet article 3 commitments give rise to tradable emission reduction units.[20] The clean development mechanism is somewhat different in that it provides for activities by developed countries that have emission commitments to take place in developing countries that do not have commitments. In recommendations to the Kyoto parties the COP of the Framework Convention has set out preliminary criteria and procedures for clean development projects. As with article 3 they limit forestry projects to afforestation and reforestation. They also provide for the designation of "operational entities" to verify and certify project activities and results. Host countries must designate a national authority for clean development projects and must choose a minimum value for crown cover, tree height, and land area to apply to green development projects.[21]

The emphasis on land use in the UN Convention to Combat Desertification (CCD),[22] which was adopted in June 1994 and entered into force on December 26,

---

1997; 37 I.L.M. 22 (1998). For a discussion, *see* K. Rosenbaum, D. Schoene, & A. Mekouar, *Climate Change and the Forest Sector,* FAO Forestry Paper 144, (FAO 2004).

[17] *Id.*, Kyoto Protocol, art. 3

[18] *Id.*, art. 3(4).

[19] Marrakesh Accords and Marrakesh Declaration, Seventh Conference of Parties to the UN Framework Convention on Climate Change, Marrakesh, Morocco, October 29 to November 9, 2001.

[20] *See* art. 6; UNFCCC Decision 16/CP.7, Guidelines for the Implementation of Article 6 of the Kyoto Protocol.

[21] UNFCCC Decision 17/CP.7; UNFCCC Decision 19/CP.9.

[22] UN Convention to Combat Desertification, 1954 U.N.T.S. 3; 33 I.L.M. 1328 (1994).

1996, can be linked to forest management. The convention defines desertification as "land degradation in arid, semi-arid and dry sub-humid areas resulting from various factors, including climatic variations and human activities."[23] The unsustainable exploitation of forest resources can contribute to land degradation and desertification. The CCD supports activities that help protect traditional knowledge and practices that may help to reduce land degradation and promote research into improved technologies for sustainable development through effective participation of local populations and communities.[24] With regard to conservation and restoration of the vegetative cover, forestry and more integrative land use and forest policies can do much to help achieve the objectives of the CCD.[25] The CCD also calls for measures to ensure integrated and sustainable management of natural resources, including forests.[26]

Sustainable forest management *cannot* be undertaken in isolation from actions for sustainable land use. There are links between forest management, land degradation, biodiversity, and climate change that need to be addressed in terms of sustainable development and poverty alleviation. Sustainable forest management requires the active participation of local communities through a system of incentives and support for sustainable livelihood alternatives.[27] The CCD stresses the global dimension of desertification and calls for increased efforts to implement national, subregional, and regional action programs to combat it, thus promoting sustainable development particularly in the dry lands of the planet.

World Trade Organization (WTO) agreements are very far from being forestry conventions, but because of the magnitude of world trade and the existence of compulsory dispute settlement, they have the power to affect forestry. The WTO's Agreement on Trade-Related Aspects of Intellectual Property Rights (TRIPS) is particularly relevant because in article 27.3 (b) it regulates traditional knowledge and biological diversity. Not only may direct attempts to protect local business run afoul of the WTO agreements, but there is reason to fear that if not properly designed some environmental, health, and safety regulations could be found to be unwarranted burdens on trade. An example in forestry is restrictions on importing planting stock.

A dispute involving Austria's Mandate Labeling Law (1992) further demonstrates the potential trade-related effects of forest law.[28] The case was brought by

---

[23] *Id.*, art. 1.

[24] *Id.*, art. 17 (c) and (f).

[25] *Id.*, art. 2.

[26] *Id.*, Annex for Africa, art. 8, and Annex for Latin America and the Caribbean, art. 4.

[27] These issues are addressed by the CCD in arts. 5, 9, 10, and 17.

[28] *See* Austria-Mandatory Labeling of Tropical Timber and Timber Products and Creation of a Quality Mark for Timber and Timber Products from Sustainable Forest Management, GATT Council, November 4, 1992, Doc. No. L/7110 of 23 October 1992.

the government of Malaysia on behalf of the Association of Southeast Asian Nations (ASEAN) contracting parties before the Council of the General Agreement of Tariffs and Trade (GATT). Although the law required that all tropical timber and products sold in Austria carry a label identifying them, it did not require mandatory labeling of other types of wood and wood products imported into Austria or produced domestically. The ASEAN charged that the Austria law was in violation of both the most-favored-nation (MFN) and national treatment provisions of GATT and was a discriminatory and unjustifiable obstacle to trade. In response, Austria amended its law to make the labeling requirement voluntary and to apply it to all kinds of timber and timber products.[29]

The International Tropical Timber Organization (ITTO) was established in 1986 as a joint body of nations producing and consuming tropical timber. It is governed by the International Tropical Timber Agreement of 1994 (ITTA).[30] Its main objective is to "provide an effective framework for consultation, international cooperation, and policy development among all members with regard to all relevant aspects of the world timber economy."[31] Other objectives are to promote sustainable management of tropical timber sources[32] and local processing of timber.[33] The agreement does not set out binding obligations of forest management; nor does it empower the ITTO to adopt binding measures. However, ITTO documents, such as guidelines for sustainable management of natural tropical forests and for the restoration, management, and rehabilitation of degraded and secondary tropical forests, embody international norms for forestry.

2.3.2 Regional and Bilateral Treaties

A person drafting a forest law cannot afford to ignore regional and bilateral treaties. Though few directly address forestry, many affect it.

Two regional treaties adopted in the last decade deal specifically with forests. First, the Regional Convention for the Management and Conservation of Natural Forest Ecosystems and the Development of Forest Plantations (Central American Forest Convention) was signed in 1993 in Guatemala City. Drafted under the auspices of the Central American Commission for Environment and Development, the Convention provides for policy and institutional reform and cooperation in

---

[29] For further discussion of the forestry implications of trade agreements and laws, *see* §10.2 below.

[30] International Tropical Timber Agreement, 33 I.L.M. 1016 (1994).

[31] *Id.*, art. 1(a).

[32] *Id.*, arts. 1(c), (d), (f), (k), (l).

[33] *Id.*, art. 1(i).

the forestry sector among the six participating countries: Costa Rica, El Salvador, Guatemala, Honduras, Nicaragua, and Panama. Second, the South African Development Community (SADC) Protocol on Forestry was adopted in Luanda in 2002 to foster cooperation between its signatories—Angola, Botswana, the Democratic Republic of Congo (DR of Congo), Lesotho, Malawi, Mauritius, Mozambique, Namibia, Seychelles, South Africa, Swaziland, Tanzania, Zambia, and Zimbabwe. The protocol sets out a common vision and approach to management of the region's forest resources in order to promote sustainable forest management and trade in forest products.

Box 2–2: Regional Agreements Affecting Mexico's Forest Management

A review of international agreements affecting forest management in Mexico illustrates the influence of regional agreements.

- Mexico is one of nineteen parties to the Convention on Nature Protection and Wildlife Preservation in the Western Hemisphere, signed in 1940 (Western Hemisphere Convention). It calls for protections for natural areas and migratory species.
- It is one of twelve members of the Working Group on Criteria and Indicators for the Conservation and Sustainable Management of Temperate and Boreal Forests, founded in June 1994 (the Montreal Process). This group has produced voluntary indicators that may influence management of Mexico's northern and high-altitude forests.
- With Canada and the United States, Mexico is party to an agreement creating the Tripartite Committee for the Conservation of Wetlands and their Migratory Birds, which implements a North American Waterfowl Management Plan.
- Mexico has signed binding bilateral agreements on environmental protection of border areas with each of its three neighbors (the United States, Belize, and Guatemala), and a migratory bird treaty with the United States.
- Finally, Mexico has signed bilateral environmental cooperation agreements with seventeen nations: Australia, Belize, Bolivia, Canada, Chile, Costa Rica, El Salvador, Finland, Germany, Great Britain, Guatemala, Japan, Nicaragua, Panama, Spain, the United States, and Venezuela. These primarily deal with joint projects and sharing of expertise rather than creation of standards, but they have had a practical effect on the capacity of the government to implement some nature protection laws.

Source: Susan Bass, *Legal Aspects of Forest Management in Mexico* (Environmental Law Institute, 1998)

In Europe the European Union (EU) standards have strongly influenced nearby nations that have ambitions to join the EU. A lawmaker working in the region would want to be aware of EU forestry-related legislation, which mainly provides for incentives for afforestation, protection of forests against fires and atmospheric pollution, and harmonization of procedures for collecting data and compiling statistics. Of particular relevance is Regulation (EC) No 2152/2003 of the European Parliament and of the Council (November 17, 2003) concerning monitoring of forests and environmental interactions in the community (the Forest Focus regulation),[34] which established a community scheme for harmonized, comprehensive, and long-term monitoring of the condition of EU forests. Also relevant are Council Directive 92/43/EEC of May 21, 1992, on the conservation of natural habitats and of wild fauna and flora,[35] Council Directive 79/409/EEC of April 2, 1979, on the conservation of wild birds,[36] and regional treaties like the 1979 Convention on the Conservation of European Wildlife and Natural Habitats (the Bern Convention)[37] and the European Landscape Convention (the Florence Convention) adopted on October 20, 2000.

Just as global trade treaties may affect forests, so too may regional trade agreements. The world's two largest timber trading partners, the United States and Canada, have argued for years over softwood timber pricing. Claiming that Canadian provinces, which own much of the nation's forests, charge below-market prices for forest concessions, the United States has placed duties on certain softwood imports; this has led to shifts in Canadian harvest levels and forest sector employment. Though Canada has with some success challenged the duties, first under the North American Free Trade Agreement (NAFTA) and then under GATT, the dispute continues.[38] It illustrates that even a domestic process like the offering of timber concessions may fall under international trade scrutiny.

A recent trade-related development that has led to bilateral agreements is the effort to suppress trade tied to illegal logging. As an example, Indonesia and the United Kingdom entered into a memorandum of understanding on illegal logging in 2002. Among other points the nations committed to reviewing their forest legislation to seek reforms to help combat the problem. For exporting nations such reforms might include clarification of land tenure rights, stronger sanctions,

---

[34] OJ L 324, 11.12.2003, pp. 1–18.

[35] OJ L 59, 8.3.1996, p. 63.

[36] OJ L 103, 25.4.1979, pp. 1–18.

[37] OJ L 38, 10.2.1982, p. 5.

[38] *See* Committee on Subsidies and Countervailing Measures: United States—Measures Affecting Imports of Softwood Lumber from Canada, Report of the Panel, Doc. No. SCM/162 of February 19, 1993.

greater law enforcement powers for foresters, or even mandatory chain-of-custody systems to trace log origin. For importing nations reforms might include authority to seize illegally sourced imports and requirements in national procurement laws to verify the sourcing of paper, furniture, and other forest-based goods.

2.3.3   Treaties with Indigenous Peoples

A significant difference between national land law and the treaty law that affects the land of Indigenous Peoples is apparent in treaties with the native populations of North America. In ordinary land law the statute of limitations would prevent a claimant from recovering land after a certain number of years, but the treaties have no such limitation and they can be applied no matter how long ago they were drawn up. As a result, large areas of land have either been returned to native populations or been the basis of monetary settlements in recent years.

In most countries treaties have not been invoked but an increasing recognition of the land rights of indigenous populations is affecting ownership of land—and therefore forest—in Australia, Bolivia, Peru, the Philippines, and South Africa, to give only a few examples. National case law as well as legislation has shown increased respect for customary law.

Treaties are influenced both by domestic law and politics and by international human rights principles. The only binding global instrument concerned with indigenous and tribal peoples' rights is International Labor Organization Convention No. 169, which has been ratified by seventeen countries.[39] The convention recognizes the rights of ownership and possession of lands that communities have traditionally occupied.[40] This right is also incorporated into article 26 of the UN Draft Declaration on the Rights of Indigenous Peoples[41] and article 18 of the Organization of American States (OAS) Proposed American Declaration on the Rights of Indigenous Peoples, both of which are currently being considered by governments and representatives of indigenous groups.[42]

At the regional level the American Convention on Human Rights has been held to apply to claims of native communities for legal recognition of their customary

[39] International Labor Organization, Convention No. 169 Concerning Indigenous and Tribal Peoples in Independent Countries, 1989.

[40] *Id.*, art. 14.

[41] *See* U.N. Draft Declaration on the Rights of Indigenous Peoples, Report of the Sub-Commission on Prevention of Discrimination and Protection of Minorities, U.N. ESCOR, 46th Session, U.N. Doc. E/CN.4/Sub2/1994/56 (1994).

[42] *See* Proposed American Declaration on the Rights of Indigenous Peoples, Inter-Am. C.H.R., 133d Session, OEA/Ser L/V/II.95.doc.7, rev. 1997 (1997).

lands. *Mayagna (Sumo) Awas Tingni Community v. Nicaragua* was a case brought by the Inter-American Commission on Human Rights seeking a determination of whether Nicaragua had violated Convention articles 1 (Obligation to Respect Rights); 2 (Domestic Legal Effects); 21 (Right to Property); and 25 (Right to Judicial Protection) because it had not demarcated the communal lands of the Awas Tingni Community, it had not adopted effective measures to ensure the rights of the community to its ancestral lands and natural resources, and it had granted a concession on community lands without the assent of the community.[43] Furthermore, the State did not ensure that there was an effective remedy for the community's concerns about its property rights.

Finding that the Nicaragua Constitution recognized the rights claimed, the Inter-American Court of Human Rights ruled that the state had violated the judicial remedy and the property right provisions of the Convention by failing to "provide effective measures for the delimitation and titling of the property of the members of the Awas Tingni Mayagna Community, in accordance with the customary law, values, customs and mores of that Community."[44]

2.3.4   Policies of International Development Organizations: The World Bank Forests Policy

Forest policies of international organizations are another type of international instrument that has significance when national forest laws are assessed and revised. A prominent example is the new World Bank Forests Policy (OP 4.36), the main features of which are summarized next.[45] Other organizations also have produced influential policy statements on forests; the policies of the Asian Development Bank and the African Development Bank, for example, are summarized in Appendix 2. Though such policies are generally directed to the operations of the organizations that publish them, they help to shape international cooperation on forests and serve as points of reference in national discussions of forest issues. In many countries such policies can thus be considered influential components of the legal and policy context for forest law.

The World Bank Forests Policy took effect on January 1, 2003. It replaced a Forestry Policy that had been in effect since 1993. The earlier policy had in essence precluded the Bank from operating in primary tropical moist forests; it was in part a response to protests about the environmental and social impact of certain Bank projects on tropical rain forests. As time passed, however, evidence accumulated

---

[43] Inter-American Court of Human Rights, *Mayagna (Sumo) Awas Tingni Community v. Nicaragua,* Series C No. 79 [2001] IACHR 9 (31 August 2001).

[44] *Id.,* pp. 68–69, 73–76.

[45] OP 4.36—Forest of November 2002 (*see* Appendix 1).

that where the Bank had disengaged because of the 1993 policy, damage to tropical forests was actually increasing. There were calls for the Bank to re-engage in this sector and fashion a new policy that would encompass principles of sustainable forest management. Together, the 2003 Policy and the accompanying Forests Strategy[46] (see Box 2–3) signaled the decision to re-engage.

Box 2–3: The World Bank Forests Strategy

The essence of the new Forests Strategy is its comprehensive view of forests as part of sustainable rural development.

The new forest strategy is founded on three "pillars":

• Harnessing the potential of forests to reduce poverty
• Integrating forests into sustainable economic development
• Protecting vital local and global forest environmental services and values

"These three aspects must be addressed *together*. . . . To be effective, the strategy demands a multisectoral approach that addresses cross-sectoral issues and takes into account impacts on forests . . . [from] outside the sector." This means that the Bank intends to take forestry into account in country assistance strategies and investment projects generally, not just forestry investments. It recognizes that much of what happens in forests and forestry depends on decisions taken outside the sector, in areas like transport, agricultural development, and public finance.

The Strategy is most specific in its approach to reducing poverty. The intent is to ensure that the rural poor have access to the forest products on which they depend for subsistence, in particular by protecting their property and usage rights. Collaborative sustainable forest management (CSFM) and participatory land-use planning will be promoted where appropriate, with particular emphasis on control over—not just use of—resources. Among other activities, support will be given to "policy and legislative reforms needed to implement 'Collaborative Forest Management', giving emphasis

---

[46] The functions of the Strategy and the Policy are different, though complementary. A World Bank Sector Strategy "outlines intent, discusses options and presents arguments for adopting particular approaches." It provides nuanced guidance on actions that should be considered in different circumstances. An Operational Policy is intended as a more concise statement of the Bank's obligations in all Bank operations covered by the policy. It provides formal and accountable safeguards that are approved by the Board. World Bank, Forest Strategy and Policy, http://web.worldbank.org/WBSITE/EXTERNAL/TOPICS/EXTARD/EXTFORESTS/0,,contentMDK:20458437~pagePK:210058~piPK:210062~theSitePK:985785,00.html.

Box 2–3 (*Continued*)

to tailoring designs to local needs."[1] A note states that plantations should not be supported in natural forest areas where the result may be to deprive the poor of forest access and that the poor should be assured an opportunity to participate.

The decision to integrate forests into sustainable development derives from the finding that recent rapid rates of deforestation are largely the side effects of poor policies in other sectors and a lack of effective governance in forestry. The specific proposals are aimed at the Bank, which, among other related issues, is to examine the effects of adjustment lending on forests. At the country level, the sustainability pillar focuses heavily on governance, in particular law enforcement, concession allocation, and forest certification.

The third pillar, protecting local and global environment values, emphasizes improved forest management outside protected areas. Governments are particularly encouraged—and will be helped—to identify critical conservation areas in all forest types. A minimum level of resources for national parks will also be supported, as will certain macroeconomic processes, such as creating markets for global and local public forest-related goods.

[1] *See* the World Bank Forest Strategy, *id.*, Appendix 2, at A–7.

Source: World Bank, *Sustaining Forests: A Development Strategy* (World Bank 2004).

The fact that the revised policy uses the word "forests" in its title, unlike the 1993 "forestry" policy demonstrates a move away from a preoccupation with extraction. The objective of the revised policy reinforces the pillars of the strategy; it is to assist borrowers to harness the potential of forests to reduce poverty in a sustainable manner, integrate forests effectively into sustainable economic development, and protect the vital local and global environmental services and values of forests.[47]

The scope of the policy has been broadened to apply to a range of "Bank-financed investment projects,"[48] specifically:

(a) projects that have or may have impacts on the health and quality of forests;

(b) projects that affect the rights and welfare of people and their . . . dependence upon or interaction with forests; and

---

[47] *See supra* n. 45, ¶1.

[48] Left out are development policy lending (environmental considerations for which are set out in OP/BP 8.60, Development Policy Lending, 2002) and debt and debt service operations. "Project" also includes projects and components funded through the Global Environment Facility.

(c) projects that aim to bring about changes in the management, protection, or utilization of natural forests or plantations, whether they are publicly, privately, or communally owned."[49]

The new policy defines "forest" more clearly while still affording flexibility and allowing reference to local perceptions in appropriate circumstances.[50] While the new policy no longer prohibits the Bank from operating in tropical rain forests, it does limit operations affecting natural habitats, especially those defined as critical in OP 4.04 on Natural Habitats, June 2001. This limitation is reflected in the requirement that, in determining the significance of any conversion or degradation, the Bank use "a precautionary approach."[51]

While the new policy no longer applies to structural adjustment loans that affect forests, Development Lending Policy (OP 8.60) 2002 requires that the Bank determine "whether specific country policies supported by the operation are likely to cause significant effects on the country's environment, forests, and other natural resources." Where such effects are deemed likely, the Bank assesses whether the country has the means in place "for reducing such adverse effects and enhancing positive effects"; where there are "significant gaps," it is the Bank's responsibility to determine how the gaps "would be addressed before or during program implementation."

The revised Forests Policy also stipulates how forests are to be addressed when World Bank Country Assistance Strategies (CAS) are drafted. The policy states that the CAS should address forests where there could be a "significant impact on forests."[52] Like development policy loans, the CAS can be critical to addressing forest issues in forest-rich countries.

---

[49] *See supra* n. 45, ¶3.

[50] *Id.* Annex A—Definitions:
(a) *Forest* is as an area of land of not less than 1.0 hectare with tree crown cover (or equivalent stocking level) of more than 10 percent that has trees with the potential to reach a minimum height of two meters at maturity *in situ*. A forest may consist of either closed forest formations, where trees of various heights and undergrowth cover a high proportion of the ground, or open forest. Young natural stands and all plantations that have yet to reach a crown density of 10 percent or tree height of two meters are included under forest, as are areas normally forming part of the forest area that are temporarily unstocked as a result of human intervention, such as harvesting, or natural causes but that are expected to revert to forest. The definition *includes* forests dedicated to forest production, protection, multiple uses, or conservation, whether formally recognized or not. The definition *excludes* areas where land uses not dependent on tree cover predominate, such as agriculture, grazing, or settlements. In countries with low forest cover, the definition may be expanded to include areas covered by trees that fall below the 10 percent threshold for canopy density but are considered forest under local conditions.

[51] *See also* OP 4.04, ¶1.

[52] *Supra* n. 45, ¶4.

Similarly, the Forests Policy makes clear that for each forest intervention an array of institutional, economic, social, and legal issues needs to be reviewed, using a range of instruments, such as environmental assessments, poverty assessments, social analyses, and public expenditure reviews. This type of review has often led the Bank and borrowers to recognize the need to couple improvements of the forest legal and institutional framework with investment or policy loans. In some cases the Bank or another international institution, such as the Food and Agriculture Organization (FAO), have provided technical and financial support for borrowers to formulate needed legislative or institutional reforms.

Perhaps the most innovative aspect of the policy revision is the requirement for certification as a condition for financing large-scale plantations, such as commercial harvesting operations. To receive financing, such an operation would have to be certified by a system acceptable to the Bank, one that had the following elements:

(1) compliance with relevant laws;
(2) recognition of and respect for any legally documented or customary land tenure and use rights and the rights of indigenous peoples and workers;
(3) measures to maintain or enhance sound and effective community relations;
(4) commitment to conserving biological diversity and ecological functions;
(5) measures to maintain or enhance environmentally sound multiple benefits accruing from the forest;
(6) prevention or minimization of adverse environmental impacts from forest use;
(7) effective forest management planning;
(8) active monitoring and assessment of forest management areas; and
(9) maintenance of critical forest areas and other natural habitats affected by the operation.

The policy also states a preference for "small-scale, community-level"[53] forest operations, calling for assessment of:

(a) the extent to which the livelihoods of local communities depend on and use trees in the project and adjacent areas;
(b) the institutional, policy, and conflict management issues involved in improving the participation of indigenous peoples and poor people in the management of the trees and forests in the project area; and
(c) forest product and forest service issues relevant to indigenous people and poor people living in or near forests in the project area and opportunities for promoting the involvement of women.[54]

---

[53] *Id.* ¶14.
[54] *See* BP 4.36, ¶6.

2.4   Criminal Law and Procedure

Criminal law and procedure are important to forests for two reasons. First, many of the crimes that might be committed in, or against, a forest are set out in the general criminal law. So are many of the powers police and other public officers need to exercise, the basis for search and arrest warrants, and the treatment of suspects and evidence. In some legal traditions it is rare to put such matters into a special law, so either existing laws must be used as they are or political and procedural steps must be taken to amend the more general law.

The second reason for paying careful attention to criminal law is that it probably expresses a general judgment about the relative severity of crimes and their appropriate punishments, as well as the proper powers of officials in enforcing the law. Unless there are very strong arguments for doing things differently in forestry, existing law is likely to define the general framework in which forest law will be enforced.[55]

2.5   Environment

Continuing questions about the relationship between environmental and forest law in part reflect the long tradition of considering forest law as environmental law for natural spaces. As an example of the questions that arise with the spread of general environmental legislation: is it necessary in certain situations for forestry to undertake an environmental impact assessment (EIA) as well as a forest management plan? There is obviously no single answer, but awareness of such questions should lead those interested in forests to examine environmental legislation for what are likely to be large impacts on forest activities. The lawmaker must do the same to determine whether particular provisions already appear in environmental laws, whether the environmental provisions are suitable (or tolerable) for forestry, and whether there are gaps between the two laws that need to be filled. Of interest to foresters might be laws on both water use and water pollution, air pollution laws, and pesticide laws. The lawmaker may also want to review laws that give government the power to pre-empt forest uses of lands, such as laws permitting the construction of mines, hydropower facilities, and roads.[56]

2.6   Wildlife

Wildlife law is often a part of forest law for a number of reasons, including the fact that forestry and wildlife officers are often part of the same department, much of organized hunting areas is officially forest, and forestry and wildlife

---

[55] For further discussion of forest offenses, *see* chapter 10.

[56] For more on environmental issues, *see* chapter 9.

share a common ecosystem. Nonetheless, because there are probably more distinct wildlife and forest laws than consolidated ones, this study does not devote much attention to wildlife.

Wildlife law cannot be ignored, however, because it often regulates the rights of hunters and animals to wander through the forest. Moreover, in the case of community forestry, nontimber products may be more important than timber. In any case, wildlife values can offer an inducement to local residents to participate in community forestry. There are also likely to be substantial wildlife-forest relationships related to enforcement because forestry and wildlife officers often have authority to enforce both laws. Wildlife is usually considered a forest product in designated forests and is subject to forest fees and licenses even if the management of wildlife is the responsibility of a separate staff.[57]

2.7 Public Administration

Much of forest law is dedicated to the management of state property, the functions of a government department, and its relations with the public. These are dealt with generally in laws on public property, concessions, public tenders, the civil service, and administrative law. As with other subjects already discussed, in some countries the general laws will obviate the need for similar provisions in forest law—indeed, there may be a very strong custom of not putting such issues into special laws. Even if the same matters deserve special treatment, how they are dealt with in general legislation is an important yardstick for how they should be dealt with in forest law. Examples are procedures for public consultations, management of separate funds (such as for reforestation or other specific activities), and rights to appeal against administrative decisions.

---

[57] Wildlife issues are covered further in §9.1.

CHAPTER 3

Forest Tenure

3.1 The Importance and Complexity of Forest Tenure

Tenure is now routinely seen as a critical variable in the sustainable management of forests. The subject figures prominently in international statements, from the Rio Forest Principles to the World Bank's Forest Strategy, where clear, secure, and long-term tenure is promoted as an inducement for responsible use and conservation. Thus, understanding the nature and role of forest tenure is important for anyone trying to evaluate and improve the legal framework for forests. The problem is that this can be surprisingly complex, particularly when broad legal statements are compared to the situation on the ground.

For example, it is convenient to group forest tenure into three categories of ownership: state, private, and customary/community (shorthand for the various ways ownership can be vested in a village, traditional authority, user group, or community-based entity).[58] Unfortunately, applying these labels to particular forests can be difficult. Moreover, used uncritically these labels can obscure significant differences in the legal rights and responsibilities that apply to forests that ostensibly fall within the same ownership category. Thus, in approaching the question of forest tenure, a number of issues should be considered at the outset:

- *Ownership may be contested.* In many countries, even where the state asserts its ownership over forests, large areas may be subject to the claims of indigenous or other community-based groups (as noted above in section 2.1). In some cases these claims are adjudicated in courts or become the basis of

---

[58] This last category has received considerable attention in recent years with the resurgence of interest in common property theory and a growing recognition of possible benefits from community-based management (*see* section 7.3, below). Some critics would argue that rights vested in a community group do not need their own category because they are simply a type of private right to be treated legally on a par with any other private right—the only distinction being that they are held by a group instead of by individuals, *see* O. Lynch, *Promoting Legal Recognition of Community-based Property Rights: Rethinking Basic Concepts,* 57 Common Property Resource Digest 3-4 (2001). Nevertheless, despite the strength of this argument, the standard practice is to distinguish between private forests owned by individuals and enterprises and those held by communities or community-based groups.

national legislation recognizing indigenous land rights, as in the Philippines or a number of Latin American countries. In other cases, the disputes may remain unresolved indefinitely, with results ranging from a state of uneasy standoff and confusion to open and violent conflict.

- *Legal ownership may not be reflected in de facto control.* Throughout the world there are forest areas where the presence of the state is so weak that the operative tenure rules are those of the local community even when the state is the *de jure* owner. In other cases, the presence of the state may disrupt traditional forest management institutions without providing an effective alternative, so that open access prevails: neither the state nor the traditional system is effectively in control. A similar outcome may occur where traditional institutions, though formally holding rights to the forest, have become dysfunctional or are no longer seen as legitimate by local people.

- *Tenure may be unclear because records are incomplete or contradictory.* Often it is simply unclear whether an area falls within a state forest or not. Sometimes the demarcation of forest boundaries was never completed or was done badly. Sometimes the situation results from competition between state agencies: for example, revenue and forestry departments in Indian states often disagree about the boundary between their jurisdictions; in Turkey, forest and agricultural cadastres often do not match.

- *It may sometimes be difficult to distinguish between categories.* Determining where to draw the line between state, private, and customary/community categories can be difficult in some contexts, and quite dissimilar arrangements may be lumped together in a single category. For example, many forests in China, like most agricultural land, are owned by collectives. Yet given the heavy presence of the state in the governance of collectives, is it meaningful to place such forests in the "customary/community" category, or are they some sort of hybrid?

- *Tenure may be allocated among multiple persons.* Identifying someone as the "owner" of a forest only tells part of the story of the tenure status of that forest. As with any other type of property, different rights over forests—rights of access, management, harvest, and so on—may be allocated among any number of persons or entities who are not the legal owners. Thus looking at the question of ownership alone may not reveal who has some of the most powerful rights. Again, this can play out in a number of ways. In Ghana for example, many forests are owned by "stools" (traditional authorities), but the state holds the power to manage those forests and allocate rights to harvest their resources. The opposite scenario can also occur—sometimes long-term lessees or concessionaires of land owned by the state may have such extensive contractual rights that for all intents and purposes the forest could be classified as private.

- *Tree tenure may differ from land tenure.* As a variant on the previous point, ownership of forest land may not carry legal power over the trees on it if in a particular legal system land tenure and tree tenure are separable. Some customary systems, for example, firmly recognize individual ownership of trees but rights to the land under them may be subject to reallocation. In forestry-related development projects, tree tenure has on occasion been used to avoid dealing directly with confusing or unsatisfactory land tenure systems. Typically the customary land authorities agree to give rights to participants in a forestry project to harvest the trees. Sometimes in women's development projects tree tenure is used to give women engaged in forestry projects the ownership of trees even though their husbands may own the land. Tree tenure is usually thought of in terms of the incentive it offers for forestry activities, but where there is a third party, such as a landlord, the granting of rights to plant trees may have the unwanted effect of causing the landlord to prohibit tree-planting. Before specific rights in trees are created, there must be a good understanding of the interests of all the possible parties.

If an assessment of the forest legal framework is to be grounded in reality, the important topic of tenure needs to be approached with such qualifications in mind.

3.2   Designation of State Forests

Though state forests may be obtained through purchase, conquest, or succession to royal forests (themselves obtained through conquest), the most distinctive method is for the state to designate state land or identify land that is presumed not to belong to anybody else. There are a number of increasingly sophisticated techniques for designating state forests.

Superficially the simplest way to create a state forest is to define "forest" and provide that whatever land fits the definition is deemed to be state forest. This is done, for instance, in the Code forestier (2001) of the Republic of Gabon. Though it is a rather crude way of cutting off other rights, it has the apparent advantage of speed where delay appears to invite further degradation of forest—but it has practical disadvantages. The greatest is that because the state forests are not demarcated or even very precisely described, it is difficult to manage or defend them. In Gabon a forest is defined as an area with a plant cover that provides wood or nonagricultural plant products and which shelters wildlife and directly or indirectly affects the soil, climate, or water supply.[59] This is unlikely to keep

---

[59] Loi No 016/01 du 31 décembre 2001 portant Code forestier en République Gabonaise, art. 4.

new, much less habitual, users off the state forest. Once they are there, it is difficult to remove them or severely restrict their activities. And as a matter of justice, land described as state forest is more than likely to be customary land.

A somewhat more sophisticated procedure is to apply the same technique only to state lands that are registered, as at least those that have not been allotted or granted to any other person. The forest law in the Democratic Republic of Congo (DRC)[60] is an example; it defines the state forest domain as those forested lands (defined similarly to Gabon) belonging to the state or to public bodies. As a statement of intention, this approach is superior to nationalizing all forests if in fact the state land is not claimed by other parties. But unless it is rapidly followed by demarcation, it will have about the same effect as the previous method, especially where there is no central office that registers state land and keeps track of which state entity is responsible for each parcel.

Deliberate designation of identified parcels of land as state forest should be different because it offers an opportunity to first examine competing claims. In fact, a procedure for examining claims is extremely common. Implemented properly, though, it is also necessarily laborious, which is probably why countries like Gabon and the DRC have taken shortcuts.

The procedure for designating state forests in Tanzania's forest law is typical. The Tanzania Forests Act (2002) allows "forest," defined as land having 10 percent tree cover (like the FAO definition) or 50 percent shrub or tree regeneration cover, to be designated as a national forest reserve.[61] The proposed designation is publicized, local meetings are held, and persons with customary or other claims to the area are invited to make their claims known. Where there are claims, an investigator is appointed to determine their validity.[62] The investigator may recommend—and by implication the Minister may decide—to modify rights or to extinguish them upon payment of compensation; modify the proposal so as not to impair the rights; or abandon the proposal where the rights are of overriding importance to the livelihood of the holders.[63] Interestingly, one way the proposal may be modified is to establish a community forest.

One way to avoid deterioration of the forest or the arrival of new claimants while claims are being settled is the temporary declaration of a state forest, effective immediately but subject to claims being settled in a fixed time. This approach is also used in many nonforest situations, such as public (eminent domain-type) takings.

---

[60] Loi No 011/2002 du 29 août 2002 portant Code forestier.

[61] *See* Forest Act (2002) (Act No. 7 of 2002), sec. 2.

[62] *See id.* § 24(1).

[63] *See id.* § 24(2).

Countries in Central and Eastern Europe and the former Soviet Union typically designated specified areas as state forests, creating a cadastre or similar system, through nationalization without regard to prior rights. Lands thus identified became part of a forest estate ("forest fund") managed by the administration. Because the law usually reserves to the highest administrative authorities the power to remove land from the estate, removal is rare. However, some of these countries have begun to address the issue of prior rights through restitution as well as other measures.

Important practical matters that arise with any system of creating forest reserves are the proper demarcation and recording of the areas. The Tanzanian Forest Act, for instance, requires the Director of Forestry to demarcate a reserve within a year of its creation.[64] Record-keeping may be complicated by the existence of two (or more) systems of recording forest and other land. Unless there is good communication between the systems, entries are likely to be incompatible.

3.3 Redesignation of State Forests to Nonforest Status

The creation of a state forest, no matter how carefully done, cannot be the last word. As different needs arise, the character of the forest may change and new alternatives, such as nonstate management, may be possible. A principal problem for the legislator is to define the conditions of permissible de-reservation so as not to vitiate the intent of the law while allowing enough flexibility to meet legitimate future needs.

One way of doing this is to require the same procedure for de-reservation as for reservation, though the two decisions are not precisely balanced: Previous usage rights are not as likely to be cut off by de-reservation, but the interest in establishing and maintaining a reserve may be viewed as longer-term and thus weightier than the interest in using the land for mining, farming, or grazing. But even without a mathematical equivalence, the use of the same procedure at least has the appearance of rough justice. In all cases, ensuring transparency and public participation are crucial to the designation process.

Minor adjustments of reserve borders are often allowed without much formality. The wisdom of this has to be judged in terms of country practice: Can administrators or ministers be trusted to keep such adjustments to the small scale intended? If not, the more tedious process of settlement and reservation should be used. Naturally, the process of publication, consultation, and decision-making should be proportionately easier as the area becomes smaller.

---

[64] *See id.* § 28(1).

All cases of de-reservation must take into account the reliance people place on the status of the forest. In particular, licenses and concessions may be granted and community forest agreements entered into in areas that may one day be excluded from the forest. The normal way to deal with these would be to cancel them, giving compensation in cash or in kind, especially where money and effort has been expended. Where the rights of subsistence users have been recognized or at least tolerated in the reserve, those rights may not stand up to formal property claims. These situations need careful scrutiny and may require specific protections in the de-reservation process.

It is not unusual, though far from universal, for countries to impose a significantly higher threshold on decisions to convert forest land to nonforest uses than on decisions to designate forests in the first place. Often these provisions are latter-day additions to the law, adopted when there is growing public concern about deforestation. They may be a reaction to the widespread phenomenon of politicians or officials treating forest land as a "bank" of land available for periodic conversion to accommodate encroachers or developers within their jurisdictions. Attempts to curb this behavior might take such forms as

- requiring approval of a different branch of government for conversion (for example, a legislature or the chief executive) or, in a federal or decentralized system, approval from the central government;
- imposing a standard of no net loss of forest land, so that any conversion to nonforest use must be accompanied by afforestation or forest classification activities elsewhere; or
- using EIA-type procedures to scrutinize the environmental consequences of any proposed conversion.

India offers a good illustration of these techniques, and some of the difficulties with them (see Box 3–1).

Turkey is another country where legal standards for allowing or prohibiting the conversion of forest land to nonforest uses have been the subject of heated controversies, particularly where the land is near major cities.[65]

In short, the issue of when and how to allow conversion of forest land to nonforest uses is fraught with difficulties and demands an often perilous balancing act. A conservative approach may seem warranted given rapidly accelerating loss of forest cover and the pressures on administrators to relinquish land for political or financial gain. But too rigid an approach can result in unfair treatment of local populations, especially where it perpetuates the classification of land as forest

---

[65] *See* Box 2–1 on the treatment of forests in Turkey's Constitution.

Box 3–1: India's Forest Conservation Act and the Conversion of Forest Land

In the Indian constitutional system forests were originally a State subject, and thus most authority for their management was vested in State governments. The Indian Forest Act (1927), which with some variations is the basis for State forest laws, puts no apparent limits on the discretion of State forest administrators to de-reserve a forest. In the late 1970s, however, forests were shifted to the Concurrent list of the Indian Constitution, and in the last two decades the Central Government has increasingly intervened in forest management. The paramount example of this is the 1980 Forest Conservation Act (FCA). Directed at the problem of the rapid conversion of forest lands to nonforest uses, the FCA essentially removes the decision to allow or legalize such conversion from the hands of State forest officials to the central government.

In its original form the FCA prohibited State governments from changing any reserved forest to a nonreserved status, and from allowing any forest land to be used for any nonforest purpose without the prior approval of the central government. In 1988 two more prohibitions were added: (i) no forest land may be assigned by lease or otherwise to any person or entity not "owned, managed or controlled" by the Government; and (ii) no forest land may be cleared of natural-growth trees for the purposes of using that land for reforestation without the prior approval of the Central Government. Extensive rules and guidelines have been promulgated under the FCA, and a procedure put in place at the State level to channel requests to the center for permission. Detailed guidelines for assessing the costs and benefits associated with requests for the diversion of forest lands to other uses have also been formulated, establishing something resembling environmental impact assessment.

The FCA has been credited with slowing the rate of forest land conversion, but it has also been a target of intense controversy, primarily because application of the FCA slows down legitimate development activities at the local level. Indeed, the courts have interpreted the Act so expansively that some observers consider it a threat to activities carried out under India's Joint Forest Management programs and contrary to the spirit of local government laws intended to vest greater authority over natural resources in village *panchayats*. Whether or not the criticism is justified, it demonstrates the difficulties inherent in balancing different interests.

Source: Information gathered by the authors.

even where it has been used informally for generations for agricultural or other purposes. The users often have little hope of acquiring secure rights over the land so long as it remains within the forest estate. The problem is exacerbated where the legal definition of forest has little to do with what actually exists on the ground in terms of tree cover, the potential of the land for forestry, or the importance of keeping the land as forest.

3.4   Private Forest Tenure

The initial question about private forest law is whether forest legislation even applies to private forest. The Forest Code (1999) of the Kyrgyz Republic, like the laws of several other Commonwealth of Independent States (CIS) countries, provides for private plantations and does not prohibit private natural forest, although neither is contemplated. As far as can be determined, forest on private land would not *be* forest unless the land was officially so declared. It would thus escape regulation—and protection—altogether. A number of other forestry laws eliminate doubt by explicitly declaring that they apply to private forests.[66] In other countries, such as Gabon, forests are defined in such a way as to make them state property, so that, intentionally or not, privately owned forests are excluded.

If land, financial resources, and enterprises are to be mobilized for forestry, it is probable that legal silence will not be enough to attract them from the private sector. A number of legislative provisions are discussed below as possible incentives to private forestry. For tenure purposes the most important is to avoid definitions of forest that make all forests state property. Where there has been a long tradition of state ownership of all land, the law needs to state explicitly that private forestry is allowed so as to overcome doubts that would deter investors.

In some cases, especially where the underlying land is subject to customary ownership, an individual cannot own forest, whether planted or natural. Here leases may be used to create a legal basis for private forestry. Where state land is involved, concessions, if permissible and for a long enough period, may have the same effect.

3.5   Customary or Community-Based Tenure

A great deal of attention over the last two decades has been devoted to the problem of recognizing or strengthening the rights of local communities over forest areas on which they depend. The tendency of many land laws to negate such rights or leave them uncertain and thus vulnerable was alluded to in section 2.1 above, but in some countries recent reforms provide legal mechanisms

---

[66] *See* Dominican Republic, Código Forestal (1999), art. 20.

for communities or indigenous groups to assert or obtain confirmation of their rights over land.

In some parts of the world, such as many African countries, the formal legal system has long recognized customary title over forests, for example in the Central African Republic.[67] Where the lands subject to such title are clearly identified, the customary title is exclusive or at least superior to other kinds of title, and the authorities empowered to grant and adjudicate customary titles are clearly identified, customary title can be a sound basis for forestry.

Even where the legitimacy of customary titles is unchallenged, however, problems can arise to complicate sustainable forest management. A major one is simply determining what the customary law is at a given place and time. Customary law is not written, and even good anthropological records of customary principles and decisions do fully reflect the evolution of customary law, the differences in law among communities in the same country, and the differences of opinion about the law within a community. An example of the last problem arose in Lesotho, where most people believed that the customary authorities became the owners of trees planted on customary land. What appeared to be more informed opinion held that the customary authorities neither owned the trees nor had the right to take them—but the existence of the belief was a significant obstacle to planting trees.

Although customary law is quite adaptable, it is probably not a good basis for a forest plantation. Full-fledged customary law systems often have two characteristics that need to be taken into account in forestry development: (1) They may prohibit nonmembers, those outside the customary group, from acquiring land, and (2) land that is allocated for individual or family use may be subject to reallocation. The most common solution to the first problem is a long lease, usually on the basis of a law that specifically allows the leasing of customary land.[68] The second problem is not so easily disposed of because it concerns internal rules of the customary system. Where there are no specific rules for forestry, an ironic possibility is that the forest tenure of outsiders may be more secure than that of indigenous group members.

The number of countries where customary ownership is well-established within the national legal framework is limited. In most countries the interaction between customary and state law can be highly problematic. Many countries have dual and overlapping systems of customary and statutory tenure that promote

---

[67] *See* Forest Law No 90-003 (1990), § 15,which stipulates that local populations can keep exercising their customary rights at no charge as long as they respect the dispositions of the law, the regulations, and the customary rules. The law does not intend to modify customary rights existing before independence.

[68] *See,* for example, Fiji, Native Land Regulations (1985).

disputes between competing claimants to the same land. This undermines the security of both customary and statutory tenure.

Conflict can also arise between the ideas of ownership and of use. Customary ownership as such, especially of forest, is often not recognized while certain usage rights are. If in fact the customary users do not regard themselves as owners, this may be a good practical solution. More often, though, the rights that are recognized are much less than what people thought they had. This is typified in forest settlement procedures, where usage rights have historically been viewed in the most limited way—often, for instance, excluding commercial timber rights. Such limited usage rights are too narrow to support community forestry where the sale of timber is an objective.

Reforms in recent decades to address the weak tenurial status of local communities can be grouped into two categories. One type of reform (see section 2.1) has been to recognize long-standing ownership claims by defined groups over particular territories. A spectrum of less far-reaching reforms involves arrangements in which local groups are given greater rights to manage and benefit from forests without the state relinquishing its claims to their ownership. The comanagement, joint management, leasehold, and other arrangements now often found in forestry laws and regulations fall into this second category. Because it is convenient to discuss these types of reforms together in terms of their tenure, governance, and management dimensions, detailed discussion is deferred to section 7.3.

PART TWO

Forest Management

CHAPTER 4

Public Forestry

4.1 Classification

Forestry legislation often provides for the classification of public forests into different categories of use and protection, but how the classifications are made varies enormously.

The broadest classifications are sometimes made through statute. Statutory action is only appropriate where the classification is intended to be long-term and difficult to change, as when national parks are designated or other areas need strong protection.

Often the law allows the executive to do the classifying, but who in the executive has this power also varies. The law may vest powers in the head of state, the head of government, the minister responsible for forestry, the head of the forest management agency, or a lower-level civil servant. The authority may be centralized, assigned to regional divisions of the national government, or assigned to subnational governments.

There are no simple rules of thumb for where power should vest; much depends on the local context. Generally, the law should assign to higher national officials classifications that are long-term, that affect important national interests, and that reflect national policies. Where more than one agency might have claim to classify forest, as where the Environment Ministry manages land classified as park and the Agriculture Ministry land classified as commercial forest, the law may call for joint classification or give the authority to an official who is superior to both agencies. The law can assign to lower-level or local officials classifications that may need to be adjusted often or that reflect local concerns. The law can give bureaucrats the power to make classifications that should be insulated from political winds, and it can give politicians the power to make or review classifications as a check on a bureaucracy captured by special interests.

Similarly, procedures for classification can vary enormously. A common method is to include classifications in the proposal for creating the forest. This has the advantage of clarifying the proposal. Another common method is to allow for subclassifications inside an already established area. For example, the law may allow the forest management agency to establish plantations, wildlife reserves, hunting areas, ecotourism areas, or research units within an existing state forest. Other legislation, such as Estonia's forest law,[69] provides for classification as an output of the management plan. This range of options reflects trade-offs between speed and flexibility on the one hand and stable forest protection on the other.

Older laws tend to have simple classification procedures. The authority may have to do little more than publish the classification. Modern laws often require more elaborate procedures, such as preparing environmental impact assessments and giving affected persons the opportunity to comment.

Criteria for classification may be mandatory, generally addressing the suitability of the site for a use, or permissive, generally reflecting the intention of the forest manager. For example, many laws specify that stream banks, slopes of certain steepness, and other such areas shall necessarily be classified as "protection forests," which are then subjected to stricter utilization restrictions. The Indonesian Forestry Act,[70] on the other hand, provides directly for the classification of forests according to their intended use. This may be practical but it gives no assurance that sites selected will be suitable for the uses specified.

Classification and management restrictions overlap where areas are defined in terms of required or prohibited practices. This is essentially a matter of drafting, although logically an area classification should correspond to an overall management objective rather than a specific action, such as not cutting trees.

4.2   Management Planning

Management planning is central to modern renewable resource management and is an important entry point for participation and transparency. It is most likely to be a legal requirement for public forest, but in many parts of the world planning requirements also apply to private forests.

Every forester learns to plan. Indeed, management planning is a hallmark of forestry, and it distinguishes foresters from those who merely log the land and leave it. What, then, is the role of the law in management planning?

4.2.1   Common Legal Issues

There are some common issues the law may address—always keeping in mind that planning requirements must be adapted to local capacity and must reflect the type of forest, the use to be made of the plan, and its legal significance. This practical approach is especially critical in countries where public resources for

---

[69] *See* Forest Act of 9 December 1998, ch. 2.

[70] Chapter II, Act No 41 of 1999, on Forestry Affairs, September 30, 1999.

forestry have been severely reduced. In the worst cases the law forces forest agencies and contractors to make overly elaborate plans rather than pursuing simpler, more practical alternatives. There plans take years to produce. Meanwhile legal exploitation of forests is impossible, and illegal logging, the only kind possible, escapes all control.

4.2.1.1 Specifying the Broad Objectives of Forest Management

Almost every modern forest law somewhere lays out objectives for forest management. In part this is a way to acknowledge international norms.[71] It is also a way to direct the forest bureaucracy to be broad-minded, taking into account more than economic factors. Some foresters argue that well-chosen, outcome-focused objectives can encourage good forestry more effectively than mandating particular forest practices.[72]

How the objectives are described can affect how much flexibility the forest agency has, sometimes in ways that nonforesters do not anticipate. For example, in terms of timber, the law could direct the agency's plan to provide for sustainable use—allowing for considerable flexibility. It could also direct the agency to manage for the maximum sustainable volume on lands devoted to timber production. This would constrain the rotation length on each stand and might actually make timber production less financially rewarding. Going even further, the law could direct the agency to provide for a set annual harvest of timber, to assure the stability of local economies. This would constrain the timing of harvests on a collection of stands near each forest-dependent community. It might reduce the initial rate of harvesting but give the agency incentive to classify more land for timber production.

4.2.1.2 The Power to Classify the Forest

Some countries vest the basic power to classify forest in the forest agency via management plans (see section 4.1). Even if the law provides other means for basic classification, as a practical matter a forest plan will need to draw finer distinctions. The law may simply state that the plan will control forest use, leaving it to the plan's authors to ascribe particular uses to particular areas. The law may list special classes of forest use, such as "Wildlife Conservation Area"; the plan's

---

[71] *See,* for example, Mozambique, Forest Law (1999), art.1; Peru, Reglamento de la Ley Forestal y Fauna Forestal (2000); Senegal, Décret 98/164 (1998), § R.11 (establishing that the plan is a programming in time and space that aims for as much forest-related economic, social, cultural, and environmental benefit as possible).

[72] *See* C. Upton & S. Bass, *Forest Certification Handbook,* 42 (St. Lucie Press 1996).

author may adopt a class and state special powers that apply there, such as the power to assess fines for disturbing habitat. The law may also require classification of certain areas, such as steep slopes, and restrict the authority of the forest agency there, for example, prohibiting timber harvest.

4.2.1.3 The Geographic Scale of Planning

Some laws call for initial national or regional forest planning.[73] Some call for more detailed planning on a smaller scale but still large enough to assure sustainable and predictable flows of forest resources to local communities, with still more detailed operational planning for lands where management operations will take place in the coming year.

4.2.1.4 The Temporal Scope of Planning[74]

How far into the future must plans look? And how often must plans be revised? Large-scale plans must look decades ahead to ensure sustainability. The law may require that plans for a commercial timber area specify harvest activities for at least the length of a typical rotation and perhaps longer, so that mills and loggers will feel secure in investing in equipment. It may be possible to limit local operational plans to just the coming year, on the assumption that larger-scale plans have dealt with longer-term issues.

Ideally, the management agency should revise large-scale plans every ten to twenty years—more often if new information or changed circumstances require. Whether the law dictates this should depend on local context and capacity.

4.2.1.5 Plan Content Generally

Essential elements of a forest management plan would be an estimate of the standing resource, its rate of exploitation and growth, specific local objectives for which it is being managed, and the management measures necessary to achieve them. This is the core of resource management; without the resource it can fairly be predicted that other values will not be realized.

Some countries produce plans based on tree girth that seem to contain little else, and that is all the law requires. A more prescriptive law may require much

---

[73] Guinea, Law 99/013 (22.06.1999), art. 5 (national forest planning replaced by regional or local plans); Gabon, Forest Law 01/16/PR (31.12.2001), art. 42 (Unité forestière d'aménagement).

[74] Cameroon, Forest Law (1994): plans must be updated periodically. Plan requirements are less comprehensive for communal and private forests than in state forests; Gabon's Forest Law (2001) gives rules for revision of management planning in regional units.

more than consideration of timber yields. It may require economic and social analyses. It may give special weight to the impact on neighboring populations, especially traditional inhabitants. Increasingly, laws call for environmental values to be recognized in management plans, or they require a separate EIA either as precedent for the plan or before decisions pursuant to the plan. The list of natural science issues the plan could examine grows with our understanding of the forest. While soil and water conservation are traditional and biological diversity is becoming common, for instance, what about climate change?

These effects cannot be quantified the way tree growth is; they may require multidisciplinary analysis. Sometimes the law may need to tie forest planning into national economic or social planning. The law might direct the plan's authors to consult with branches of government concerned with economic, social, or environmental affairs. Where the plan is linked to an EIA, the law may call for an environmental agency to review the plan.

If usage rights are significant, or if community resource management is expected to play a significant role in the forest, the law may call for planners to do a more careful assessment of existing rights and how they are exercised, and to arrive at management objectives shared by the community. Laws often imply this by requiring that a community forest management plan be in the form of an agreement. Agencies often respond to such requirements by drafting standard agreements, which may lack local relevance—another demonstration that well-intended laws may be empty if agencies lack the ability or will to implement them.

4.2.1.6 The Process of Planning

Who is responsible for writing the plan and who participates in its preparation?[75] In countries that grant long-term concessions, the law often gives the burden of writing the management plan to the concessionaire, subject to government review.

Since the Rio Declaration was adopted in 1992, with its Principle 10 on public involvement, public participation has been the international norm in environmental decision-making.[76] The World Bank's Forest Strategy reiterates this standard. Planning is the stage where fundamental management decisions are taken. It is also the stage where it is most natural to take account of interests outside the

---

[75] The Gambia, Forest Act (1998): management plans are mandatory for all categories of forest ownership. Forest owners are responsible for drawing up the plans. *See also* Tanzania, Forest Act (2002).

[76] *See* Rio Declaration on Environment and Development, U.N. Doc. A/CONF.151/26, 31 ILM (1992).

forestry profession. The law may require a variety of forms of public participation. Approval of a national forest management plan usually requires at least the opinion of the forestry advisory council or a similar body. Some laws, such as article 17 of Kosovo's Forest Law (2003) require the government to publish plans in draft and solicit public comment.

Laws promoting community forestry or local control may call for the planner to adopt a plan in agreement or close consultation with local groups. A plan drawn up through a collaborative process is almost certain to be less technical than one created by a single organization. One way to professionalize the result of a user-sponsored plan is to require that it be prepared by a professional. Peru's forestry regulation, for example, stipulates that management plans be prepared by licensed professionals; their submission is the joint responsibility of the concessionaire and the professional.[77] In other countries ultimately the plan is issued unilaterally even though the results of consultation must be taken into consideration.

The law may sometimes relax the technical requirements of a forest management plan for a community forest.[78] Lawmakers may see technical requirements as a barrier to community participation and fear that if they do not participate fully communities will ignore forest plans.

4.2.1.7 The Legal Effect of the Plan

Where the country manages its forest through concessions, a national plan may be the basis for forest licensing decisions. The law may provide that licenses must be consistent with the plan or that no license may be issued unless a plan is in place.[79] This can be problematic if the kinds of license vary significantly.

For both large concessions and community forests, a management plan may essentially be a contract for management. In both cases, the plan is either the basis for granting rights or a condition of their becoming effective. The latter option may be dangerous if there is pressure to begin logging—and collecting revenue—immediately. The management plan, on the other hand, can protect a concessionaire against changes in regulations that would defeat its expectations.

Management plans may also form the legal basis for regulating forest operations, particularly where a number of licensees or users are regulated in this way. There are at least two good reasons for using the management plan

---

[77] *See* Peru, Decreto Supremo No. 014/01/AG 2001, arts. 58–66.

[78] *See* Lesotho, Forest Act (1998), § 17. *See also* The Gambia, Forest Act (1998) and Tanzania, Forest Act (2002).

[79] *See* Guinea, Law No. 99, § 42: exploitation should always respect the management plan; and § 59: when trees to be felled are covered by a management plan, a license for felling can only be issued if felling is consistent with the plan.

for this: (1) It creates a logical connection between the objectives of management and the means to be used. This should help limit the use of restrictions that are the result of history rather than study. (2) When the management plan is the basis of regulation, consultations on the plan help develop consensus on both the need for regulations and their content.

Where the government manages all or part of the forest directly, including noncommercial lands, the law should specify to what degree the plan binds the government. On the one hand, the government should be able to act outside the plan to respond to imminent threats to life or property, such as forest fires. On the other hand, if the law does not somehow bind the government to follow its plans, the plans have little purpose. When the government wishes to depart from a plan, the law should ordinarily require it to first draft a revised plan following standard planning procedures.

4.2.1.8 Providing for Transitions to a New Planning Regime

If a country has no plans in place, the law may first require annual local operational plans, phasing in a requirement for longer-term and larger-scale plans. Eventually, the law should prohibit all harvests or other irreversible actions unless they are undertaken pursuant to an approved management plan.

4.2.2 Forest Inventories

Forest inventories are essential tools for management planning. As natural regeneration is a centerpiece of silvicultural practice, particularly in long-term forest concessions in highly variable tropical forests, inventorying forests is essential for designing, and authorizing, annual plans and annual harvesting volumes. It also forms the baseline for monitoring performance, forest control, and inspection and has extensive impact on preventing and halting illegal logging and the associated trade.

Inventories in certified forests in Bolivia have demonstrated that they are a worthwhile investment with significant economic return. Inventories have supported

- an increase in forest productivity from two or three cubic meters to twelve cubic meters per hectare, because inventories make it easier to identify species of commercial value and incorporate them into annual harvest plans; some lesser-known species have gained market share domestically and internationally.
- a decrease in the cost of harvest operations, because planning and species mapping allow for more efficient harvest practices.
- a substantial increase in the cost-effectiveness of forest road investments.

Forest operators use inventories to design marketing and business plans. Inventories have also proved valuable in attracting investments and justifying loans to operators.

Unfortunately, because their benefits are often indirect, inventories and data collecting can become the stepchildren of forest management. Regulations for forest inventories within a flexible framework will remind legislators and donors of the importance of good data. They will also prevent foresters from making management decisions without enough information.

Besides mandating inventories the lawmaker will want to address the availability of inventory data. One option is to give the government access to data collected by concession holders, to both improve future planning and ensure that the conditions of the concession are met. The law can deal with this through regulation or through conditions in concessions contracts.

Another option is for the law, despite the general benefits of disclosure and transparency, to restrict public access to some data. Inventory data on timber volumes in protected areas may create political pressure to open them for harvest. Data indicating the quality or presence of wildlife habitat would be invaluable to poachers. Carefully targeted exceptions to disclosure can protect data like these.[80]

4.3   Concessions and Licensing

Exploitation of public forests is allowed primarily through concessions and licenses. These are not so much distinct categories as general descriptions of methods; their boundaries blend. Within a country, methods for allocating resources may have any of a number of names: concessions, contracts, agreements, sales, licenses, permits. These may be terms of art the meanings of which are independent of forest law.

Factors that distinguish exploitation categories are (1) duration; (2) geographic scope; (3) management or infrastructure obligations; (4) exclusivity; (5) resources covered; (6) eligibility; and (7) nature of payment.

In general, the concession is a long-term authorization, usually related to timber, that covers a large area. In return for the right to exploit the forest, the concessionaire often must take on such management duties as reforestation, construction and maintenance of roads and other infrastructure, and planning. The concessionaire gets exclusive use of such forest resources as timber, perhaps with exceptions for noncommercial community use. Occasionally the law will

---

[80] *See* § 8.1 for further discussion of disclosure and reasons to withhold certain data.

allow concessions exclusively for such nontimber uses as hunting or recreation. A concession is usually granted to a business entity rather than an individual, and there may be restrictions on the form of business, its ownership, and its minimum assets. It usually calls for payment to the government based on measures such as the amount of land involved and the volume of timber harvested, but there also may be requirements for posting of completion bonds, payments to local communities, provision of local employment, or creation of assets for public use, ranging from recreation facilities to local schools and clinics.

In Gabon, for example, a concession is issued for at least one rotation, with no specific upper limit, and the area covered may be from 50,000 to 200,000 hectares.[81] In Ontario, Canada, where concessions are called sustainable forest licenses, the law does not place a maximum geographic scope on them but does limit the basic term to twenty years with possible five-year extensions. For the right to harvest, the license holder is responsible for managing the forest, which includes obligations to inventory and plan.[82]

Lesser timber harvest contracts usually go under names like licenses, and sales. In Gabon the maximum area covered by a license is 50,000 hectares and licenses are only granted to nationals.[83] In Ontario the category below sustainable forest license is called a forest resource license. Again, the law sets no geographic maximum on these licenses, but they are limited to five years with one-year extensions possible. The license holder may take on some management obligations or pay the Minister a management fee.[84] In many countries conditions attached to large concessions and lesser contracts are similar, so it is hard to draw sharp distinctions between them.

At the bottom of the scale, countries with strong capacity to police the forest or have strong traditions of regulation may grant short-term licenses or permits allowing people to collect small amounts of wood, for as little as a season or even a day. Area and volume may be limited. The only "management obligation" would be careful harvest. As a way to collect data, the licensee might have to report the amount of wood taken. The license would probably not be exclusive. It might be limited to noncommercial use by individuals, for a flat payment or a small fee based on the amount harvested.

Lawmakers must understand the effect of general laws on forest concessions. Many countries have concessions or procurement laws that apply to all government

---

[81] *See* Gabon, Code forestier (2001), art. 97.

[82] *See* Ontario (Canada), Crown Forest Sustainability Act (1994), § 26.

[83] *See* Gabon, Code forestier (2001), art. 96.

[84] *See supra* n. 82, § 27.

entities.[85] In a country with a general concession law that applies to forests, the law-maker must find ways to integrate the general requirements and particular needs of forest management like EIAs and the need to negotiate agreements with local communities.

4.3.1 Allocation Criteria, Procedures, and Conditions

4.3.1.1 Process Considerations

Forest law, perhaps in conjunction with national procurement law, provides the framework for choosing the best candidate for rights to be granted in public forests. This important function is not as obvious as it seems. Indeed, older forestry laws and regulations are essentially silent as to what procedures, criteria, and so on should govern the awarding of forestry contracts. The general trend in recent years, however, has been to spell out in considerable detail preliminary steps for awarding of a contract, sometimes in the principal legislation, sometimes in regulations, most often in a combination of the two.

Why is this desirable? One reason is simply that in many parts of the world, the granting of forestry concessions has been notoriously secretive, often conducted at high political levels on an ad hoc basis. In recent years concession arrangements have been at the center of high-profile corruption scandals and concern about forest governance and the depletion of tropical forests. Not infrequently foresters find that concessions are presented to them as a fait accompli by their political superiors. Spelling out the process cannot solve this problem, but it may

- Inject some degree of transparency and accountability into decision-making.
- Provide a level playing field for potential contractors.
- Ensure that technical experts are involved in the decision-making process, rather than simply finding decisions foisted on them.
- Ensure that decisions are made in terms of technical criteria and standards.
- Ensure that the rights of third parties and the public at large are taken into account.

A well-ordered, consistent process of evaluating and granting contracts is one way to reduce the chaos and conflict that has emerged in countries where carelessness, or worse, has led to the issuing of overlapping concessions, or to the complete or partial disregard of use rights over parts of the concession area.

---

[85] In a number of civil law countries the concession for use of public land is a peculiar legal instrument, usually governed by a law that applies to all kinds of concession, except that the forest concession is usually governed by a separate forest law.

4.3.1.2 Qualifications

As a matter of principle, state management of forests implies a long-term approach and a maximization of benefits to the entire nation. When a license or concession is used to transfer substantial responsibility for the forest, the same objectives should govern the arrangement—the licensee should be a partner, not just a buyer. The qualifications of the licensee will therefore be as important as the amount to be paid, and the contract is likely to be a complicated one, subject to adjustment over time.

Laws may spell out in detail the minimum qualifications of applicants to allow some prescreening. A favorite criterion is nationality. There are few tropical countries, for example (Gabon is an exception) where 100 percent foreign ownership of a concessionaire is allowed. Setting limits on foreign ownership is something that is tried in many fields of activity; it is also an area littered with loopholes. For example, percentage limits on foreign shareholding often do not prevent foreign investors from acquiring controlling interests in a company through other means.

Another common qualification criterion is whether or not a prospective concessionaire has other concessions in the country. Governments may want to ensure that not too much of the country's forest estate ends up in a single set of hands. Again, it is difficult to avoid the loopholes that abound in this area. In one country where single concessions are limited to 150,000 hectares, for example, companies acting through shells have managed to acquire small concessions that cumulatively exceed the limit.

The law may specify the type of business organization that may hold a concession. Because concessions are so long-term, the government may prefer that the holder be a corporation rather than an individual or partnership.

The law may require the would-be concessionaire to post a bond with the application or bid. The bond would be forfeit if the government offered the concession and the applicant declined. Most firms meet that requirement with a letter of credit from a bank or a guarantee from an insurer. The true benefit of the bonding requirement is that it invites an objective vote of confidence from a financial institution about the applicant's reliability.

Some laws speak of the qualifications of a forest licensee in terms of honesty, competence, and previous record. This may not always be effective, but it at least expresses the wishes of the legislature and may provide a useful standard for reviewing information about the applicant and judging results after the fact. A related method is to entrust a tender committee or the like with the task of determining the qualifications of applicants and the acceptability of a proposal. In both cases it is difficult to set objective criteria for judging candidates without their being arbitrary—if they are not in fact drawn up to exclude certain candidates and favor others. This is an area that depends greatly not so much on the text of the law itself as on the judgment and integrity of those administering the law. The law can help by at least requiring certain information to be submitted, such as the owners, officers and proposed key staff of a company, corporate and individual experience, and basic financial information.

The law may direct the forest agency to keep a list of those debarred from future concessions because they have violated conditions of past concessions, been convicted of forest-related crimes, are in arrears on payment of forest-related fees or taxes, or are otherwise clearly unsuitable as concessionaires. Allowing people to be removed from the list if they reform (for example, by paying taxes owed or going a specified number of years without new violations) can be an incentive for better behavior. However, debarment can encourage many of the same avoidance tactics and abuses as other character-related bidding limits.

The technical requirements for an application obviously depend on what is being sought. For large-scale harvesting, a serious management plan, processing and marketing plans, and later detailed logging and road plans will be required. Preparing these demands both an investment and knowledge of the forest. In some countries the government prepares the initial inventory before offering the concession. In many others this task falls to the would-be concessionaire. A prospecting or similar preliminary permit is one way to authorize the necessary exploration but it does not solve the real problem, which is that the applicant will clearly expect to receive a concession at the end of his prospecting but the forest-owner will not wish to commit to that without a detailed proposal. One way of handling this would be to reimburse some or all preparation expense of competing applicants, but this is never done. It is probable that some harvesting, official or unofficial, during the prospecting phase covers preparation costs.

For technical qualifications, requirements may need to be nuanced, with different qualifications applying in different situations. For example, where community-based management is encouraged, different standards may apply than in areas where large-scale plantation management and logging is envisioned.

4.3.1.3   Bidding or Administrative Grants

Procedures for competitive bidding are increasingly finding their way into the legislation and regulations of forest-rich countries. Cameroon's 1994 law is a notable early example; such details can also be found in the recent law of the DR of Congo, among others.

In drafting regulations for an auction and bidding system, it is necessary to deal with relatively mechanical things, such as the content of a call for bids, the form and content of bids, timing, and so on. The professional qualifications and independence of the auctioneer are also important to spell out.

Perhaps more challenging is trying to define how and when, if ever, government may use noneconomic criteria to distinguish between competing bids. It may be, for example, that a country wants to give more weight to bidders that are not already concessionaires, create a preference for domestic businesses, or take into account certain nonquantifiable characteristics of the bidding entity. For example, Ghana requires applicants for timber rights to incorporate in their bids proposals to assist in "addressing social needs of the communities who have interest" in the concerned area.[86] This makes it possible to evaluate bids on the basis of the willingness of applicants to accept social obligations. Whether factoring in noneconomic criteria always makes economic sense may be debatable, but from a legal point of view the challenge is to draft such clauses or exceptions so that they do not act as loopholes that defeat the entire point of competitive bidding.

In some contexts, due to a lack of information, prevailing market conditions, or special government objectives, an auction system may not be the best approach. The challenge for drafters then is to try to define circumstances in which government may abandon this approach and rely on administrative grants. Of course, even if administrative grants are used, the usual concerns about transparency, fairness and accountability would still apply.

4.3.1.4 Public Access to Information and Right to Comment

North American countries have elaborate procedures to ensure that the public has access to the process of awarding contracts for public forest land, at least for contracts of any appreciable size. Whether these standards are everywhere appropriate may be debatable, but it is important that some basic access to information is guaranteed, that the process be at least minimally transparent, and that community concerns are taken into account. Because auctions are often done through sealed bids, the law may at least guarantee the bidders themselves the right to examine all bids before the government awards the contract. Increasingly, forestry legislation requires public notice and opportunity to comment at least when management plans or EIAs are being prepared and when large individual concessions are granted.

4.3.1.5 Authority and Conditions

At the heart of the concession is the authority it grants and the conditions it imposes on the concessionaire. The concession contract will spell these out, but statute or regulation should provide general guidance for the forest agency about

---

[86] Ghana, Timber Rights Act (1997), § 3(3).

what conditions to include. Not all relevant issues can reasonably be detailed fully in the forest law because the real conditions for a major undertaking like a forest concession need to be negotiated. Even the framework is very difficult to articulate in a law because the important elements in a concession may change over the years. But the forest law does need to establish a suitable context within which such decisions can be made.

The concession must specify the basic exploitation rights: the resources the concessionaire may harvest, the area covered, and the duration of the concession. Even if the concession is primarily directed at one commercial resource (usually timber), the government may grant the concessionaire reasonable use of other forest resources incidental to its primary objective (such as gravel for roads of land for log yards and mills) or may give it general control over entry and use of the forest.

However long the concession, the possibility of renewal will arise. Concessionaires will argue for preference for the incumbent. In some cases, a right of first refusal or a presumption of renewal absent good cause to deny it is reasonable. However, the law must be careful to prevent a license designed for temporary operations in small areas from being extended to allow large-scale, long-term operations without the obligations that usually accompany large concessions.

The contract may detail requirements for planning and good forest practices. It may set deadlines for completion of plans and reforestation after harvest. Although these may simply reflect regulatory requirements, putting them in the contract allows the government to seek additional remedies (for example, forfeiture of performance bonds or cancellation of contracts) if the conditions are not met.

The law may also

- Limit the transferability of the concession; the government will not want to expend effort prequalifying one bidder only to have the concession sold to a less capable firm.
- Require the concessionaire to post a performance bond to ensure that taxes and fees are paid and plans, infrastructure, and other concession requirements completed.
- Exempt the concessionaire from import duties for heavy equipment and other capital investments, and perhaps also for fuel and other imported supplies. The lawmaker must draft these exemptions carefully to prevent them from becoming a license to import far more than the business of the concession requires and sell the excess.
- Require the concessionaire to supply benefits to the local community or economy, such as constructing processing facilities, hiring and training local labor, or even negotiating agreements for sharing income, benefits, or

access to the forest with local communities. The law may wish to clarify ownership of any improvements that the concessionaire makes to forest or community lands.

- Specify how much the concessionaire must pay the government. In a competitive bidding situation, the auction will establish the basic payment, but to make the bids comparable the law will need to describe how the payment is measured. Most simply, the law could require bids to be in the form of an annual fee.[87] The law may also direct the government to determine a reserve or minimum bid, perhaps based on the area covered by the concession or on market prices of wood, to prevent the government from being seriously cheated. The law may also require concessionaires to pay more than just the bid or basic fee—stumpage fees based on the volume and species of wood harvested, for example. It might specify higher fees for logs and sawn wood that is exported, perhaps with incentives for local processing.

No matter how perfect a concession contract is, it will require active oversight, so the law may discuss reporting and monitoring. It is always a reasonable question whether a forest administration is capable of managing the complexities of overseeing work done under the contract. If there are real doubts about the technical competence and discipline of the organization, it is probable that the country will fail to gain the expected benefits.

The law may address the requirements or conditions that relate to the release or confidentiality of reported data. The concessionaire will want to keep some of its information private for business reasons, but there is a public interest in making much of the data public. For example, the local community may be interested in data relevant to environmental impacts or information on how the concessionaire has met promises to hire local workers. Publicizing any arrearages on taxes or fees may create an incentive for the concessionaire to keep current. The law may therefore wish to create a presumption that all data required to be submitted to the government is public and craft narrow exemptions for data whose disclosure would threaten trade secrets or promote environmental harm. The law, as noted, may want to make the concession contract itself public.

Finally, the forest law may address many issues common to contracts generally: dispute resolution, contract amendment, termination (perhaps provision for the government to buy out the concessionaire), response to both foreseeable and unforeseen risks, and penalties in case of breach, such as liquidated damages.

---

[87] Among the alternatives are fees based on the area of land actually harvested each year or on the volume harvested.

Termination can be particularly sensitive issue. In theory termination allows the government to withdraw if things go badly, but the advantage of this flexibility must be weighed against the likelihood that an insecure concessionaire will pursue a very short-term program, or that the power to cancel may not offer any protection because it will never be taken seriously. In general it is less risky to limit concessions to shorter periods until there is sufficient capacity to supervise bigger contracts. The forest, after all, will still be there in ten years as long as it receives the minimum protection in the meantime.

4.3.1.6 Inventorying Existing Rights

A critical point in issuing concessions or other contracts related to state forests is determining who other than the government may have rights to the resources in question.

Part of the difficulty is the vagueness with which national laws treat the question of local rights. The Basic Forestry Act of Indonesia, for example, says in essence that "customary rights of forest communities will be respected unless the national interest requires otherwise."[88] In Suriname the rights of communities in the interior are to be respected "as much as possible."[89] Such vague formulations make it difficult even for the most conscientious contracting parties to determine what rights are legally recognizable and need to be taken into account. The Indian Forest Act (1927), the model for many British colonial forest acts, has an elaborate procedure for settling local rights when government forests are created, but in India, as elsewhere, colonial officials may have applied the procedures half-heartedly, local people may not have understood their options, and there is no clear procedure for updating the rights as conditions change. Now some of previously accepted "rights" are so old they bear little resemblance to how communities and forests actually interact in the modern world.

The laws of some countries attempt to make it clear how to deal with similar problems. In the Philippines, for example, the Rules and Regulations Governing the Industrial Forest Management Program (IFMA) anticipate that applications for management agreements may be made in areas where claims for Ancestral Domain status are likely to be made in the future. The regulations stipulate that:

> Those areas verified by the appropriate office of the DENR [Department of Environmental and Natural Resources] to be actually occupied by indigenous cultural communities under a claim of time immemorial possession shall likewise not be open to applications for IFMA without the prior

---

[88] *See* Indonesia, Act No 41 of 1999, on Forestry Affairs, September 30, 1999, art. 4.

[89] Suriname, Forest Management Act, September 18, 1992.

informed consent and express and written agreement of the occupants, which shall be obtained in accordance with customary law where appropriate, or until the claim shall have been resolved.[90]

Ideally, the forest law should mandate creation and maintenance of a public registry of concessions. An integrated system has been tried in some contexts, with concessions registered in land registries rather than kept separately by forestry departments. This is the approach envisioned by Suriname's Forest Management Act (1992), which states that the concession will not take effect unless it has been registered. This helps ensure against the issuing of overlapping contracts, or contracts that conflict with pre-existing rights to land.

4.3.1.7 Approval or Ratification

Where the law describes careful standards and transparent processes for selecting concession areas and concessionaires, and where these standards and processes are widely honored, it may not matter who has the power to sign the concession. The law may give that authority to a senior official in the forest agency or to the minister with responsibility for forestry.

Where the granting of a concession affects rights beyond traditional forest use, the law may call for signatures of officials from more than one ministry—the assent of the agriculture ministry, for example, if the concession will affect agricultural practices; the trade minister, if it grants special import or export rights; or the mines authority if it affects access to mineral rights.

Where the concession in effect transfers a public property right into private hands, there may be traditional or constitutional reasons to require higher-level approval, such as action by the legislature, the head of government, or the head of state.

Requiring multiple or high-level approvals can act as a check on arbitrary action by the forest authority, but the more officials that must sign the concession, the more vulnerable the process is to delay, and corruption.

4.3.1.8 Smaller Grants

For less important timber harvest licenses (smaller areas, shorter duration), the law may require basic information about the applicant and its plans. Normally the government should have already prepared a management plan as the basis for its licensing policy: if not, the law may require the licensee to do the same degree of planning. A legal impasse can occur where the law requires that the forest

---

[90] *See* Philippines, Department of Environment and Natural Resources (DENR) Administrative Order No. 04, Series of 1997, § 6.

administration prepare the plan, but it does not have the means to do it. The law must be realistic, but realism may well mean no exploitation of resources: if a forest administration is not able to carry out basic management planning, it is not likely to be able to supervise licensees properly. If, on the other hand, the required plans are too elaborate, there is also a good case for changing the requirement.

Very small wood harvest permits, often limited to local operators, can be granted without much formality, but the law should require basic planning (at least recognition of resource availability) before these are issued. Probably the only exception should be established uses, whose curtailment rather than continuation should reasonably be based on planning.

4.3.2 Forest Practices

Because public forest is public land, there is a rich body of regulations that governs what forest users may and must do and their relations with each other as they use the forest. Similar provisions may be found in license conditions, concession agreements, management plans, and local bylaws.

No matter where the provisions appear, the activities regulated as they relate to logging are complex, subject to change with circumstances and over time, and therefore difficult to regulate effectively. Some flexibility is necessary. At the same time, there needs to be some predictability. Substantial investments are made on the basis of the regulations, and they may apply not only to a single user (in which case a contract might do) but to multiple users, from local inhabitants to forest industries that use or provide forest roads. One approach to promote both flexibility and stability is to regulate practices in terms of desired outcomes rather than specific methods.[91]

4.3.2.1 Roads

Forest roads are a vexing issue. Building a road in an isolated area is an economic boon that makes agriculture more profitable and may make life more convenient. But by drawing people into the forest a road may hasten the overexploitation, if not the destruction, of its resources.

Because many forests are remote, any roads are likely to be built there expressly for forest purposes, though they may then be used for others. Because of their size and power, forest vehicles mean unusually heavy wear on the roads that they use. These facts may be reflected in forest legislation or addressed in EIAs, and they certainly need to be reflected in forest operational policy.

---

[91] Society of American Foresters, Briefing on Forestry Issues, March 2006.

Concessionaires usually have the right to build the forest roads they need—even in some cases[92] to build them over the land of others and over public land outside the concession area. They may have to allow third parties to use their roads, which of course implies even greater wear. In that case, the sharing of maintenance costs may be covered.[93] The concessionaire may have the right to exclude third parties other than for specified uses.[94] There is a clear public interest in the quality and routing of logging roads, in the interest both of other users and of minimizing their environmental impact, especially erosion. Specifications may be found in regulations[95] or in concession agreements; in the DRC providing roads for local use is one of the conditions to be elaborated in concession agreements.[96]

4.3.2.2   Harvesting Practices

Except where clearing a forest for replanting or other purposes is envisaged, the control of logging is essential to proper management. The traditional regulation of logging is by species, minimum size, or age and the nature of the terrain, especially slopes and proximity to water courses. It is possible to regulate what machinery may be used to limit the damage caused.[97] If no finer regulation is contemplated, writing this into the law may be as good a way as any to ensure adherence to minimum standards. As a general proposition, however, many factors go into good harvesting practices, so a way to evaluate them comprehensively in each situation would be desirable. Yet a long-term logging agreement requires predictable conditions. Reconciling these dimensions has led to a variety of solutions.

One solution that is very common is to require that every tree be marked by a forest official before harvesting. This has the advantage of allowing all factors to be professionally judged tree by tree. The disadvantage, of course, is the cost of proceeding so meticulously.

Another is to put the goals of management in law and to specify harvesting practices to achieve those goals in plans. As management planning has become more common in forestry, specific shorter-term working plans have been a

---

[92] *See* Democratic Republic of Congo, Code forestier (2002), art. 103; Gabon, Code forestier (2001), art. 142.

[93] *See* Peru, Reglamento de la Ley Forestal y de Fauna Silvestre (2001), art. 93.

[94] *See* Gabon, Code forestier (2001), art. 143.

[95] *See* Nicaragua, Resolución No. 07-02, arts. 25–26.

[96] *See* Democratic Republic of the Congo, Code forestier, art. 89.

[97] Sabah Forest Rules (1969), Rules 20B(2), (7) and (8).

natural complement.[98] These may include not only the area and kind and quantity of trees to be cut but also such measures as plans of extraction routes or special requirements for steep slopes. Even in the absence of an annual plan, annual cutting authorizations may be required to maintain oversight of longer-term licenses.

A method of prescribing complex harvesting practices without too rigid a formulation is the logging code of practice, which is spreading from Australia throughout the Pacific.[99] A code of practice can be applied by regulation or as a license condition.[100]

4.4　Nontimber Forest Products

Nontimber forest products traditionally refer to nontimber vegetation such as secondary wood products but can also include earth, stones, and gravel, wildlife, and such services as tourism. Grazing and shifting cultivation are not "products" but they may be considered to be. The use of public forests for mining, roads, power lines, and similar construction also needs to be considered at some point.

Nontimber forest products may be subject to usage rights or historic rights of public access. They also may be under the jurisdiction of ministries that are not sensitive to forestry issues. Even if there are no jurisdictional disputes, how nontimber products are treated will depend greatly on the relative importance of different products and uses, and the potential for revenue and for damage to the forest resource and, as always, on the capacity of the State to regulate them.

One of the problems in distinguishing between nontimber products that deserve regulation and those that do not is that an apparently minor product may turn out to be significant, or an occasional forest use may become much more common. In such cases, if the legal tradition permits, it is useful to give the forest agency the power to license and otherwise regulate the taking of forest products beyond those specifically named in the statute.[101] An alternative to licensing could be to give the forest agency power to declare closed seasons and areas.

Another distinction is common in Soviet-influenced legislation, where there is a public right of forest access, even on private forest, to, e.g., gather berries, mushrooms, and medicinal plants. However, in some countries the public may be

---

[98] *See supra* n. 97, art. 3.

[99] J. Fingleton, *Resolving Conflicts Between Custom and Official Forestry Law in the Southwestern Pacific* 44 UNASYLVA 175 (1993).

[100] *See* Vanuatu, Forestry Act (2001), § 43; the state of Victoria (Australia), Conservation, Forests and Lands Act (1987), §§ 31–40 and Sustainable Forests (Timber) Act (2004), § 49 (audit of compliance with codes of practice).

[101] Mexico, Ley General de Desarrollo Forestal Sustentable, February 21, 2003, arts. 55, 97, and 100.

excluded from these activities on private land if the owner posts the area.[102] Estonia provides that any owner that has incurred expenses to improve production of nontimber products can charge for their taking.[103]

Whether or not an activity is subject to licensing or fees, the forest manager needs to be able to regulate activities in new planting areas, especially if they are threatened by grazing; in areas or at times of fire danger; and for similar reasons. Though this is sometimes done by zoning forests into protection areas where public access and grazing are restricted, that does not fully meet the need to protect production areas when circumstances so require.

Care must be taken to preserve public usage rights in timber licenses and concessions where that is appropriate. This may mean not only reserving the rights in the agreement but also establishing conditions to facilitate their exercise. Otherwise the control and responsibility that the licensee or concessionaire normally exercises may inadvertently give it the power to exclude other users. Where the concession is very large, it is likely that agriculture, grazing, and many other activities will take place in what is officially classified as forest, and these have to be addressed. Yet there must be reasonable authority to exclude the public from certain areas to prevent injuries from logging and damage to regeneration areas. (One way of managing nontimber uses in a concession area is to allow sublicensing by the concessionaire.[104])

Forest law often regulates hunting and fishing. Even if they are regulated separately, enforcement of hunting and fishing law is entrusted to forest officers as often as more specialized forces. This offers considerable economy in covering large areas. Where the activity takes place in a public forest, forest officers are probably the only means of effective enforcement.

The traditional treatment of forests as residual stocks of public land has meant that use for roads, mines, power lines, and military purposes has been permitted without due consideration of the forest values being sacrificed. Often the mine, for example, is entitled to both take timber for itself and clear forest for construction. One way to ensure balance when nonforest projects are undertaken is to require payment for all forest resources damaged, destroyed, or used. These uses may require a forest license, as in Namibia,[105] or simply attract the payment of fees and royalties. It is always necessary in assessing forest legislation to see what mining, road, power, and other acts provide in this respect.

---

[102] Latvia, Forest Act, February 24, 2000, §§ 5 and 16.

[103] Estonia, Forest Act (1998), § 32(2).

[104] Peru, Ley Forestal y de Fauna Silvestre (2001), art. 14.

[105] Namibia, Forest Act (2001), §§ 29 and 30.

CHAPTER 5

Private Forestry

The role of private forestry ranges from nil to over 80 percent of forest production in some countries. In many countries private forestry has never been significant and, even when land has been privatized, the state has often retained the forests. In much of Africa individual land ownership is relatively limited, so that the closest approach to private forestry is usually community forestry (although South Africa and Swaziland, among other countries, have extensive private plantations). More recently the values of farm forestry and of private capital and management have increased official interest in private forestry.

As a relatively long-term investment vulnerable to disease, fire, and other threats, private forestry is often thought to need special encouragement. A number of obstacles to private forestry may need to be removed or compensated for if a private forest policy is to succeed.

5.1 Incentives

Where most forest and potential forest land is owned or controlled by the state, making some available for private forestry is the most significant incentive that can be offered. The Lao People's Democratic Republic (Lao PDR) provides grants of state land to farmers, villages, and cooperatives if they accept the obligation to improve or restore the forest.[106] A plantation agreement may be used to allocate state land for commercial or community plantations.[107] Provisions for agroforestry may also be seen as incentives to private forestry, though the term of the agroforester is usually short-term.

The fact that land grants or leases are not necessarily limited to afforestation tracts causes much dissatisfaction when public land is allocated for private forestry. There is a plentiful history of forested land taken with an obligation to plant but then neglected after the original timber was cut. The World Bank does not finance plantations on existing natural forest; there is little reason for states

---

[106] Lao PDR, Decree on the Management and Use of Forests and Forested Land, November 3, 1993, arts. 3–5.

[107] Malawi, Forest Act (1997), § 36; Sabah (Malaysia), Forest Enactment (1968), § 15(1A).

to do so either. One way to limit such abuses is to require full royalty payments regardless of the future use of the forest. If there is an obligation to reforest, it can then be enforced and policed successively.

Although they are seldom under full control of the forest law, taxes can greatly influence private forestry. The income from small forest holdings tends to come in lumps, perhaps years apart, coinciding with harvests. Demands for annual taxes discourage noncommercial thinning, environmentally beneficial long rotations and other long-term practices.

To offset this, tax legislation often offers more favorable treatment to forestry than it would otherwise enjoy. Reducing or deferring property taxes for forestland is common in countries where tenure is sufficiently settled to support real-property taxes. As an example, the state of Oregon in the United States taxes all forest land at a lower-than-market rate; "small tracts" of less than 5,000 acres (about 2,000 hectares) enjoy an 80 percent reduction of the land tax.[108] At harvest, Oregon recoups the difference using a severance or stumpage tax based on harvest volume, at rates calculated to approximate the unpaid property tax. The state thus takes on some of the risk of fire, insects, disease, or storm damage to the timber.

In some countries in transition to private ownership and a market economy, the tax on private forest harvests exists only as a vestige of the stumpage fee charged for cutting on state lands. This demands careful examination to see what purpose it serves and the extent to which it burdens private forestry.

Another real property tax incentive is to defer payment of land transfer or inheritance taxes until harvest. A very simple one is not to tax forested land at all.

All property tax provisions are subject to abuse. Without careful controls it is relatively easy to cheat the government over the amount of stumpage—far easier than to cheat the government over the amount of acreage. In forests where only a few trees have real commercial value, it may be easy to deceive the government about whether any harvest has occurred at all.

Some owners will be tempted to take advantage of tax reductions when they have no intent to manage the land for forest cover over the long run. The owner may be simply waiting for the right time to sell or convert the land to agriculture. Tax reductions should therefore carry a penalty (for example, payment of back taxes at the standard rate, plus interest) if an owner or buyer fails to reforest the land or converts it to nonforest use after the harvest.

Governments can also use income tax reduction as an incentive. The costs of forest planting and maintenance, which might ordinarily be treated as a capital investment, may instead be treated as current expense to be deducted from

---

[108] *See* http://www.oregon.gov/DOR/TIMBER/how-forestland.shtml.

current income, or there may be a tax credit for what is spent on reforestation. If the investment is considered a capital transaction, accelerated depreciation may allows it to be deducted in the early years of the rotation. Finally, income on sale may be treated as a capital gain and taxed at a lower rate than ordinary business income.[109]

Export taxes and duties also influence private forest investments. Reducing export fees can expand the market for forest products.

Forestry tax issues can be daunting. As a U.S. Forest Service publication says, "Most tax accountants are not familiar with all of the special provisions available for private forest landowners. The tax code is very complex and these special provisions are quite obscure. Hence, you need to be aware of them so that you can inform your tax accountant."[110] The same admonition would apply to forest law researchers in any country.

To protect the property interest of the forest owner, some countries specify civil remedies for timber trespass (the removal or destruction of trees on a property without the owner's permission). A typical civil remedy—the market value of the trees taken—might not adequately reflect the harm done. If the trees are relatively young, as when a neighbor allows cattle to graze in a regenerating forest, the law may direct the courts to award the owner the cost of restoring the lost trees.[111] If the trees are older and restoration is not practical, as when a logger strays over a property boundary, the law may award the owner double or triple the market value of the trees.[112] This both helps to capture the environmental damage and promotes respect for property boundaries.

A number of countries have outright cash subsidies for private forestry, in particular reforestation. New Zealand provides for agreements that run with the land in exchange for loans that may be progressively forgiven as planting and silvicultural conditions are fulfilled.[113] Provision may also be made for subsidies for particular operations.[114] Though progressive payments have the advantage of

---

[109] *See* http://www.fs.fed.us/r8/spf/coop/taxation/ for examples of favorable income tax treatment.

[110] *See id.*

[111] *See* Kosovo, Forest Law (2003), § 28.2.

[112] *See* Code of Virginia (USA), § 55-332(B).

[113] New Zealand, Forestry Encouragement Act (1962).

[114] *See* Chile, Decreto 192, Reglamento para el Pago de las Bonificaciones Forestales 1998, amended 2000, 2001; Walloon Region (Belgium), Arrêté du Gouvernement wallon relatif à l'octroi d'une subvention aux propriétaires particuliers pour l'éclaircie et le débardage au cheval en peuplements feuillus et résineux.

reducing the risk of noncompliance, or absconding with the money, they also imply more laborious approval and monitoring of each activity.

The law can encourage private forestry by providing information; this is usually done by creating extension services that offer management advice. The law can also mandate government sponsorship of research stations and forestry schools to help build local knowledge and capacity.

The law may permit small owners to organize cooperatives for purchasing and marketing, which can explore actions like branding or certification that unsophisticated owners would be unlikely to pursue individually. The law could even create and financially support a national private forestry marketing board.

5.2   Forest Use Obligations

The obligations the law places on private forestry may range from none at all to stringent rules that essentially duplicate the controls over public forestry. The primary purpose is to assure sustainable use of the forest resource, with special attention to the public benefits and harm that can result from forest use or neglect. Secondary reasons may be to raise revenue and protect the property interests of other forest owners.

Private ownership is supposed to give the owner incentive to care for the land, and it does, to a point, but the incentives have distinct limits. Because they tend to be economic, they ignore values that the market values poorly, such as environmental quality. Because they tend to have relatively short planning horizons due to the time-value of money, they give less weight to long-term benefits. Unless the law returns the benefits and costs to the owner, incentives bypass benefits granted or harms inflicted on others, such as positive or negative effects on water quality downstream. Like all market incentives, they depend on knowledge, and the owner may not be particularly sophisticated about the costs and benefits of forest management.

To address sustainable use, the law may specify procedural or substantive terms for forest management. The least stringent procedural requirement is for notice before or after timber harvests. The notice gives the forest agency information useful for assuring compliance with any substantive requirements. The tax collector may also appreciate notice.

More formidable is the requirement of consent in the form of a permit to harvest. A number of countries subject private forest harvest to permits, even if no fees are charged. The legal reformer should scrutinize permit requirements to see what purpose they serve. Some obligations of private forestry are more remnants of previous systems than expressions of deliberate policy. But in some cases, like Malaysia, a removal permit is required to avoid confusion between state and private timber,[115] and even recent forest acts designed for liberal economies require authorizations for logging on private land.[116]

The next step up in stringency is to require a management plan. In Latin America planning requirements are very common, and plans must be prepared by a professional forester.[117] Intermediate operations may not need a plan.[118] Some countries may allow small holdings to draw up simpler plans.[119] As they shift to a mixed economy, some countries have retained a very elaborate system of management planning. This can be a greater burden than the forest resource can economically bear, whatever its ownership. In some countries, like Latvia, this has been alleviated by encouraging planning but not requiring it for private holdings, most of which are small.

Clearing land and often less drastic logging may still require an EIA or similar evaluation.[120] Sometimes forestry officials' review of such actions can be considered sufficient; where there is no general environmental legislation it will necessarily suffice. Where there is such legislation, it needs to be reviewed in conjunction with forest legislation to avoid conflicts and ensure coordinated application of national policies.

Some forest laws require that each tree to be cut, even on private holdings, be marked by the forest administration.[121] Whether this is useful depends on the value of the resource, the damage that might be done by logging, and the capacity of the state to respond quickly to marking requests. A fee is usually charged to cover the cost of the state's action.

The law generally calls for these kinds of procedural steps in order to assure compliance with substantive standards, although the law may impose such standards independent of particular procedures. Typical standards may forbid cutting trees below a certain size (usually expressed as girth or diameter at breast height); restrict cutting near water; or require steps to assure regeneration, such as retention of seed trees. There may be rules to protect vegetation on steep slopes and fragile soils. Certain trees may be protected, but usually

---

[115] Malaysia, National Forestry Act (1984), §§ 41 and 42.

[116] Latvia, Forestry Law (2000), §§ 12 and 39; Nicaragua, Ley de Conservación, Fomento y Desarrollo Sostenible del Sector Forestal No. 462 of 2003, art. 21.

[117] El Salvador, Ley Forestal (2002), arts. 8–9.

[118] *Id.* art. 10.

[119] Benin, Décret No. 96/271, art. 80.

[120] Costa Rica, Ley Forestal (1996), art. 19.

[121] Kosovo, Forest Law (2003), art. 12.3.

plantation products are exempted.[122] As with public forestry, to promote flexibility, it may be wise to write standards in terms of outcomes rather than required techniques.

The private forest owner, like the private vineyard owner, may not be free to plant what he or she wants.[123] This may be more than compensated by subsidizing what can be planted.[124]

General seed, plant protection, and pesticide legislation is likely to apply to forest planting and vegetation management actions. The forest lawmaker should review these laws to ensure that products and processes that are useful to forestry are properly evaluated. One way to do this is to have separate panels of experts for decisions affecting forestry, or to have a forestry representative on any relevant committee.

Taken in total, the law may provide for the adoption of of regulations for private lands that are as sophisticated as those for public forests. It bears repeating, however, that in most countries private forest rules are much simpler, if they exist at all. Where forest agency capacity is low, attention to large public tracts pays greater rewards than attention to small private holdings.

Section 5.1 already introduced the topic of harvest taxes. Some countries assess yield, severance, or stumpage taxes on private wood harvested. Administering them means the forest agency must keep close tabs on private land management activities. They are harder to assess and collect than land taxes. A country looking for forest revenue might find it easier to tax wood, regardless of origin, at the mill or at export.

Forest owners have a clear interest in preventing fires and pests, so the obligation to collaborate in actions to control them cannot be considered simply a burden. It is nonetheless important that it be an obligation, because the failure of one owner to participate can cause disproportionate damage to neighbors. Sometimes the actions required are spelled out in detail.[125] There may be requirements or encouragement to form local fire management committees.[126] In fire-prone areas the law may restrict forest work during fire seasons or require logging operations

---

[122] Nicaragua, Ley de Conservación, Fomento y Desarrollo Sostenible del Sector Forestal No. 462 of 2003, art. 19.

[123] France, Décret No. 2003-237 of 2003 relatif aux plantations d'essences forestières et modifiant certaines dispositions du code rural.

[124] Portugal, Portaria No. 533-F/2000 on support to forest plants and seeds, and controls over the quality of planting material in commerce; Ecuador, Acuerdo No. 3 Norma de Semillas Forestales, January 16, 2004.

[125] France, Arrêté of 28.5.2003 relatif à la lutte contre *anoplohora glabripennis*.

[126] Uruguay, Ley Forestal, December 28, 1987, art. 8.

to have basic fire-fighting equipment on hand to deal with small blazes. Loggers may be required to dispose of logging waste in a way that reduces fire risk. The law may also regulate the use of prescriptive burns.

The law may create a general obligation to report the presence of pests and to follow official instructions on their eradication,[127] but joint preventive action would seem to be equally valid. The forest agency may be given the power to enter private forests to inspect for and respond to serious threats. For example, article 27 of Kosovo's Forest Law allows the forest agency to inspect for conditions that might encourage fire, pests, disease, or invasive species. The agency may order the owner to abate the problem, or if necessary abate the nuisance and bill the owner.

5.3 Controls and Obstacles

Controls on private forestry may be bearable and reasonable, or not. Obstacles as used here refers to factors that make private forestry on any scale impossible.

The greatest obstacle to private forestry arises from uncertainty about legal status. First, the lack of private forestry in socialist economies has given rise to an extensive definition of state forest in transitional legislation. This is fairly simple to deal with if private land ownership is generally allowed and government is ready to welcome private forestry. It is sufficient to review laws that define forest as state property and clarify that every such provision applies only to forest on state land. If the normal tenure is leasehold, state forest should include only land that has not been leased, unless the lease itself so provides.

Second, and less tractable, is the lack of recognition of customary tenure. When statutory titles are issued for customary land, the statutory owner cannot be sure that the customary owners will not oust him, by force if necessary. Yet customary title alone will be a very unsafe basis for forest activities.

A related tenure issue is the uncertainty of land boundaries. Boundaries in rural areas are often located by reference to impermanent landmarks, if they are surveyed at all. To remove some of the uncertainty, the law can direct the government to maintain official cadastral records, locate and mark permanent survey reference points, and enforce penalties for disturbing survey marks.

Fragmentation of forest property is another obstacle to the sustainability of private forestry. The problem seems to be most acute in former socialist countries where land has been returned to descendants of former owners. Many "forests" of only five and ten hectares have appeared, causing serious management concerns. Some countries have avoided this by not privatizing forest, but where the land has already been privatized it is probably too late to change. There are

---

[127] Mexico, Reglamento de la Ley Forestal, September 23, 1998, arts. 89 and 90.

possibilities of managing numerous holdings as a whole and achieving a critical size, but only if owners are willing to join such an arrangement. In many countries the new owners do not yet have enough confidence in cooperatives and similar arrangements to trust their land to one. Similarly, land consolidation laws are politically difficult to propose and in any case are not a solution for many small holdings but only for fragmentation of single holdings.

Another obstacle to private forestry might be called legal instability. Where environmental and tax regulations change unpredictably, long-term investment will be profoundly discouraged. This can create a real dilemma when private forestry is first legalized because some new provisions are bound to be less than perfect. Still, it is more the overall legal climate than single regulatory changes that usually influences private forestry. It is then necessary to take serious account of investors' opinions only when changes are made.

Finally, another obstacle to private forestry is poor management of public forests and the consequent supply of cheap or free (stolen) wood. Even when woodlots might make sense in terms of local costs and incomes, they will not be planted if the leakage of fuel wood from public forests is not controlled.

5.4   Plantations

Plantations have most of the characteristics of forests generally, with the notable exception of biological diversity. Economically, they exaggerate the general forest characteristic of a long wait for revenue after the initial investment, and the investment in plantations is commonly much greater than natural forest regeneration and tending. A new plantation may have no revenue at all for many years; an established private forest normally has an income yield from mature stands even as younger ones are growing. Because of these differences plantations are often given special treatment in the manner of both their acquisition and their regulation.

5.4.1   Definitions

A threshold issue is what a plantation is. If someone takes old farmland and plants trees in careful rows, that clearly is a plantation. But what if an owner harvests in a natural forest and then plants or sows seeds of some high-valued trees to increase their prevalence in the regenerating forest? What if a farmer plants a windbreak, or a community plants trees along a roadside?

Depending on the policy the law seeks to promote, definitions of planting or other limits on application may differ. A law seeking to encourage restoration of forest cover might apply only to lands larger than a minimum area that have not had forest cover for some time or that have been put to non-forest uses. A law seeking to promote silviculture generally might apply to most plantings, including windbreaks and roadside plantings, but perhaps not to orchards, trees on city streets, and ornamental plantings. A law seeking to control introduction of exotic species might apply to every kind of planting.

5.4.2   Encouraging Plantations

Direct subsidies or tax benefits unavailable for natural forest operations are often used to encourage forest planting.[128] This has had several unintended effects. One is that plantations are often proposed in natural forest areas and clearance of the natural forest is justified by the benefits of the plantation (for example, production of timber suitable for local processing). Even if the benefits are sufficient, it is necessary to ensure that the proposed tree-planter does not abandon the project after having logged the natural forest. Even on bare land the existence of sufficient incentives may lead to initial subsidized planting followed by subsequent neglect. The balance of incentives and the choice of recipients is obviously a delicate matter.

Still, plantations often must be encouraged. Here are some typical incentives:

- *Public land leases and licenses:* Forest law may allow public land to be used for private plantations. Congo has a very liberal provision that allows any physical person and any Congolese company by planting trees on the nonpermanent state forest domain to obtain both ownership of the trees and use of the land.[129] Both rights are transferable. Other countries provide for leases, licenses, or concessions to use state land for plantation purposes. Individual conditions can be built into the agreement for each plantation, which seems prudent when dealing with public land claims.
- *Provision of planting stock:* The law may direct the forest agency to establish tree nurseries and see seedlings to landowners at low cost. Nurseries both encourage planting and provide employment in rural areas.
- *Relaxation of private forestry controls:* The rights and obligations that generally influence private forestry also influence investments in private plantations. Obligations that are too burdensome may discourage planting in the first place. The public benefits that forest regulations are designed to protect might then never arise to be protected. Although the law may wish to strike a balance, some countries simply exempt plantations from controls that apply to natural forests.[130] Where there is reason to fear the effects of poor management, the right to harvest can be tied to forest practice rules, such as the obligation to follow general codes of logging practice.[131]

---

[128] Costa Rica, Ley Forestal (1996), § 29, providing for tax benefits and subsidies.

[129] Republic of Congo, Loi forestière, art. 36.

[130] El Salvador, Ley Forestal (2002), art. 16.

[131] Fiji, Forest Decree (1992), § 12.

- *Right to harvest:* The most difficult issue of rights and obligations is balancing the right to harvest a plantation with controls over logging. The complication arises because even in a private plantation there is a strong public interest in watershed conservation, wildlife habitat, possible carbon sequestration, and other interests that may arise. The plantation owner wants certainty of harvest; the state wants to retain flexibility. How this is dealt with depends on factors that will differ in different countries, such as how much land area is under plantation, how scarce forest habitat is, how much the state wishes to encourage forest planting, and how acceptable land-use regulations are generally. There are also differences in individual plantations, such as whether the area was planted due to a reforestation obligation, whether incentives were received, whether the plantation is part of an industrial development, and whether the land is public or private.

One way of reassuring the plantation owner in the last case is a simple exemption from the requirement of a logging permit,[132] which need not bar all regulation of forest management. Costa Rica had as part of its plantation incentive system a management plan that governed the conditions of logging. Though the present forest law simply exempts plantations from logging, transport, processing, and export licenses, it retains the condition of the management plan for existing plantations.[133]

A more articulated regulatory system is found in the state of New South Wales, Australia, where a new plantation requires authorization but there is a right to harvest in accordance with a legislated code of practice. An authorized plantation is protected from changes in the code of practice and is eligible for compensation if operations are restricted for reasons of wildlife protection.[134] Malawi also gives plantation owners the right to harvest the crop.[135]

In the United States population growth has led to construction of residences in previously rural and forested areas. Many states have adopted "right to farm" laws that bar new neighbors from going to court to limit farm and forest operations. For example, Oregon's law[136] bars most nuisance claims against forestry activities, including road construction, harvest, or pesticide use, if they comply with regulations.

---

[132] *See supra* n. 130.

[133] Costa Rica, Ley Forestal (1996), art. 28; Namibia, Forest Act (2001), sec. 31.

[134] New South Wales (Australia), Plantations and Reafforestation Act (1999).

[135] Malawi, Forest Act 1997, § 37.

[136] Oregon (USA) Revised Statutes, §§ 30.930–30.947.

5.4.3   Regulating Plantations

- *Location:* The law may discourage or withhold benefits from plantations based on location or the state of the land before planting. Determining and controlling the appropriate location of forest planting is not simple. There may be reasons to treat afforestation, reforestation, and enrichment planting differently, but they are not so easily distinguished when a law is being drafted. Even a new plantation on essentially bare land may involve some residual clearing. An easier activity to regulate is the replacement of a natural forest with different species.[137] An example is found in the Irish Planning and Development Act (2000)[138] controlling the "replacement of broadleaf high forest by conifer species"; it is not forbidden but may require planning permission.

- *Permits for plantation:* Not all countries offer open-ended encouragement to forest plantations. In Southern Africa, where there is stiff competition between forest plantations and other vegetation for water, plantations require permission.[139] Even where planting is not limited, some record of plantations is likely to be useful if plantation produce enjoys different treatment from natural forest produce or if subsidies or tax credits are to be granted.

- *Limits on species:* The law may wish to restrict the species of trees that people can plant,[140] or replacement of a natural forest with a different species. In many areas the most profitable species to plant are exotics. The law may restrict which exotics may be planted or require clearance before new ones are introduced. An emerging issue is the use of genetically engineered planting stock—trees modified for faster growth, better quality fiber, or resistance to insects and disease. The environmental concerns about such trees may eventually lead to more widespread regulation of their use.

---

[137] *See supra* n. 101, art. 85.

[138] § 4(1)(i).

[139] Plantations are a "stream flow reducing activity" under the South African Water Act (1998), §§ 21(d), 22(1)(b), 36; for plantations of over 15 hectares in Namibia, *see* Forest Act (2001), § 23.

[140] Nicaragua, Ley Forestal (2003), § 25; *see* Benin, Law on Environment 98-030 (1999), § 56: forests must be protected against introduction of unadapted species.

PART THREE

Institutional Arrangements

CHAPTER 6

Public Institutions

Forestry institutions seem to be evolving rapidly. The standard forestry department operating in relative isolation and having sole responsibility for "forestry" is becoming rarer. The range of issues that must be considered has broadened, the constituencies concerned have both broadened and become more vocal, and there is greater need for forestry to justify itself both in the fight for public resources and as the discipline that should manage forest lands.

6.1 Roles of Minister and Forest Department

An issue that seems peculiar to forestry, at least among the natural resources, is the degree to which the responsible minister should be able to exercise his or her own judgment. It is often argued that because ministers are easily swayed by politics or corruption, reducing ministerial discretion will lead to better forestry. In particular cases this may be true; carried too far, it has the significant disadvantage that flexibility to meet new circumstances is lost.

One way to reduce aberrant decision-making without losing too much flexibility is to tie decisions, such as permissible harvests, to logical processes the results of which are to a degree binding. This is true of management plans, the potential contents of which may be very open but which constrain both official and private forest activities once adopted. As discussed in section 4.2, however, plans that are too complex and expensive will not be honored if adopted and the system will break down. A simpler but still useful measure is annual harvesting limits, with no cutting permit issued if it would breach the limit. The applicant would need to wait until the following year or buy out another's rights.

6.2 Coordinating Bodies

As the criteria for forest management have become enriched by biological diversity, recreational opportunities, integrated land-use planning, and greater recognition of traditional rights and general public interests, the capacity or willingness of forest departments to consider all relevant factors has been stretched. The range of participation in forestry decisions has been broadened with both public and interministerial participation on advisory bodies. This has been taken to such a level of complexity in Turkey that an environment and forestry assembly of

300 members has been created. It meets in plenary session every four years and in committees as necessary.[141]

Even as forestry institutions proliferate, nonforest institutions, especially those dealing with the environment, are also dealing with forestry in certain respects. National environmental councils may have a role in coordinating the activities of sectoral ministries. Peru has a clearly articulated structure of this sort. There is a national environmental management "system," of which the lead agency is the national environmental council.[142] The council's role is to "plan, promote, co-ordinate, regulate, enforce and oversee."[143] The national natural resource institute is still responsible for resources, including forestry, but is directed to provide reports and adopt measures necessary to minimize and control adverse environmental impacts.[144] Conflicts between agencies, such as the environmental council and the natural resources institute, may be brought to the tribunal for the resolution of environmental disputes.[145]

Other interministerial matters in which forestry interests are involved are water management, plant health, pesticides, biodiversity, and climate change. In all cases it is wise to ensure that the enabling legislation does not create conflicts or, where conflicts are inevitable, provides a sensible means of resolving them. Where decisions affecting forestry are made in other institutions, there should be a way to ensure that important forestry concerns are heard. This may entail representation on a coordinating or decision-making body (such as a pesticide registration body) or simply advance notice of proposed decisions. This is something that needs to be analyzed case by case.

A notable feature of the 1996 Bolivian forestry law is the creation of the Forest Superintendency (*Superintendencia Forestal*) as an independent technical, administrative, and economic agency. Empowered to grant 21 million hectares of

---

[141] *See* Turkey, Regulation on Environment and Forestry Assembly (2004).

[142] Peru, Ley marco del sistema nacional de gestión ambiental, Ley no. 28245 (2004), arts. 2 and 7.

[143] *Id.* art. 8:

El CONAM tiene por finalidad planificar, promover, coordinar, normar, sancionar y supervisar las acciones orientadas a la protección ambiental y contribuir a la conservación del patrimonio natural; controlar y velar el cumplimiento de las obligaciones ambientales; dirimir y solucionar las controversias entre las entidades públicas; y ejecutar las acciones derivadas de las funciones otorgadas por la presente Ley, su ley de creación y las normas modificatorias y complementarias.

[144] Peru, Decreto Supremo Nº 008-2005-PCM, Aprueba el Reglamento de la Ley Nº 28245, art. 11.

[145] *Id.* art. 12.

forest concessions, this government agency, whose structure incorporates civil society participation, has separate and balanced power in the forest sector. The creation of the Forest Superintendency meets the need for effective forest law enforcement, control, and supervision through activities that respond to and comply with the Bolivian forest code. The activities include collecting area-based forestry taxes as well as granting concessions. To prevent untoward political influence and corruption, the appointments of Senior Officers of the Forest Superintendency transcend electoral terms; the appointment of the Forest Superintendent is thus not affected by changes in administrations. The Superintendent is appointed for a six-year term by the president from a short list proposed by the Bolivian Congress. As head of a politically independent agency, the Forest Superintendent can only be removed by a Federal Court order and is responsible for managing the budget allocated directly by the central government. This process has attracted high-quality professionals who have demonstrated leadership, operational effectiveness, and transparency.

There is, however, potential for conflicts of interest. The Forest Superintendency grants concessions, collects forest fees, and approves management plans, while also being responsible for enforcing the laws regulating these concessions, especially those governing forest management plans, control, and supervision of forest products transportation, storage, processing, and trade. Such responsibilities as collecting taxes and approving forest management plans might be shifted to a Forest agency that in addition to serving as a policy unit could be responsible for other areas, such as approval of management plans and tax collection. In Peru, for example, granting forest concessions is the responsibility of an ad hoc and fixed-term Forest Commission, specifically set up to manage the concession-granting process.

6.3   Structures for Public Participation

Participation in planning, in community forestry, and generally is discussed in sections 4.2, 7.3, and 9.2. Structures for participation often have other roles, however. The forest advisory council, which at national and local levels is probably the typical body, is a good example. Some advisory councils do not really provide for public participation; essentially they are gatherings of forestry staff or other public officials.[146] Others include both official and nongovernmental members, the latter of which may include experts and representatives of public interests.[147]

---

[146] Vanuatu, Forestry Act (2001), § 6, schd. 1.

[147] Fiji, Forest Decree (1992), § 4; Namibia, Forest Act (2001), § 2.

Though it is not in the nature of advisory bodies to have decisional powers, some decision-making bodies have public members, such as the program committees of the forestry and wildlife funds in Cameroon.[148] Some advisory bodies have considerable legal force behind their advice, as in South Africa, where "The Minister must consider and respond to the advice provided to him or her by the Council."[149] In Nicaragua the national forestry commission, which has a substantial nongovernmental membership, has the power to approve the forest policy proposed by the ministry.[150]

Advisory bodies may also be weightier depending on the subjects on which they advise. A Minister who must submit certain questions for advice and publicize the recommendations of the committee is likely to cultivate good relations with the committee and the constituencies of its members. Some committees are also empowered to investigate and report without being asked.[151] Where the committee is limited to questions chosen by the minister, its power is correspondingly reduced.

6.4 Forest Commissions and Outsourcing

There is a general tendency in public administration to seek new ways to carry out public business. Governments are selling public enterprises (airports and highways as well as forests) to the private sector, outsourcing tasks to the private sector, and changing the legal and management structure of public institutions to a more "corporate" form.

Of the many varieties of reform in the forestry sector, the forest commission has been most significant. Reportedly beginning in Great Britain in 1919, it has replaced the traditional forest department in several common law countries. The British Forest Commissioners have the power to manage and use the forest estate entrusted to them[152] but not to buy or sell land. They depend on the minister for that.[153]

In Africa an early example was the Forestry Commission of Zimbabwe (then Southern Rhodesia), established in 1954.[154] The commission is a corporation

---

[148] Cameroon, Décret no. 96/237/PM of 1996 fixant les modalités de fonctionnement des Fonds Spéciaux etc., arts. 15–19; Tanzania, Forest Act (2002), § 29, schd. 2.

[149] South Africa, National Forests Act (1998), § 33(3).

[150] Nicaragua, Ley de Conservación, Fomento y Desarrollo Sostenible del Sector Forestal No. 462 of 2003, art. 5.

[151] Namibia, Forest Act (2001), § 3(c).

[152] United Kingdom, Forestry Act (1967), § 1.

[153] *Id.* § 39.

[154] Zimbabwe, Forest Act cap. 19:05, § 4.

subject to the direction of the minister.[155] It can buy and sell land and, with the consent of the minister, borrow money.[156]

Among the arguments in favor of forest commissions is their efficiency and their ability to act without political considerations, but it is doubtful that either has been borne out in practice in developing countries. Commissions are also sometimes able to avoid civil service salary limits, which makes them attractive to foresters and should allow them to recruit and motivate better staff.

A novel movement in recent years has been to engage private entities in traditional government functions.[157] In 1999 in an effort to reduce illegal logging Cambodia retained an international NGO to monitor its forest operations. This arrangement collapsed in 2003. At present a private consulting firm is auditing the Cambodian government's reporting of forest crime. Ecuador's *Vigilancia Verde* program formalized a role for civil society in timber transport inspections. In 2002 Ecuador tried to outsource many inspection functions to an international consulting firm, but the effort ran into legal hurdles. Opponents challenged the government's authority to delegate enforcement powers to a private business. The Republic of Congo has a private firm tracking logs and Papua New Guinea has privatized monitoring of timber exports. Legislation can clarify the authority of governments to delegate these roles, the duty of timber harvesters to cooperate with private monitors, and the power of any private monitors to collect fees, seize contraband, or arrest violators. This area is likely to engage lawmakers more in the future.

6.5   State Forest Corporations

Because the management of state production forests presents some of the same challenges as management of a private forest, many states have adopted the corporate form. Latvia has reduced the forest administration to a small policy unit, a compliance service, and the State Forest Corporation, which manages but does not own the state forests. The corporation is required to operate on a commercial basis. The next step in this process can be seen in Fiji where Fiji Hardwood

---

[155] *Id.* §§ 4, 12.

[156] *Id.* §§ 11, 21, and schd. 2. *See also* Sudan, National Forests Corporation Act (1989); Papua New Guinea, Forestry Act (1994), § 5.

[157] The discussion in this paragraph is drawn from A. Contreras and E. Peter, eds., *Best Practices for Improving Law Compliance in the Forestry Sector,* FAO Forestry Paper 145 (FAO 2005), ftp://ftp.fao.org/docrep/fao/008/a0146e/a0146e00.pdf; and A. de la Rochefordière, *Excluding Illegal Timber: Border Controls and Procurement—Making the System Work* (Royal Institute of International Affairs 2003), http://www.chathamhouse .org.uk/pdf/research/sdp/BorderControlsJan04.pdf.

Corporation has been converted into a "privatized company," which means that it can have private shareholders.[158]

While these experiments in public land management are going on, there has been a concerted effort to get the state out of logging and sawmilling. In the former socialist countries this has gone along with general economic and legal reform. One of the perhaps unintended consequences of privatization has been the creation of companies entirely staffed by former state employees to carry out functions like forest inventory and planning. Having only the forest administration as a client and no corporate culture, these companies do not have a bright future, and making use of their services mandatory for forest users is not likely to promote efficiency.

---

[158] Fiji, Mahogany Act (2003), §§ 2 and 3.

CHAPTER 7

Decentralization and Devolution

7.1 Similarities and Distinctions

This chapter addresses the legal aspects of two relatively recent trends in forest governance: decentralization of forest administration to local governments or administrative units, and devolution of rights and responsibilities over local forests to groups of local stakeholders, referred to variously as communities, community-based groups, management committees, or user groups (see Box 7–1).

These two topics are closely related; sometimes they may overlap to such an extent that they are difficult to differentiate. Both decentralization and devolution (as that term is used here) represent efforts to move forest management and decision-making closer to the forests themselves and to the people who in one way or another depend on them or interact with them regularly. They reflect a recognition that forest governance is enhanced if it is informed by local knowledge and if it engages the active attention and support of local people, whether these are public officials or private citizens. Thus they stem from a common conviction that almost everywhere forest administration and ownership have suffered from over-centralization. The result of this is that forestry authorities often lack the capacity to implement laws and programs effectively, and local actors feel disengaged from, if not antagonistic to, forest governance structures.

It is important, however, to draw some distinctions, or at least be alert to the ways decentralization and devolution agendas may diverge on the ground. Decentralization is in essence about restructuring government and enhancing the powers and capacities of local *public* administration. Community-based management is about strengthening the rights of different configurations of local, often non-governmental, *private* actors. Though these can be, and often are, mutually reinforcing processes, there is no reason they cannot proceed independently, and that has happened in various parts of the world.

For example, the fact that forest decision-making is relocated to a lower level of government is no guarantee that the interests of forest-dependent communities within that territorial unit will be looked after any more than they were before—though well-functioning democratic processes may increase the likelihood of this outcome. Among other factors, decentralization of forestry administration usually involves territorial units that are larger or differently configured than areas typically managed, or suitable for active management, by local groups of users or communities as traditionally defined. In a few cases, the structure of local government may be such that the territories and membership of the smallest administrative unit and a "traditional" forest-dependent community may be very similar, so that vesting powers in and allocating benefits to one or the other has virtually the same social and legal consequences. Because this is the exception rather than the rule, however, actively engaging local users even in a decentralized system may require an additional step. Some West African forest laws, for example, provide first for the decentralization of some administrative authority over forests to the commune level, and then allow for the possibility of commune administrations entering into site-specific management contracts with local user groups.

Another phenomenon is that community-based management is often a feature of the sectoral strategy of centralized forest administrations even as it is being advocated as part of overall government reform in support of decentralization. Too often these two processes are not carefully synchronized, either as policy or in practice. Specialized committees like forest protection committees, though supported by forest departments of the central government, may find themselves in an awkward relationship with local governments. Throughout the history of Joint Forest Management (JFM) in India, for example, there has been serious debate about the extent to which forest user committees should be independent of or subsumed by democratically elected village *panchayats*. Those in favor of independence have sometimes argued that both the special needs of vulnerable sections of society (women, tribes, scheduled castes—those most dependent on forests) and the national interest in maintaining forests would be jeopardized if the management were turned over to faction-ridden, corrupt local democracies. Failure to do so, others counter, would demonstrate how thin the commitment is to the ideal of local democracy.

In short, decentralization of forest governance and the promotion of forest management by community-based groups, while overlapping to a large extent, are not synonymous.

7.2 Decentralization

Decentralization is usually a phenomenon that affects government as a whole; it does not affect forestry more than other sectors. Nevertheless, it sometimes has consequences or unintended effects that are best appreciated sector by sector.

A common, and with a little care avoidable, problem is confusion between sweeping general decentralization laws and the centralist orientation of sectoral laws, new as well as old. Sometimes central bureaucracies attempt to use their influence over sectoral legislation to try to carve out exceptions to the general rule. These attempts have on occasion been abetted by international advisors, who tend to be specialists taking the perspective of their sector.

Box 7–1: Decentralization and Forest Administration in Bolivia

Bolivia provides a particularly interesting example of how decentralization of forestry administration has been reflected in the law, and how decentralization can grant even stronger rights to local user groups and communities. In 1994 the Popular Participation Law formally introduced political-administrative decentralization in Bolivia. Two years later the Agrarian Reform and the Forestry Law were approved, both conceived within the new decentralized context.[1] The 1996 Forest Law incorporated two mechanisms to stimulate democratization of access to forest resources:

- Indigenous Peoples have an exclusive right to use the forest resources within their territories, which are recognized legally with the new Agrarian Reform Law of 1996. According to this law, indigenous claims over land are considered to be titled after the appropriate land surveys and title assignments.
- Local forest user groups can benefit from forest concessions within areas declared as municipal forest reserves, which represent up to 20 percent of public forest within each municipal jurisdiction. Most of the indigenous groups located in lowlands Bolivia have the right to claim the lands that they consider are needed to guarantee their subsistence, though the claim must be assessed by the National Institute of Agrarian Reform (*Instituto Nacional de Reforma Agraria* or INRA).

The 1996 Forest Law granted forest management responsibilities to prefectures (art. 24), and municipalities (art. 25). The main prefecture responsibilities are to implement programs of public investment related to the forestry sector at the departmental level and create programs for strengthening the institutional capacities of municipalities. Municipal governments have been assigned such functions as monitoring logging activities and inspecting raw material supply and processing programs. They are also in charge of delimiting municipal forest reserves, allocating them to local user associations (*Asociacion Social del Lugar* or ASLs) (art. 31), and helping the associations with forest management. Municipalities are expected to create forestry municipal units (*Unidades Forestales Municipales* or UFMs) and maintain them by assigning them an annual share of forest taxes: 25 percent of forest extraction and conversion.[2]

[1] P. Pachego & D. Pachego, presentation, *Decentralization and Community Forestry: Main Approaches and Their Implications in the Lowlands of Bolivia*, Oaxaca, Mexico, Aug. 9–13, 2004 (Intl. Assoc. Study of Common Property, Tenth Biennial Conf.). http://dlc.dlib.indiana .edu/archive/00001460/00/Pacheco_Decentralization_040512_Paper472a.pdf.

[2] According to article 38 of the 1996 Forest Law, forest revenues are distributed as followed: (i) prefectures (35%), (ii) municipalities (25%), National Forest Development Fund (10%), and forestry superintendence (30%).

A common reason for wishing to retain central control over forestry is that even in forest poor countries it is a source of revenue. If not enough of the revenue is reinvested, the forest will deteriorate—and local governments are often viewed as short-sighted revenue-seekers. Since many experiments in decentralization have not been accompanied by corresponding shifts in public revenues, there is an understandable temptation to milk the revenue sources that are available locally.

A more serious problem than conflicting laws and policies is whether provincial or local governments have the capacity to administer and legislate for forests. In part, this again relates to financial resources and the ability to hire and train the necessary staff.

Decentralization is very recent; experience necessarily takes time to acquire. Moreover, local governments tend to be weaker than the national government in negotiation, law enforcement, and other functions needed for managing large forest resources. This may justify decentralized bodies calling upon central resources (or being forced to do so) when they deal with concessions and other major transactions.

Another concern is that local governments are more insulated than national governments from international norms, which have been a major force for progressive reform of forest management. In local areas with large amounts of forest, the relative contribution of the forest to the economy is likely to be more obvious than on the national level, and economic uses of the forest are likely to carry greater weight. Issues like biodiversity or carbon sequestration are thus likely to lose priority when there is decentralization. To minimize these problems, the central government can retain the role of setting general goals of management and minimum standards for forest practices. It can also retain an auditing or oversight function.

Yet there are good reasons for forestry to be selected for decentralization even if other matters are not. In principle decentralization should bring decision-making closer to the people, helping to satisfy a generally accepted need for popular participation in decision-making. Much of forest administration is also inextricable from land-use regulation, which is typically a local responsibility even in relatively centralized systems.

The transfer of responsibilities needs to be, but often is not, accompanied by the transfer of sufficient financial resources to fulfill the responsibilities. Often in developing countries ministries of finance resist transferring adequate funds to territorial administrations, even where those funds consist essentially of forest-related taxes and forest services fees from a particular area. Different options have been tested:

- Allocation by the state of a lump sum to cover permanent responsibilities that are transferred to a territorial administration. The lump sum can be fixed for a few years in order to assess how forests are being managed and how the funds are administered.

- Creation of a revolving fund financed from resources from international development partners and some forest-related taxes and fees. Territorial administrations benefit from the fund under specified conditions. The funds could be allocated for education, health, infrastructure, and other matters related to building local communities—such as forestry.
- Creation of an adjustment system to enable administrations of territories where forest resources are less abundant to benefit more from the rotation fund. This approach amounts to a mutual aid fund system between "rich" and "poor" forest administrations.

Local administrations often lack the qualified staff they need to achieve their mandate. As an initial response, the transfer of responsibilities should be accompanied by an interim transfer of staff from the central to the territorial administrations. Transferred staff would help local authorities manage forest lands and resources and improve their management capacity. In Burkina Faso and Mali, for instance, the decentralization law specifies the appointment and training of territorial administration staff.

Naturally, civil servants may be reluctant to transfer from central to territorial administrations for two reasons: First, they fear that they will lose powers and responsibilities as a consequence of the transfer and, second, territorial civil services are generally considered less remunerative and prestigious in terms of status and career opportunities. For this reason, the *Commission nationale de la décentralisation* created in Burkina Faso to supervise decentralization has recommended that the status of the national civil service be the reference for drafting territorial civil service status, so that both national and territorial staff will have similar rights and obligations.

7.3   Devolution to Community-Based Groups

To avoid problems that come with too much centralization, devolution has become a popular option.

7.3.1   Growth in Community-Based Approaches in Forest Law

In the last two decades local people and rural communities have assumed increasing prominence in national forest management legislation, regulation, and strategies. In policies and in the design of ground-level interventions, terms like community forestry, community-based forest management (CFM), comanagement, joint management, collaborative management, devolution, and participatory local forest management have all become commonplace. The World Bank's Forest Strategy in fact calls for support to "policy and legislative reforms needed to implement CFM, giving emphasis to tailoring designs to local needs."[159]

Until lately national forestry and land laws have not typically encouraged the participation of local people in forest management. Indeed, in many parts of the world the trend until recently was to assert government legal control over forest resources at the expense of local populations. While there has often been some legal recognition of limited use, usually for subsistence purposes, most laws provided little scope for local people to play a meaningful part in the planning, management, and allocation of the forest resources on which they may have depended for generations—and which, in some cases, they may have actively managed and protected in accordance with long-standing traditional rules.

In recent years, however, in the wake of widespread experimentation with and rhetorical endorsement of community-based management, mechanisms for granting or recognizing the rights of local groups to participate in forest management are now common features of laws governing forests.

The main impetus for promoting greater local involvement in management may come from any of several different directions[160]:

- It may originate from a conviction that local management leads to more effective conservation, protection, and afforestation.
- It may be intended to help enhance local livelihoods.
- It may be driven by local demands for the recognition of long-standing land claims, especially where indigenous groups are asserting historical claims.
- It may be related to governance reform in general, especially promotion of local democratic institutions.

Because the mix of motivations varies greatly from place to place, the design of participatory forest management approaches takes many different forms depending on the goals of participation, how participation is to be structured, and who should participate. At one end of the spectrum of approaches (perhaps with the greatest number of examples) are narrowly defined participatory processes with a time-bound sectoral agenda driven primarily by the national forestry department. In such models, the rights, benefits, and decision-making powers of the groups participating are relatively limited. At the other end are models that

---

[159] *See supra* n. 46. The Bank Forest Strategy is discussed and cited in the opening chapter.

[160] J. Arnold, *Managing Forests as Common Property* (FAO 1998).

seek to nest management within a vision of local democracy that vests decision-making power and ownership in local communities, with foresters playing only a technical advisory role.

Legal changes that have enhanced the opportunity for local involvement have taken such forms as

- **Management of selected state forest areas turned over to local user groups.** Nepal's 1993 Forest Act is well-known: A Forest User Group is formed by the people themselves. In consultation with the forest department, they draw up a management plan. They are then entrusted with the responsibility for managing the forest according to the plan. Ownership of the land remains with the state, and the Forest Department has the right of veto if management rules are transgressed, but the User Group has the right to harvest and benefit from all products listed in the management plan.

- **Joint management or comanagement of state forest land.** This differs from the first approach only in the sense that the role of the forest department in management is more clearly spelled out. JFM in India pioneered the idea of agreements between forest departments and local groups in which management responsibilities and benefits are shared. The structure of these agreements differed, with a variety of formulas and conditions and with schedules that vary significantly from state to state. Forms of comanagement are found all over the world, from the Philippines to Canada (British Columbia) to South Africa to Mexico, either spelled out in forestry statutes or effected through regulation.

- **Limited rights of access and use permitted in state-owned protected areas or buffer zones.** Not specifically a forest management model, this refers to the fact that in protected-area legislation in many parts of the world (most notably in Latin America but elsewhere as well), there are increasing examples of people being given limited access and use rights either in the protected areas themselves or in buffer zones around them.

- **State land leased for forestry purposes.** This is an approach used in the Philippines, Nepal, and a number of other countries, with permitted lessees being either individuals or local groups. These are often seen by governments as a way to get degraded land replanted (as in Nepal, Sri Lanka, Uganda, or Vietnam), although they may also be considered for productive, well-stocked forest (as in the Kyrgyz Republic). The Philippines has transferred some lands formerly under timber license to local communities. The management agreements specifically allow for timber harvesting, although there is currently a moratorium.

- **Local management of community or privately owned land.** In recent years, some countries have given increasing recognition to the historical land or territorial claims of local peoples. The Indigenous Peoples' Rights Act (1997) in the Philippines is an example, and the rights of indigenous communities figure prominently in several Latin American laws. Australia, Canada, South Africa, and several countries in Central and Eastern Europe, among others, are restoring the lands of dispossessed communities and individuals, some of which bear natural forests or commercial plantations. In other cases, communal ownership of some forest land has long been recognized by law, and forest laws have provided tools for community-based management, as in parts of Austria and Switzerland.

- **Local benefits granted without direct control.** Sometimes the central forest administration does not wish to vest control in the hands of the community but wishes to grant it some share of benefits. The Kosovo Forest Law (2003) actually centralized administration, shifting management control from regional state enterprises and municipalities to the new central Forest Agency. In return, the law[161] grants the municipalities 20 percent of the revenues from timber harvest licenses. In the United States 25 percent of receipts from the national forests go to state governments to be used for schools and roads in the jurisdictions where the forest is located.[162]

Despite the fact that legal provisions in support of community-based management are now widespread, their implementation often lags far behind due to an absence of political will, weak capacities of both local and government partners, and the technical, social, and economic challenges of making local management a sustainable success. Moreover, as will be explored below, none of these legal innovations is perfect, and in many places the laws are poorly drafted or riddled with contradictions. There is, however, an unmistakable trend in the national laws toward greater local management of forests.

7.3.2 Defining the "Community"

Even where the law is clear that the "community" is granted certain rights and responsibilities, it often does not make clear just what constitutes a community.

7.3.2.1 Models for Defining the Management Group

Who are the rights holders? How do they govern themselves? And how do they fit into the larger governance sphere? The difficulties of defining what is a community or an appropriate community-based group for purposes of local management

---

[161] Kosovo, Forest Law, § 21.5(b).

[162] 16 U.S.C. § 500 (2004).

strategies have been extensively debated in development and social science litera-ture. For legal drafters, finding a way through these difficulties is both essential and unavoidable for one simple reason: if a law is to vest or recognize rights and responsibilities in a group or entity, it obviously needs to identify, or provide a process for identifying, who or what that group or entity is.

In recent laws and regulations, we find a variety of different models:

- *The user group model:* This is epitomized by the Nepal Forest Law (1993). In theory, it is a self-identifying group of households united by a common interest in a particular resource, often based on historical practice. Again in theory, there need be no convergence between such groups and other local community identities and institutions or administrative arrangements. In Nepal, for example, the law states that user groups may straddle *panchayat* (local government) boundaries and that households can be members of more than one user group.
- *The adjacent community model:* This may be very similar to the user group model except that there is an attempt to define beforehand the pool of eligible participants by reference to geographical limitations. Thus, some JFM resolutions in India talk in terms of villages adjacent to a forest as the predefined unit from which forest protection committees may emerge.
- *Indigenous or community land-holding model:* Here (again in theory) the impetus is quite different from the first two models. Local resource manage-ment in this model is incident to the deeper struggle by local people for self-determination based on historically verifiable notions of community identity and territorial control. The Mozambique Land Law and the Philippines Indigenous Peoples' Rights Act are two recent examples. Both laws contain elaborate procedures by which groups identify themselves and negotiate their territorial limits with adjoining people and the government. To varying degrees land tenure and management within identified areas are recognized as being governed by the customary law of the identified community.
- *Local government model:* Finally, local management may be part of a wider agenda of decentralization, and laws may vest resource management rights in local governments. The extent to which these governments repre-sent a local vision of community or can serve as a platform for true local participation varies significantly. Ribot has shown how in West Africa much of the decentralization of forest and land management has not been accompanied by downward accountability to the people themselves.[163]

---

[163] J. Ribot, *Democratic Decentralization of Natural Resources: Institutionalizing Popular Participation* (World Resources Institute 2002).

There are, however, at least potentially more positive examples. The Tanzanian land, forestry, and local government laws, taken together, represent a potential merging of robust local democracy with the assertion of community property rights over local resources.[164]

Looking across this crude typology of often overlapping legal approaches, we can identify recurring problem areas and issues associated with several or all of them, which are discussed next.

7.3.2.2 Membership Criteria

Because community-based forestry is intended at least in part to enhance local livelihoods, the criteria for the composition of an eligible forest user group become very important. Group formation should not be a vehicle that allows outsiders to acquire interests in a local forest to the detriment of local people. Appropriately, therefore, forest laws sometimes impose requirements to ensure that membership is based on residency either for all group members or for a very high percentage of them. The laws may leave open the possibility for groups to invite outsiders to participate as investors or to contract with outsiders for service.

Yet care also needs to be taken to ensure that membership criteria are not unduly limited or unfairly exclusionary. In some countries agreements are fashioned between the government and "people's organizations" that may represent only a fraction of the community. Problems can also arise where definitions of user or other forest management groups result in the exclusion of some persons who may have a legitimate stake in the forest. The classic examples are cases where secondary or transient users of a resource suddenly find their access cut off by a comanagement agreement between a local group and a forest department—a problem that from the beginning has beset JFM in India. While this type of exclusion may be driven by politics and power grabs, it is exacerbated by a tendency to resort to simplistic one-to-one legal relationships between narrowly defined communities and particular resources. Local groups may themselves seize upon the opportunity the laws provide to exclude long-term but distant users.

Laws can help reduce the possibility of this happening by setting out a careful process of identifying all those with legitimate interests in the resource. A number of laws, for example, require public consultation and open access to information before an area is assigned to a particular group. Of course, accommodating diverse and distant stakeholders within a well-functioning, cohesive management group may not be feasible; as a practical matter, some uses of the contracted area may

---

[164] L. Alden Wily, *Forest Law in Eastern and Southern Africa:Moving Towards a Community-Based Forest Future?* UNASYLVA, No. 203, Vol. 51 (2000).

need to be cut off or relocated if forest management is to succeed. In this respect, creation of a "community forest" is no different than creation of a forest reserve: some disruption of traditional rights or practices may be unavoidable, but laws also need to provide for satisfactory mitigation measures.

7.3.2.3 Legal Status and Institutional Forms

Most countries trying to promote greater local involvement provide for formation or recognition of local legal entities (villages, societies, committees, forest user groups, cooperatives, and so on) for participation in community and smallholder forestry. Depending on the country, the mechanisms may be created by the forestry law itself or by general laws of association. Status as a legal entity is usually necessary for community-based groups to engage in economic activities, open bank accounts, own property, sue and be sued, and contract with outsiders.

It is increasingly recognized that such mechanisms need to be both socially appropriate and easy for people to use. Imposition on people of institutional arrangements that are out of step with their traditions, their aspirations, and their capacities can *disable* rather than *enable* participation. Unfortunately, the framers of some laws that are otherwise supportive of participation failed to take this fully into account, and instead require local groups to adopt organizational forms that are too complex, alien to a local situation, and expensive to establish. This may lead to the creation of legal entities that have little legitimacy among their members, allowing more sophisticated group members opportunities to gain advantage by manipulating unfamiliar legal forms. This phenomenon is now well documented in Australia and Papua-New Guinea[165]; in connection with the Communal Property Associations Act in South Africa[166]; for native corporations in Alaska[167]; and for community-based forest management in Uttarakhand, India.[168] It can also seriously delay initiation of local management if the process of getting the legal entity registered is too lengthy.

Law drafters and governments often prefer community management groups to look more or less the same in terms of make up, structure, size, and jurisdictional

---

[165] J. Fingleton, *Legal Recognition of Indigenous Groups,* FAO Legal Paper Online No. 1 (FAO 1998).

[166] T. Cousins & D. Hornby, *Leaping the Fissures: Bridging the Gap Between Paper and Real Practice in Setting Up Common Property Institutions in Land Reform in South Africa* (CASS/PLAAS 2000).

[167] H. Jacobs, & B. Hirsch, *Indigenous Land Tenure and Land Use in Alaska: Community Impacts of the Alaska Native Claims Settlement Act* (Land Tenure Center, U. Wis.-Madison 1998).

[168] M. Sarin, N. Singh, N. Sundar, & R. Bhogal, *Devolution as a Threat to Democratic Decision-making in Forestry? Findings from Three States in India* (ODI 2003).

areas. Imposing such a vision, however, can come at the cost of the diversity. It can be particularly counter-productive where one of the goals has been to build on institutions and management arrangements that have in fact been working. Hence, some laws avoid spelling out detailed governance structures and processes that eligible groups would need to comply with. They favor a more flexible approach that allows groups, for example, to resolve conflicts according to customary law and to define decision-making roles as they see fit, subject to minimum standards of transparency and accountability.

7.3.2.4   Deciding on the Area

Just as the criteria for membership in a group should be fair and applied transparently, so should the process for determining the area over which a particular group will have rights. If the boundaries of the management area are defined inappropriately, some people who traditionally use the area may be excluded.

Aside from the problem of fairness between neighboring communities, there is also a need to put in place an open and responsive process by which the government receives, considers, and decides upon the requests of community groups for areas to be assigned to them. In many parts of the world, the most frequent problem is not that excessively large areas are granted to groups, but that *no* area or *the wrong* area is assigned, often with no explanation and little or no consultation with a claimant group. In other words, local people have essentially no say in the process. Some laws try to reduce this problem by requiring that decisions be open and given within a specified time period; that reasons for rejection be given in writing; and that there be a process of public consultation.

The area allocated and the rights to it need to be sufficiently well defined to make the group's jurisdiction clear. It has been argued that too much certainty is not necessarily compatible with a certain tolerance among neighboring groups in traditional lifestyles, and that attempting to demarcate areas creates conflict that could otherwise be avoided. This may be true in some situations, and the lawmaker has to be sensitive to the possibility, but it seems likely that demarcation will be increasingly needed as populations grow and other users (industrial logging, commercial agriculture) impinge on the traditional space.

7.3.3   The Nature, Scope, and Security of Rights

7.3.3.1   Benefits

Sustained involvement by local people in forest management requires that they see clear benefits to their livelihoods from the involvement. Where the benefits are not clear, or where the responsibilities of participants to protect and conserve resources outweigh the benefits they receive, they have little incentive to participate.

Internationally, some legal frameworks designed to promote community-based management fail to observe this principle. After creating a mechanism by which groups can acquire rights over local forests, they then severely restrict the types of activities or forest utilization the groups can engage in. For example, some laws put great emphasis on community groups protecting forests but offer them little prospect to actually realize any significant monetary or other livelihood benefits from the forest they protect. Other laws[169] put no significant restrictions on the types of benefits that can be enjoyed as long as they are within the strictures of the agreed management plan.

Of course, not every forest area is suitable for a community-based management approach that involves significant utilization. Particularly sensitive ecosystems and habitats, for example, may not lend themselves to this approach (though even in such settings, there is often more scope for local involvement than is typically appreciated). However, this is better analyzed by looking at the local context, rather than by overly broad application of uniform and restrictive rules.

7.3.3.2   Management and Control

In older forest laws, management planning was viewed as a technical exercise undertaken by foresters, with no consultation required or contemplated. Moreover, in practice, planning criteria and objectives have until relatively recently focused mainly on trees. Social functions, water production, and biodiversity values of forests and nonwood forest products were generally underemphasized.

Management of local forests by and for local people requires a new approach. Most laws supporting community-based management now provide for some sort of local planning process for community or locally managed forests. The plan then serves as the basis for the agreement between the government and the group.

However, even in some new laws what is striking is the extent to which government hangs on to the decision-making function. Often regulations about comanagement continue to vest almost all management decisions in government. Such a top-down approach increases the risk that management choices will be made that do not reflect the actual priorities and needs of local people, or take into account their direct knowledge of the resource. Critics also point out that these planning requirements are often highly complex, requiring expertise to prepare that only a trained forester can provide. As one observer of Nepal commented: "The writing of FUG [forest user group] constitutions is a forest ranger's task,

---

[169] *See supra* n. 9.

since it requires the rigid use of legal language and the establishment of an inventory and a maximum sustainable yield."[170] In other cases management options may be preempted by the need to link local plans to regional forestry objectives, about which local people are likely to have little say.

In response to concerns like these, some analysts argue that laws need to be reformed to reflect a more sensible approach to defining the scope of "local" decisions, with a more rigorous and narrower identification of the priorities that might justify outside interference. Ribot, for example, calls for setting "minimal environmental standards" against which local management activities can be judged, rather than imposing complex planning requirements.[171] A number of recent laws (see § 4.2 above), such as those from Tanzania and the Gambia, have introduced simplified planning procedures in the context of community management to ensure greater local ownership of the decision made.

Quite a few laws worldwide also prescribe how the community is to use the proceeds of economic activities—that is, a certain percent must be reinvested into protection or reforestation or community development activities. It may be desirable to target some of the benefits on community needs, in order to maintain the spirit of a community-based enterprise, but reducing the flexibility of group members to decide for themselves how to use the benefits can also undermine incentives. A proper balance must be sought.

7.3.3.3   Security of Rights

Although the nature of the rights local people have with respect to the resource can vary considerably from model to model, one principle should apply in any context: if for an individual community effort is to be successful, it must not only provide a realistic hope of significant benefits, it must instill confidence that the rights to those benefits are secure. This principle applies however limited or extensive the rights granted may be.

Security is, of course, in part a state of mind. Where relations between community and government have traditionally been good, local people might feel secure enough to undertake management simply on the basis of a promise from local officials. Sometimes a sense of security is derived from the fact that a particular management arrangement is part of a donor-funded project and thus unlikely to be derailed as long as funds flow—a type of security that may prove to

---

[170] H. Tanaka, *Forest Management Plans for Collective Forest Managers in Developing Countries: A Review of Constraints and Promising Experience* (FAO 2002).

[171] J. Ribot, paper, *Decentralization Without Representation: Rural Authority and Popular Participation in Sahelian Forestry* (FAO Tech. Consultation on Decent., Rome, Dec. 16–18, 1997).

be illusory over time. In other situations, communities may not feel secure no matter how carefully and strongly their rights are set forth in legal documents.[172] Some indicators of insecurity to look for in a law are the following:

- *The threat of unilateral termination or changes in midstream.* The security of a local management arrangement is often weakened by apparently wide government powers to terminate the arrangement. The grounds for termination may be poorly defined or vaguely spelled out, with the result that a significant amount of discretionary power is vested in a government agent. Fisheries comanagement in Sri Lanka is a case in point: the Minister is given wide discretion to terminate an agreement for any reason. At the heart of this phenomenon is a lingering tendency to treat community management arrangements as a favor bestowed by government rather than a legally binding agreement. Where a community group contests termination, the law may limit recourse to levels of officials within the relevant ministry, which is like vesting the power to arbitrate contract disputes in one of the parties to a contract.

A number of recent laws have included provisions to reduce the potential for inappropriate termination. Sometimes, termination requires the payment of compensation. Other laws now contain much clearer criteria for determining whether a serious breach has occurred that would allow the government to take disciplinary action, and spell out steps for inquiry, notice, and review.[173]

Insecurity arising from the unilateral actions of government may not apply simply at the level of individual local arrangements—it can permeate the legal framework for local management. Government forestry policy changes in Nepal and Lao PDR, for example, are often cited as examples of government back-tracking that could make it difficult for those who agreed to participate when the rules of the game were more favorable to effectively realize any benefits. In India, despite several attempts to amend the Forest Act (1927) to provide a firm legal basis for joint forest management, the program continues to be a creation of state government notifications and administrative orders. While this does offer opportunities for flexibility in responding to experiences and problems encountered, it also fosters a sense among some government officials that the rights of participants are

---

[172] J. Lindsay, *Creating Legal Space for Community-based Management: Principles and Dilemmas,* in *Decentralization and Devolution of Forest Management in Asia and the Pacific* (T. Enters, B. Patrick, P. Durs, & M. Victor, eds., FAO and RECOFTC 2000).

[173] The Gambia Forest Act (1998).

malleable and temporary and can be changed unilaterally if government decides conditions warrant.[174]

- **Short duration of rights.** A sense of security is naturally undercut to the extent the rights do not last long. This arises in some leasing or comanagement arrangements where the terms imposed are so short that they call into question whether the benefits of participation can be fully realized by those incurring the initial costs. Rights need to be extended enough that a group feels real commitment to the area it manages and feels secure about investing time and effort into it. Theoretically, this sense of security is maximized if the rights are perpetual—that is, the group actually owns the resource or has some other type of open-ended arrangement that will continue indefinitely, subject to revocation perhaps, but only in cases of extreme abuse or abandonment. Not all countries are ready to use such an approach in participatory forestry contexts, though it may be a long-range goal and is being used with apparent success in a number of places. If rights are to be in force only for a specified time—as in co-management arrangements or community forestry leases—care should be taken to ensure that agreements are at least as long as is realistically required to reap the benefits of participation. Some of India's JFM programs, for example, prescribe terms of between five and ten years. Such provisions (which are fairly typical of comanagement in other countries as well) may create the impression of a one-shot approach that could undermine the community sense of ownership of the resources and undermined its long-term commitment to management.

- **Unclear rights to exclude others from the resource and enforce rules against outsiders.** The right to exclude is a classic property right. Local rights holders need to be able to control the access of outsiders to the resource and to call upon government to help enforce this right as would any other private property owner (see also "Enforceability of Rights" below). Yet a number of laws that allow for community-based management do not make clear the right to exclude. The definition of who is an "outsider" is in itself a difficult question, as will be discussed below. "Exclusivity" does not mean that there are no people outside the group responsible for management that might have rights that need to be respected. Distant or sporadic users of a resource may have legitimate historical claims. "Exclusive" also does not mean that resources cannot be shared—simply that the group that holds the right should be involved in the decision to share. Finally, "exclusive" does not mean "exclusionary"—it

---

[174] *See* Lindsay, *supra* n. 14.

does not mean that community members who want to participate in management can be unfairly excluded from the group.

What exclusivity does mean is that once the holders of rights have been defined, other users cannot be imposed on the group against its will. Government, for example, cannot assign rights to others over the same resource (such as giving cutting licenses for a community forest to outsiders). It also means that government needs to recognize the power of the community group to apply its rules to outsiders, and where necessary to assist in enforcement and protection of the group's rights from outside interference.

- *Enforceability of rights:* A common complaint among those participating in community-based management is that they have no clear power to directly apprehend outsider violators or to sanction members of their own group who violate the rules. One response to this problem has been to spell out in the law that whenever someone violates the approved management plan for a community-based forest management area, that person is in effect committing an offense under the forestry law. Another is to explicitly give power to community members (or specially designated members) to act as forest guards, with authority equivalent to any other forest guard under the forestry law.

Box 7–2 (see next page) presents a checklist against which community-based forestry arrangements, as expressed in laws, regulations, or individual agreements, can be tested with respect to the security they provide to rights-holders.

Box 7–2: Security in the Context of Community-based Forest Management

1. **Security requires that there be clarity as to what the rights are.** Confusion about the rights of a group and the rights of individuals within that group can significantly undermine the effectiveness and enthusiasm with which those rights are exercised.
2. **Security requires certainty that rights cannot be taken away or changed unilaterally and unfairly.** In almost any situation, of course, there are circumstances where rights can be taken away or diminished, but conditions for doing so need to be fair and clearly spelled out, with fair and transparent procedures for doing so, and the issue of compensation needs to be addressed.
3. **Security is enhanced if rights endure either in perpetuity or for a period clearly spelled out and long enough for the benefits of participation to be fully realized.** If rights are to be in force only for a particular period—as in some comanagement arrangements or community forestry leases care should be taken to ensure that agreements are made for at least as long as is realistically required to reap the benefits of participation.
4. **Security means that rights need to be enforceable against the state (including local government).** The legal system has to recognize that the state has an obligation to respect those rights.
5. **Security requires that the rights be exclusive.** The holders of rights need to be able to exclude or control the access of outsiders to the resource over which they have rights.
6. A corollary to exclusivity is that **there must be certainty both about the boundaries of the resources to which the rights apply and about who is entitled to claim membership in the group.**
7. Another corollary where comanagement concerns government land is that the **government entity entering into the agreement must have clear authority to do so.** An agreement should only reflect government promises that the responsible authority is empowered to fulfill.
8. **Security requires that the law recognize the holder of the rights.** The law should provide a way for the holder of the rights to acquire a legal personality, with the capacity to take a wide range of steps, such as applying for credits and subsidies, entering into contracts with outsiders, or collecting fees.
9. Finally, and perhaps most daunting, security requires **accessible, affordable, and fair avenues for seeking protection of the rights,** solving disputes, and appealing decisions of government officials.

Source: J. Lindsay, *Creating Legal Space for Community-based Management: Principles and Dilemmas,* in *Decentralization and Devolution of Forest Management in Asia and the Pacific* (T. Enters, B. Patrick, P. Durst, & M. Victor, eds., FAO and RECOFTC 2000).

CHAPTER **8**

Good Governance

Though legislation alone cannot ensure good governance, it can establish certain prerequisites, such as "to provide scope for meaningful participation in forest decision-making; to increase the stake that people have in sustainable management; to improve the transparency and accountability of forest institutions; and to set forth rules that are coherent, realistic and comprehensive."[175] By this measure, good governance is intimately related to the subjects of decentralization and devolution already discussed. This chapter will address more general aspects of good governance—specifically, transparency and disclosure, public participation, and accountability—and then consider the lawmaker's role in combating illegal acts and corruption.

8.1   Transparency and Disclosure

Transparency means allowing stakeholders to see what is happening in forest administration. The idea is that governments, businesses, and individuals will be much less likely to act against prevailing norms, social or legal, if those acts are open to scrutiny.[176]

---

[175] *See* J. Lindsay, A. Mekouar, & L. Christy, *Why Law Matters: Design Principles for Strengthening the Role of Forestry Legislation in Reducing Illegal Activities and Corrupt Practices,* 11 FAO Legal Papers Online No 27 (FAO 2002), http://www.fao.org/legal/prs-ol/lpo27.pdf.

[176] For some thoughts on transparency in forestry, *see* the report prepared by Global Witness, *Forest Law Enforcement in Cameroon,* 1st Summary Report of the Independent Observer, May—November 2001, (Global Witness 2002), http://www.globalwitness.org/reports/show.php/en.00027.html. One of the Recommendations of the African Forest Law Enforcement and Governance (AFLEG) Ministerial Conference in 2003 is specific to transparency:

—Improve access to information through strengthening local, national and regional mechanisms for sharing and exchanging information on forest management (for example, concession agreements, concession maps production and export data for timber and non-timber products, tax payment by logging companies, report on forest infractions etc.);

—Establish a public accessible centralized data based/register system for each sub region for violation of forestry laws to serve as a tool for monitoring industrial forest companies activities;

—Develop mechanisms to conduct independent forest assessment and monitoring (for example, independent observer in Cameroon);

The first step toward transparency is making the legal norms freely available to the public. Some countries fail to publish their forest laws. Agencies claim to act pursuant to regulations that no one outside the agency has seen. Ideally countries should publish all their laws. If this is not done as a matter of course, the forest law should require that forest regulations be published before they become effective, and agency rules can allow public inspection of compilations of regulations at forest agency offices.

If a country does not have a general law concerning public access to government documents, or if that general law does not serve forest administration well, the forest law may specify what agency documents the public should be allowed to inspect. These could include forest management plans, environmental assessments, inventory data, concessions contracts, records of concessions payments due and received, and community management agreements. Indeed, the law could with limited exceptions make all forest administration documents public. The exceptions might include disclosures that would hamper law enforcement (for example, duty assignments for forest inspectors who conduct surprise visits to concession sites); lead to environmental harm (population surveys of animals subject to poaching); violate personal privacy without good cause (medical records from the agency's first aid station); or, in rare cases, affect national security (maps of roads in a forest near a contested border).

There are a number of examples of document disclosure provisions in recent forest laws. Nicaragua's *Ley de Conservaciòn, Fomento y Desarrollo Sostenible del Sector Forestal* (2003) creates a national public registry of forest-related information, including management plans, inventories, and permits.[177] Kosovo's Forest Law (2003) requires the forest agency and ministry to make available rules, plans, and inventories.[178] In contrast, the Tanzanian Forest Act (2002) allows but does not require forest officials to release information to the public.[179]

For information to be useful, it must be understandable. Where the agency is preparing public documents like management plans and environmental studies, the law may reasonably require the agency to write in a style suitable for a general audience. For example, in the United States, the regulatory framework for environmental impact assessment requires that assessments be in plain language

---

—Ensure effective participation of civil society, indigenous and local communities in the policy development process and their implementation;
—Develop and encourage mechanisms that compel accountability from government and the forest companies operating concessions.

[177] Art. 8.

[178] Arts. 17 and 35.

[179] § 7.

so that the public and decision-makers can readily understand them.[180] In countries with multiple languages, the law might require the agency to provide copies of plans and studies in the local language.

Private businesses will want protection for confidential business information submitted to the government, such as prospecting data submitted to back a request for a concession. Such information could be of value to competitors also seeking the concession. This is a tricky area because local communities and the public often have an interest in access to these data. One approach is to allow protection from disclosure for a narrow range of items, such as prospecting reports; require the business to request protection for each document; and require the government to make public the reason for granting the request. Another approach is to allow disclosure after sufficient time has passed. Liberia's Forest Act (2000) creates a two-year limit on confidentiality of prospecting data submitted to the government.[181]

The law can mandate disclosure about forest agency administration. Even in cultures where people are reluctant to disclose financial or internal organizational data, disclosure of agency organization, job descriptions, staffing levels, senior staff backgrounds, budgets, revenues, purchases, and salaries can prompt healthy questions about work levels, ghost employees, and the standards of living enjoyed by presumably honest government workers. Organization charts can help citizens and civil society groups locate the proper official to answer inquiries or field complaints.

Besides disclosure of government documents, the law can require certain personal disclosures of senior officials. For example, Ghana's Forestry Commission Act[182] requires members to disclose if they have an interest in matters before the commission and if so to recuse themselves. The Indian Forest Act (1927) has a prohibition on forest officers having business interests in the sector unless they have written permission from the government.[183] As an alternative to a prohibition, the law could require forest officers to file annual disclosures of business interests and senior officers to disclose significant gifts or payments they or their families receive—again, a step short of an outright prohibition.

Though transparency is a matter of information, not regulation or punishment, transparency measures are often the most controversial part of a proposed forest

---

[180] 40 C.F.R. § 1502.8.

[181] § 152.

[182] *See* art. 7.

[183] *See* art. 75.

law, particularly within the forest administration. The reality is that despite strong efforts to empower communities and civil society, the forest administration will often have far more influence than the public over forest law reform. Forest officials may tolerate efforts to make rules and plans public, but they tend to more defensive about information that might invade their privacy or shed light on personal malfeasance.

The result is that powerful transparency provisions are still rare, though the drafter can find ideas and models in some European and North American instruments. The Aarhus Convention promotes and ensures the role of the public in making decisions about the environment.[184] The United States Freedom of Information Act is a general transparency law, complex but containing useful ideas.[185]

8.2   Public Participation

Availability of information sets the stage for public participation. The forest administration may be expert in the technical aspects of forestry, but the public knows its own values and needs. Without public participation the forest administration will be far less responsive to those needs. Public participation also helps foster a sense of ownership of forest law and policy. Without public support, forest laws are difficult to enforce.[186]

Opportunities for public participation opportunities from simple public notice of pending agency action with no special procedure for the public to intervene all the way to requirements that the agency get the consent of an affected group before proceeding. On the spectrum between these two options are requirements to accept comments from the public and to actively seek comments or consult with affected interests.

A number of international bodies and intergovernmental organizations have recognized the right of the public to participate in decisions that affect them. For example, the World Bank has noted its support for a process of free, prior, and informed consultation with affected communities that leads to their acceptance of a project.[187] The World Commission on Dams has supported the right to consent

---

[184] *See* UN Economic Commission of Europe's Convention on Access to Information, Public Participation in Decision-Making and Access to Justice in Environmental Matters of June 25, 1998, 38 ILM 517 (1999), art. 3(9).

[185] 5 U.S.C. § 552 (2004).

[186] *See* Principle 4 in Lindsay *et al., supra* n. 17.

[187] *See., e.g.,* World Bank, *Draft World Bank Group Management Response to the Extractive Industries Review,* 9–11, June 4, 2004; World Bank, Draft Operational Policy on Indigenous Peoples (OP 4.10), 2004.

of affected indigenous and tribal peoples, guided by their customary laws and practices and by national laws.[188] Several countries have their own laws embodying this principle. For instance, in the Philippines the Indigenous Peoples' Rights Act (1997) requires free, prior, and informed consent for exploration, development, and use of natural resources, among other activities.

The Philippine example illustrates that drafters may have to look outside the forest laws to understand how public participation is to be structured. Administrative procedure laws, EIA laws, and procurement laws are common sources of public participation requirements for forestry. The drafter should take care to make the forest law consistent with the procedural requirements in other laws.

Public participation can take place at various levels and with varying degrees of formality. National and state or provincial advisory councils are probably the most common form of participation for forest policy-making. The membership and powers of such groups can vary widely. Members may be chosen by a minister or by the groups they represent; they may be limited to public officials or open to the forest industry, professions, NGOs, and customary right-holders. They may have the power to initiate provisions, or only to review items submitted by the minister. They may have the right to comment on policies, national plans, legislation, and regulations.

An example of a rather powerful council with public representation is the Forestry Commission created by Ghana's Forestry Commission Act (1999). More than an advisory body, it oversees administration of forestry throughout the country. It has the power to regulate private forestry and manage the public forest reserves, although it must follow the minister in matters of policy. It is composed of a chairman; the chief executive of the Commission; representatives of the National House of Chiefs, the timber trade and industry, the wildlife trade and industry, the Ghana Institute of Professional Foresters, NGOs involved in forest and wildlife management, and the Lands Commission; and three other persons with financial, commercial, or managerial experience who are nominated by the minister, at least one of whom must be a woman.

The law can provide opportunities for the public in general to participate at a variety of points, including rulemaking, awarding concessions, planning, and classifying land. For example, the Liberian Forest Act (2000) requires the forest agency to publish a draft of any proposed regulations and allow 60 days of public comment before the agency submits the regulations to its board of directors for further comment.[189] The Draft Liberian Act Creating the Public

---

[188] World Commission on Dams, *Dams and Development: A New Framework for Decision-Making,* 112, 281 (Earthscan 2000).

[189] § 183.

Procurement and Concessions Commission requires agencies to hold a stakeholder forum before awarding a concession.[190] The Tanzanian Forest Act (2002) requires the government to consult with local stakeholders in preparing management plans.[191] The Kosovo Forest Law (2003) requires the agency to release drafts of management plans and accept public comment for 60 days.[192] The Indian Forest Act (1927) requires public notice and opportunity to raise objections before the government can constitute a reserved forest.[193] The Forest Law (2000) of the Congo has a similar process for classifying forests, and it places local representatives on the commission that reviews require objections and claims of rights.[194]

As a rule, where public participation is a matter of consultation rather than consent, it has more potential to influence the agency when it happens early in the decision-making process. For example, a requirement that an agency consult with the public before inviting bids on a concession is likely to be more influential than a requirement that the agency consult before signing the contract. A requirement that an agency hold a forum on the scope of impacts it plans to cover in an EIA will probably have more influence than a requirement that the agency hold a forum after it has completed the assessment—although the law could well require both.

For any public participation process, a free and interested press and an active civil society increase the likelihood that the public will take advantage of the right.

At the community level, the right to be meaningfully consulted may expand into a right to participate in management of the resource. In this sense, participation blends in with community forestry.[195] There may also be local management or advisory boards for single forests on which local residents sit.

8.3 Accountability

Accountability means holding people responsible for their actions. Consequences may attach if the action is unlawful or simply bad, all things considered. The latter may not be a legal standard, but the law can create mechanisms that encourage such scrutiny.

---

[190] §§ 90 and 91.

[191] *See* § 13(1).

[192] Art. 17.

[193] §§ 4–22.

[194] Arts 15–20.

[195] *See* § 7.3 above.

Box 8–1: Stakeholder Participation in Reform and Modernization of the Peruvian Forestry Sector

The need for technical and political support to confront the significant challenges of implementing new forest legislation in Peru's uncertain political environment prompted the Minister of Agriculture in 2001 to promote establishment of a broad-based civil society and private sector stakeholder forum. It was later named the Roundtable for Forest Dialogue and Consensus (*Mesa de Dialogo y Concertacion Forestal,* MDCF). The MDCF organized the main forest actors in formulating contemporary forest policy in Peru. The complex challenges inherent in leading forest sector reform and modernization were the drivers for the Peruvian government to foster public participation, rather than an interest in promoting democratic principles and the right to be informed and consulted.

Under the leadership of the MDCF, conservation NGOs, the forest industry, forest products trade organizations, indigenous communities, small loggers, and government agencies met weekly (more often as needed) to work on a consensus basis to review and propose forest policy and complementary forest legislation and to support the forest administration agency as it moved forest sector reform forward. The MDCF has played, and hopefully continues to play, a key role in sector analysis and in reviewing legislation to support forest sector reform and modernization.

By popular demand versions of this forum were established at the local level in important forest provinces where logging corporations, small loggers, local NGOs, other grasssroots organizations, indigenous groups, and local government officials provided valuable input in shaping complementary forest legislation that addressed local problems and work on resolving areas of conflict. The diverse set of actors and consensus decision-making ensured that differing interests were represented and that no single actor controlled the decision-making process. The MDCF made a difficult process possible and even sustainable. It directly proposed complementary regulations related to allocation criteria, bidding protocols, and forest fees, and helped refine monitoring of performance protocols. MDCFs proposed short lists for appointments to the Forest Commissions and at the local and national level have helped find ways to resolve conflicts about claims of customary ownership from indigenous communities. They have dealt with such issues as illegal logging and the associated trade and catalyzed the naming of an interagency commission to combat illegal logging.

Source: Information gathered by the authors.

Transparency mechanisms promote accountability. If the actions of the forest administration are open to scrutiny, many actors outside the executive can bring pressure to bear on the agency, among them players in the "national integrity system,"[196] such as the press, international donors, civil society, private businesses, the legislature, and the voters.

There are almost always informal accountability mechanisms operating within the executive arms of government. For example, environmental and agriculture agencies may have reason to keep watch over the forest agency. Transparency of forest administration encourages this kind of watchfulness.

Properly structured, decentralization can promote accountability. The key is to disperse power among actors that have an incentive to keep an eye on one another. Giving some authority to local governments or communities encourages them to build capacity and grow more able to raise concerns about actions of the central government. Retaining oversight and perhaps standard-setting authority in the regional and central government helps keep local and community governments on their toes. At the same time, local and community governments are theoretically more accountable to the people than are the agencies of the central government.

The law can use other institutional mechanisms to promote oversight and accountability. To facilitate interagency diligence, the law can create mixed panels to carry out or supervise certain actions. Under the Timber Resources Management Act (1997) of Ghana,[197] an evaluation committee made up of forest and land officials from different agencies, including the Forestry Department, the Forestry Commission, the Institute of Professional Foresters, the Lands Commission, and the Stool (community) Lands Administrator, ranks the bidders for timber contracts. Under Liberia's Act Creating the Public Procurement and Concessions Commission (2005),[198] the Inter-Ministerial Concessions Committee that oversees granting of a forest concession has seven government members, only one of whom is from a forest agency.

To keep an eye on the forest agency from within, the law can create the position of inspector general or ombudsman. Neither of these titles has a precise definition, and there is overlap in the use of the terms. An inspector general typically

---

[196] *See* J. Pope, *Confronting Corruption: The Elements of a National Integrity System* (Transparency International Source Book 2000), http://www.transparency.org/sourcebook/index.html.

[197] *See* arts. 5 and 6.

[198] *See* § 81.

investigates and prosecutes cases of waste, fraud, and abuse of power. An ombudsman typically advocates on behalf of the public in interactions with the government, but the ombudsman often has powers of investigation and a mandate to publicly criticize, if not to prosecute.

If the law creates such an officer within a forest agency, the law must grant the position some independence from the head of the agency. One approach is to forbid the head from firing or reducing the salary or budget of the inspector without permission from the head of state or the legislature. Another is to require the head to publish reasons for the dismissal. A third is for the law to set out justifiable causes for dismissal and allow the courts to review the action.

Another way to promote accountability is to vest powers of investigation in an advisory committee or board of directors for the forest agency. Any person may petition the Forest Advisory Board in Kosovo to investigate a matter related to the public administration of forests. The board must either deny the request publicly or conduct an investigation and make the results public.[199]

General matters of judicial review of agency action may be beyond the scope of the forest law, but it can create special powers of review. One way is to give citizens standing to challenge the legality of agency actions in court, and set remedies even if no monetary interest is at stake.[200] Another is to give the citizens power to enforce forest laws as private attorneys general or to bring *qui tam* actions to collect forest-related fees and taxes owed to the government.

Though matters of civil service law are usually beyond the scope of the forest law, whistleblower protections can encourage agency accountability. These provisions prevent a superior from punishing a civil servant for making a public report of illegality, waste, fraud, or abuse of power. (But although whistleblower laws probably do encourage people to speak up, it is virtually impossible for the law to protect the whistleblower from all the subtle forms of retribution available to an employer.)

Besides these institutional measures the law can promote accountability by spelling out standards against which official action can be judged. The forest law will usually state broad objectives for forest management; these become rough standards for evaluating the exercise of agency discretion. For specific actions the law can provide specific standards. For example, the law can require officials to

---

[199] *See* Kosovo Forest Law (2003), § 10.4.
[200] *Id.* § 28.3.

award forest concessions to the highest qualified bidder or can require forest managers to follow published management plans. The law can also set reasonable deadlines for agency actions, such as a time limit for processing harvest permit requests. Though it is impractical to eliminate official discretion entirely, it is wise for the law to post clear bounds on its use.

8.4 Combating Illegal Logging and Corruption

Governments have a major responsibility to suppress illegal activities.[201] Lack of enforcement, and sometimes illegal acts by the forest administration itself, are among the main factors of failure in forest regulation. Illegal activities and corruption increase investment risk and reduce the willingness of investors to implement sustainable management practices.[202] They undermine the authority of the state and deprive it of income.

Illegal action and corruption are not synonyms; lawmakers should understand the difference. Box 8–2 lists illegal activities that affect the forest sector; they go far beyond illegal logging and range far from the forest.

---

[201] In the Declaration adopted during the AFLEG Ministerial Conference, measures proposed for law enforcement and monitoring were as follows: (i) seek collective responsibility in forest law enforcement and governance at local, national, regional, and international levels; (ii) integrate the concern for sustainable development of wildlife resources and nontimber forest products in AFLEG; (iii) improve conditions of service of field staff and of enforcement services to ensure forest law enforcement and governance; (iv) develop monitoring and auditing capacity of forest and legal authorities; (v) encourage independent monitoring; (vi) encourage decentralized law enforcement and empower people and local governing bodies for forest law enforcement and governance; (vii) encourage initiatives that will lead to harmonization and implementation, in a concerted manner, of legislation in respect of management of transboundary forest resources, as well as combating forest fires.

[202] The government of Indonesia has initiated an Illegal Logging and Law Enforcement Assessment, which is supported by the World Bank/WWF Alliance, to establish a basis for specific and detailed terms of reference for prevention, detection, and suppression measures, which the national, provincial, and district governments and other stakeholders can realistically implement to reduce illegal logging in Indonesia. This initiative might also generate awareness-raising materials of two types: specific information for important target audiences such as local government officials and legislators, and more general materials that could be disseminated through public awareness programs targeted at those investing in Indonesia's forest sector or selling or consuming its products. Decentralization and its potential for the control of illegal logging is also an important focus of this activity.

Box 8–2: Illegal Activities Associated with the Forest Sector

- Harvest and Transport
  - Theft or vandalism of trees or other forest resources
  - Violation of harvest or management regulations
  - Civil wrongs, such as breach of contract
  - Illegal transport
- Sales or Processing
  - Fraud (including deceptions about grade, species, volume, origin, or certification status)
  - Violation of sales regulations
  - Violation of processing regulations
  - Sham transactions to hide profits, avoid liabilities and taxes, etc.
- Export and Import
  - Smuggling and other violations of export controls
  - Violation of import controls, including tariffs and phytosanitary laws
- Associated Crimes (which may happen any time from harvest to export)
  - Crimes linked to earlier crimes, such as receiving stolen property or being part of a criminal conspiracy
  - Evading taxes, tariffs, or fees due to the government
  - Bribery and extortion
- Abuse of Governmental Authority
  - Criminal abuse: soliciting bribes, exercising favoritism, diverting government income to personal use, etc.
  - Abuse of discretion: failing to follow required standards and procedures in administering government forests

Source: Adapted from K. Rosenbaum, *Defining Illegal Logging: What is it, and what is being done about it?* Background paper for the 44th meeting of the FAO Advisory Committee on Paper and Wood Products, Rome, May 2003.[203]

---

[203] This paper contains a more detailed list, adapted from D. Callister, *Corrupt and Illegal Activities in the Forestry Sector: Current Understandings, and Implications for World Bank Forest Policy* (draft for discussion, prepared for the World Bank Group, Forest Policy Implementation Review and Strategy Development: Analytical Studies) (1999); A. Contreras-Hermosilla, *Policy Alternatives to Improve Law Compliance in the Forest Sector* (background paper prepared for FAO meeting of experts, Rome, Jan. 2002); and D. Brack & G. Hayman, *Intergovernmental Actions on Illegal Logging: Options for Intergovernmental Action to Help Combat Illegal Logging and Illegal Trade in Timber and Forest Products* (Royal Inst. of Intl. Aff. 2001), http://www.iucn.org/places/brao/toolkiteng/Background%20Papers/RIIA%20on%20illegal%20logging.pdf.

Box 8–3: Examples of Forest-Related Corruption

Bribery
• To get a scarce resource, such as a forest concession
• To get a discretionary favor, such as to avoid prosecution for a forest offense
• To get an incidental benefit, such as rapid issuance of a harvest permit
• To impose a cost on others, such as to schedule inspection of a competitor

Favoritism and Patronage
• Self-dealing, such as awarding a contract to one's own firm
• Nepotism, such as hiring an unqualified relative as forest official
• Cronyism, such as granting a forest concession as a reward for loyalty

Kickbacks
• Payments from outsiders to officials, such as sharing excessive profits from sale of overpriced equipment to the forest agency
• Disguised payments, such as a scholarship for an official's child
• Payments from subordinates, such as a percentage of pay increases

Fraud
• Defrauding an employer, such as by placing ghost employees on the payroll
• Defrauding others in the name of the employer, such as issuing false export certificates

Source: Adapted from K. Rosenbaum, *Tools for Civil Society Action to Reduce Forest Corruption: Drawing Lessons from Transparency International* (World Bank 2005), available at http://www.profor.info/governance/FINReport.htm.

Corruption, according to Transparency International, is abuse of entrusted power for personal gain.[204] Box 8–3 lists some corrupt activities that affect the forest sector. Note that they go beyond bribery; that they can happen entirely outside of government, as when a corporate manager practices self-dealing; and that their object is not always to avoid the law. In some countries people must pay bribes to get the very services that the law requires the government to provide, such as issuance of harvest or transit permits. Where the corruption leads to actions "according to rule," it can be difficult to detect.

---

[204] *See* Transparency International's Web page, http://www.transparency.org/faqs/faq-corruption.html.

Lawmakers can design laws in ways that help reduce illegal activities and corruption:

- Avoid legislative overreaching. Do not write laws that exceed national capacity, that are more elaborate than necessary to achieve the intended policy, or that are socially unacceptable.
- Avoid unnecessary requirements for licenses or permission. These add to the burden on both government and private sector resources and invite corruption. Make sure license and control requirements serve a genuine purpose.
- Promote transparency and accountability. These serve both to deter bad acts and to make their detection easier. Where the law gives officials discretion, it should provide standards for exercise of that discretion.
- Enhance the stake of local, nongovernment interests in forest management. The law can do this both by better recognizing existing rights and by creating new opportunities for local people to benefit from forest management. Without local support, law enforcement in forest areas is difficult.
- Adopt the law using a highly participatory process. This promotes a sense of ownership of the law among stakeholders, and thus a respect for it.
- Make law enforcement mechanisms in the law effective. Set appropriate penalties and have effective enforcement powers and procedures.[205]

Illegality and corruption are complex problems that cannot be solved by legislative reform alone. Civil society and forest businesses have promoted promising initiatives such as certification,[206] corporate social responsibility programs,[207] and integrity pacts for public contracting.[208] Lawmakers should support such efforts.

---

[205] *See* Lindsay, *et al., supra* n. 28.

[206] *See* chapter 9 below.

[207] *See* the Business Principles for Countering Bribery for a model set of principles for private use, http://www.transparency.org/tools/business_principles. For an example of a corporate social responsibility program to promote transparency in the forest sector, see the Tikhvin project, http://www.tikhvinproject.ru/.

[208] *See* integrity pact page on the Transparency International web site, http://www.transparency.org/global_priorities/public_contracting/integrity_pacts.

PART FOUR

Environmental and Trade Issues

CHAPTER 9

Forest Law and the Environment

Environmental protection has traditionally been an element of forestry, both in its emphasis on conserving forests and their natural character and in accounting for environmental impacts outside the forest, especially on soil and water. Still, this was normally within the framework of forests as a productive asset managed by production specialists.

In recent years a series of influences primarily from outside the forest sector has had a substantial impact on the objectives of forestry and on the contents of forest law. In common with other sectors, forestry has been profoundly affected by the emergence of environmental awareness and by environmental legislation in the last generation. The greening of forest law has brought greater emphasis on nonfinancial values, including the protection of wilderness and esthetic values. As Cirelli and Schmithüsen note with respect to Western Europe: "Moving away from a perspective which focused on wood as a sustainable resource, forest laws are now addressing a wider range of private and public goods and values."[209]

Management plans increasingly are required to take explicit account of environmental factors.[210] EIAs also figure in forestry laws, especially in Africa.[211] Equally significantly, involvement in forest decision-making has opened up beyond forest-owners, managers, and users. Nontimber users, in particular recreational users, users of neighboring land, and the general public have gained a role in participatory structures and been accepted by the courts as interested parties. This follows the opening up of the legal processes in environmental law and greater transparency in public processes generally.

The relationship between forest and environmental law is not simply one of incorporating environmental precepts. It is of course only sensible to incorporate relevant major public policies, including environmental ones, into the considerations on which forest management is based. Where the general objectives of

---

[209] *See* M. Cirelli, F. Schmithüsen, J. Texier & T. Young, *Trends in Forestry Law in Europe and Africa* Legislative Study No. 72, 45 (FAO 2001).

[210] *See, for example,* Guinea, Code forestier (1999), art. 39.

[211] *See* Cirelli, *et al., supra* n. 51 at 88.

forest management or the contents of management plans are set out in the law, environmental objectives would in most countries have a prominent role.

But discussing EIAs in forest legislation is not so straightforward. If there is no environmental impact legislation, it might be prudent to specify that such assessments for forests be included in the act. Later, a general EIA provision would be expected to supersede the forest EIA, hopefully by explicit repeal.

Even with a separate EIA act, there may be reasons to consider providing for EIAs in the forest act. At a minimum the lawmaker should thoroughly understand the procedures under the EIA act to make sure that the forest act does not conflict. For example, if the forest act sets a 90-day deadline for reviewing requests to renew a concession, and the EIA act requires an environmental assessment before awarding a concession, there is potential for a clash. On occasion the lawmaker may want to expand the requirements in the EIA act. It may be good practice to specify an assessment of programmatic national forest plans even if the EIA act only requires assessments of concrete local actions.

It is enormously helpful for the forest agency to be sure which of its activities is subject to environmental regulation by other agencies. Whether environmental permits be required in the case of forestry (in addition to forest plans, licenses, and other approvals), and. if not, whether and how their criteria should be included in forest permits, are knotty issues (complicated by the potential for professional jealousy).

An interesting way to deal with this was chosen by Peru, which has created a tribunal to which interdepartmental conflicts of authority can be referred.[212] Another method is used in South Africa where, when an activity is to be subject to an EIA, the minister under whose jurisdiction that activity falls must agree to undertake the assessment.[213] The South African Act is very explicit, however, that any permission required is in addition to permission required under any other Act.[214] Indeed, it is often important to craft interministerial mechanisms to resolve differences between agencies charged with resource use and environmental protection. If there are no such mechanisms, an alternative course for lawmakers is to encourage the forest and environmental agencies to negotiate an ad hoc memorandum of understanding that clarifies how the environmental laws apply to forest management.

To the general environmental influences on forest law have been added two very specific influences: biological diversity and climate change.

---

[212] Peru, Decreto Supremo no. 008-2005-PCM, Reglamento de la Ley Marco del Sistema Nacional de Gestión Ambiental, art. 12.

[213] South Africa, National Environmental Management Act (1998), as amended, § 24.

[214] *Id.*, §§ 24(7) and (8).

9.1 Biological Diversity

The CBD signed at Rio de Janeiro in 1992 does not explicitly mention forests, but they are recognized as the habitat of much of the biological diversity the convention covers. They are therefore greatly affected by the general obligations to identify and monitor biological diversity as well as obligations of *in situ* conservation.

In general terms, biological diversity is appearing in national laws as a value to be protected in forest management.[215] In some cases it is to be taken into account when forest management plans are drawn up.[216] Where criteria and indicators for sustainable forest management exist, biological diversity is represented.[217]

As with an EIA, including biological diversity in forest legislation is not a simple solution to forest biodiversity issues. First, there is the matter of priority between sustainable forest production and conservation of biological diversity. For tree species this is partially addressed by restricting the clearing of natural forest and use of exotic species in plantations.[218] Many other forest practice requirements, such as limits on harvesting near streams and limits on road construction, also benefit biodiversity. For ecosystems and plant species in general, however, it is likely that a comprehensive approach to biological diversity will be required to meet the requirements of the CBD. Increasingly, countries have such legislation as well as provisions in sectoral laws.[219]

Conflict between biodiversity and forest legislation can occur unless great care is taken to avoid it. The main areas of potential conflict concern the management of reserves or protected areas and the definition of which activities are governed by biodiversity and which by forest legislation. Costa Rica has dealt with the first issue by providing that areas such as forest and wildlife reserves that form part of the national biodiversity conservation system continue to be managed by the original authorities "without prejudice to the aims for which

---

[215] Niger, Loi n. 2004–40, Regime forestier, art. 9; South Africa Forest Act, October 20ᵗ, 1998, §§ 3 and 4; R. Silva-Repetto, *Latin America*, in *Trends in Forest Law in America and Asia* (E. Kern, K. Rosenbaum, R. Silva Repetto, & T. Young, eds.), FAO Legislative Studies #66, 26 (FAO 1998); Cirelli, *et al., supra* n. 53 at 86–87.

[216] Namibia Forest Act (2001), §§ 10, 21; South Africa Forest Act (1998), §§ 3 and 4.

[217] Belgium, Flemish Region, Arrêté fixant les critères d'une gestion durable des bois situées en Région flamande, 23 June 2003, Annex, chapter V; South Africa Forest Act (1998), §§ 3 and 4.

[218] *Id.*, Belgium.

[219] Costa Rica's Ley de Biodiversidad, no. 7788 (1998), amending Ley Forestal no. 7575 (1996).

they were established."[220] Coordination and general policy is the responsibility of an interministerial council[221] and by analogous subnational institutions.[222]

The areas of application of the two laws can be a problem because forest products are without doubt a "biological resource," the taking of which is regulated by some biodiversity laws.[223] A forest is also an element of biodiversity (ecosystem) and contains species and varieties that are themselves elements of biodiversity. The solution that seems most common is to subject prospecting and taking of biological resources for purposes of research to the biodiversity law.[224] This does not completely avoid the problem where forest research and forest product research is concerned, but it would clearly exclude normal forest extraction.

Some administrative difficulties might be avoided if forest licenses were accepted as authority for forest extraction, with a provision that the licenses comply with the biodiversity law or that doubtful cases be referred to biodiversity authorities. This cautionary measure does not, however, appear to have been taken up. In fact Queensland, Australia, has chosen the opposite solution, where an authority under the Biodiscovery Act (2004) exempts the holder from the license required by other legislation, such as a forestry law.[225]

9.2 Climate Change

Climate change is now entering forest vocabulary and legislation, especially with the entry into force of the Kyoto Protocol. General references place mitigating climate change among the objectives of forest law and policy.[226] This complements broader climate policies and programs.[227] As Rosenbaum and colleagues point out, however, there is little legislation containing specific provisions for mitigating forest-based climate-change.[228]

---

[220] *Id.* art. 22.

[221] *Id.* art. 23.

[222] *Id.* art. 29.

[223] India's Biological Diversity Act (2002), § 19.

[224] *See supra* n. 61; *see also* South Africa National Environmental Management Biodiversity Act (2004).

[225] § 7.

[226] *See* Rosenbaum, *et al., supra* n. 57, at 21.

[227] Argentina, Resolución 248/2005; Paraguay, Decreto No. 14.943 por el cual se Implementa el Programa Nacional de Cambio Climático.

[228] *See* Rosenbaum, *et al., supra* n. 57, at 21.

Box 9–1: The Global Environment Facility

The CBD identifies the Global Environment Facility (GEF) as the financial mechanism of the convention, making it a major force behind the effort to protect forest-based biodiversity throughout the world. The GEF, established in 1991, has 176 member governments. Shortly after it was formed the GEF began providing financial support to eligible developing country members to protect their biodiversity, often through measures that protected important forests around the globe. In some of these cases project components included development or improvement of forest legislation.

GEF members agreed in 2002 to add land degradation to biodiversity as one of the GEF focal areas, thereby increasing the ability of the GEF to support the UN Convention to Combat Desertification and provide grant funds for activities that could have a supportive relation to protection of the world's forests. In addition to biodiversity and land degradation, climate change is also one the focal areas, along with international waters, ozone depletion, and persistent organic pollutants. With these and its mission to support various multilateral environmental agreements, the GEF has a major role in efforts to protect forests and the biodiversity within them.

Source: http://www.gefweb.org/

A party to the Kyoto Protocol is not obliged to enact legislation for forest-based mitigation; it may choose to meet its reduction obligations through emission controls and other mitigation methods. Even where forest management or plantations are used to meet the obligations, they do not need specific legislation beyond the registration and reporting requirements that apply to all relevant activities. If, however, a country wishes to attract and protect investments in forest-based mitigation, whether to meet its own obligations or as clean development investments, it will have to consider how the relevant legal interests can be defined and managed.

Ownership of the forest and of the rights deriving from its carbon-absorbing capacity does not need to be the same. Even where forests are largely private, the state could (and some states will) manage carbon absorption as a public good and distribute the benefits only in part to the forest owners or occupiers. In any given case there will be questions about how much regulation of private owners is politically or constitutionally acceptable and how much of the benefit needs to be paid to them to ensure that the program is a success.

Even where a state wished to devolve the benefits of carbon sequestration projects to forest owners, it might be constrained by fragmentation of holdings, or lack of a solid legal foundation for customary or group rights, or simply forest owner lack of negotiating capacity. One response is exemplified by Costa Rica, which conducts greenhouse gas negotiations with other parties and pays the proceeds used to facilitate carbon sequestration into a fund that in turn is used to finance projects implemented jointly with forest owners. The State of Oregon has taken another tack, acting as a broker between forest owners and those seeking forestry carbon offsets. It also finances reforestation, retaining the rights to the carbon offsets created. New South Wales, Australia, has taken the more radical step of establishing tradable interests in the carbon sequestration of forests; it may be supposed that other countries with experience in third-party reforestation agreements will follow that example.

Where state land is involved, one possibility is the example of Peru, which has included a concession for carbon sequestration among its nontimber forest concessions.[229] Because the regulations do not refer to carbon sequestration among the environmental concessions, however, the provision has probably not yet been implemented. In principle, concessions with provisions for local participation at least equal to timber concessions could be devised.

9.3   Compensation for Environmental Goods

As the Kyoto Protocol begins to generate payments related to carbon sequestration, the idea of payment for environmental services in general is likely to grow. Costa Rica's current forest law already sets aside one-third of the proceeds of a national fuel tax to compensate forest owners for the environmental services they provide.[230]

---

[229] *See supra* n. 54, art. 10.

[230] Costa Rica Ley Forestal, art. 69; Reglamento a la ley forestal, arts. 60–69; Resolución no. 042-MINAE-SINAC-FONOFIFO, 15.6.99, Manual de procedimientos para el pago de servicios ambiéntateles.

CHAPTER 10

Forest Law and Trade

10.1 Voluntary Certification

Environmental groups have targeted an array of entities that they believe have not done enough to curb deforestation, and have sought to organize consumers behind those that harvest timber in a sustainable manner. Product certification is a common method of supporting sustainable harvesting. In broad terms certification "is an economic market-based instrument which aims to raise awareness and provide incentives for both producers and consumers toward a more responsible use of forests."[231] The process of certification informs the market that the forest product has met a set of requirements demonstrating that harvesting and management of the timber is sustainable. It is a way to identify the forest product or timber as having come from a forest operation that meets a minimum standard of good practice, from both an environmental and a social standpoint. The benefits are especially clear when consumers are willing to pay a premium for products that they associate with sustainable environmental and social practices.

Further, "forest certification" is usually understood as an external testament that a forest is managed in accordance with certain environmental and social standards. Because a major incentive for forest owners to seek certification is to enhance their ability to sell to clients who market to environmentally conscious customers, a primary objective of a certification system is credibility with consumers. At the same time, forest owners naturally wish to be judged on the factors they consider most important for sustainable and profitable forest management. They are also concerned about the cost of certification.

Perhaps the best known certification system operates under the umbrella of the Forest Stewardship Council (FSC), an international nongovernmental ("multistakeholder") organization with numerous national chapters that sets standards and accredits certifying agencies. The system is voluntary, although the FSC has agreements with some major manufacturers and distributors that require forest products to be certified under the FSC. The FSC system can be considered the reference standard for forest certification, but it is not without criticism, in particular because of its costs and for allowing noncompliant certifications the time to come into compliance.

---

[231] *See* Upton & Bass, *supra* n. 72, p. 42.

In addition to FSC certification, a country can run its own certification program or at least create a system for accrediting certifying agencies. These agencies could be FSC-accredited international or local organizations, non-FSC voluntary organizations, or new entities set up under the legislation that provides for accreditation. In fact FSC operates through what it terms institutional elements, which have the task of producing national and regional standards for certification. FSC requires that these standards be developed through "a consultative process by an FSC working group, or be recommended by an FSC working group as having had adequate consultation."[232]

A number of countries have provided for voluntary accreditation in their forest legislation, although forest certification processes do not necessarily require that national legislation be enacted. Peru, for example, provides for registration of certifying bodies and offers participating concessionaires a 25 percent reduction in forest fees and exemption from official inspections.[233] Costa Rica and South Africa, among others, have gone further by adopting or providing for criteria and indicators of sustainable forest management to be the basis of a certification system; in South Africa their breach may also be an offense.[234] Also noteworthy is the Forestry Law (1996) of Bolivia, which states that third-party certification may serve as a substitute for governmental audits of concessions on public forestland.

Russia is unusual in providing for mandatory certification of forest resources, to be carried out by the federal forestry agency.[235] An agency official has vigorously defended the system against criticism that this would amount to self-certification (all forests being state-owned) and thus lacks credibility.[236] He also said that the private international certification organizations were not very knowledgeable about Russia and were largely motivated by the profitable market for certification in Russia. He pointed out that Russian certification would be much cheaper than international.

Even though most certification is voluntary, there is a clear, although not indispensable, role for supporting legislation. The World Bank Forests Policy

---

[232] *See* FSC Process Guidelines for Developing Regional Certification Standards.

[233] Peru, Ley 27308, Ley Forestal y de la Fauna Silvestre (2000), arts. 6(c) and 32; Decreto supremo no. 014-2001-AG, Reglamento de la Ley Forestal y de la Fauna Silvestre (2001), arts. 11(f), 87(g), (j), 88(f), 336(h), 340, and 351; *see also* Georgia, Forest Code (1999), art. 94.

[234] Costa Rica, Decreto no. 25721-MINAE, Reglamento de la Lay Forestal (1996), art. 26; Decreto no. 27388-MINAE, Principios, Criterios y Indicadores para el Manejo Forestal y la Certificación en Costa Rica (1998), as amended by Decreto no. 27998-MINAE (1999); South Africa, National Forests Act (1998), § 4.

[235] Russia, Forest Code (1997), art. 71.

[236] Interview with Evgeny Kuzmichov, Associate Director, Federal Forest Agency, http://www.forest.ru/eng/sustainable_forestry/certification/rcn3.html.

notes that most acceptable certification systems require "compliance with national laws." The standards of certification are subject to a process of reconciliation of a variety of interests. As environmental and social concerns become more prominent, there is likely to be increasing pressure to include forests that might not voluntarily participate. Even a certificate with elements that differ from the more popular forms could have some weight, both with distributors that are not committed to a particular certificate and in influencing the application of international standards to national forests. Depending upon their elements, some purely national systems might also be seen as a step toward internationally

---

Box 10–1: Eliminating Disincentives to Certification

One issue tied to compliance with national laws that has emerged with environmental certification systems, such as ISO 14000, seems likely to emerge with forest certification as well. Many systems require that producers keep internal records demonstrating compliance with certification standards or, where problems occur, documenting efforts to restore compliance. Some require regular audits to demonstrate compliance. The fact that the forest administration might use those records in enforcement proceedings to show violations of national law could be a disincentive to participate in certification programs.

In response, jurisdictions have taken two approaches to environmental certification. One is to create a privilege that prevents the government from using certification records and self-audits in enforcement proceedings,[237] though the privilege does not usually apply when the government alleges criminal or intentional violation of the law. The other approach is to promise reductions or waivers in penalties if the violator itself reports the violation.[238] Typically, this approach would require the violator to have discovered the violation as part of a self-audit, to have taken prompt steps to cure it, and to cooperate fully with any later government investigation and inspections.

Source: ISO 14000, http://www.iso.org/iso/en/iso9000-14000/index.html.

---

[237] For examples of environmental audit privileges in U.S. states, *see* Col. Rev. Stat., §§ 13-25-126.5; Mich. Natural Res. & Envtl. Prot. Act (1994), part 148; Or. Rev. Stat., § 468.963. These provisions are quite complex and could be simplified for most forestry purposes.

[238] For an example of this kind of penalty reduction policy in the environmental field, *see* the U.S. Environmental Protection Agency's policy on audits, http://www.epa.gov/compliance/incentives/auditing/auditpolicy.html.

recognized certification. Indeed, it is not unusual for operators to seek a second certificate when the national one has limited acceptance.

Legislation that recognizes local certification bodies would not normally interfere with their acceptance by FSC or external markets unless it forced the legislation to adopt incompatible standards. Provisions like those of Costa Rica or South Africa that empower the executive to establish criteria and indicators as a basis for certification not only fills this lacuna, it also puts the executive in a position to bring national proposals into the discussion of international standards.[239] Costa Rica permits foreign entities to be registered as certifiers, which seems advisable where there is doubt about how to proceed with certification, since at first the necessary experience may not be available locally. Where the definition of national certification standards is too closely controlled by the government, on the other hand, gaining international recognition may be difficult, especially from FSC, which insists on a multistakeholder approach[240] and the involvement of FSC steering committees.[241]

Certification schemes generally require that certain measures be taken before they allow their label to be affixed to a product entering the market. Wood products need labels that assure consumers that their purchases come from forests that adhere to these measures. Labeling requires tracing the wood product from the forest to the customer, which depends on a secure, reliable chain of custody.[242] Chain of custody is described as "the link between buyers and sellers from the forest to the point of final sale."[243] Because determining the chain of custody identifies the entities that are engaged at each point of transfer of the timber, it reinforces the likelihood that timber can be certified as sustainably harvested. The identity of entities in the chain can be useful information for those charged with enforcing forest law, enabling a correlation between the ability to produce certified timber and respect for national and local law.[244] This market-based mechanism is thus highly supportive of local law enforcement.

---

[239] *See supra,* n. 76.

[240] Draft papers, Forest Certification in Developing and Transitioning Societies, http://www.yale.edu/forestcertification/symposium/index.html.

[241] *See supra* n. 74.

[242] "Certification in Indonesia: A Briefing." Down to Earth, June 2001 Newsletter, http://dte.gn.apc.org.

[243] *See id.*

[244] A chain of custody *system* is different from an *assessment* of the chain of custody. The former sets out the steps by which the product is traced. The latter sets out how that system is being operated. *See* Upton & Bass, *See* C. Upton & S. Bass, *Forest Certification Handbook,* 42 (St. Lucie Press 1996) *supra* n. 15, § 4.1.1, at 99.

As with labeling, proposals for certification also require consideration of international standards and trade. Developing countries have expressed concern that if certification sets up impediments to the free flow of timber, it could act as a trade barrier. At the same time, for many products over many years, the International Standards Organization (ISO) and other standard-setting bodies have set standards acceptable under the WTO Agreements. They have also established standards for the types of management systems sustainable forests should have in place. Using a harmonized approach, via a certified system, can give both producer and consumer certainty.

For these reasons, where the certification approach is being harmonized among forest producers and consumers, it can alleviate some concerns about trade barriers. But the same approach can be threatened if there is a plethora of conflicting certification systems. To the extent possible, international organizations and governments should work together to support a harmonized approach to certification.

Certification also highlights the important relationship between markets and local law enforcement. Some people tout certification systems, coupled with chain of custody systems, as a solution to illegal logging, but such systems, although helpful, are still vulnerable to fraud and corrupt influences.

Where there is no reliable chain of custody, the credibility of the certified wood product—and hence the system of certification—would be damaged if illegal harvesting is unchecked, especially if illegal products enter the stream of commerce. The importance of this relationship is heightened by the fact that many critics of certification contend that illegal logging is continuing in most parts of the world. Some have asserted that it is very difficult to keep out unsustainably harvested timber, and that the higher price for certified wood keeps other wood attractive to consumers.

The only sure way to address the issue is to strictly enforce the law. Governments should seek to integrated effective enforcement of the law with appropriate market mechanisms, given the urgency with which forests globally are being depleted. Each year more of the world's forests come under certification schemes. Certification can lead to sustainable forest management when combined with sound policies and legal and institutional approaches.

10.2   International Trade

Most nations subscribe to instruments that support the free flow of goods, including timber, in international trade. The International Tropical Timber Organization and the Intergovernmental Forum on Forests (and the successor United Nations Forum on Forests) have both stated that national standards, certification, and labeling schemes should not discriminate with respect to imports and exports of wood and wood products. It has also been noted in the WTO that ensuring a level playing field for forest products should not interfere with efforts to ensure sustainable forest management, but that further work is necessary to achieve these objectives.[245] The WTO also seeks to progressively reduce tariffs on products like timber, and to eliminate protectionism.

There has been a range of motives for countries imposing measures viewed by some as trade restrictive, such as timber export bans and taxes, among them the need to decrease deforestation and achieve both environmental and economic objectives. Numerous timber-producing countries have banned export of raw or semi-processed logs, often with the stated purposes of encouraging domestic processing industries and reducing overexploitation of natural resources. Some have viewed these measures as essentially protective and therefore contrary to principles of free trade. At the same time, whether these measures are valid can depend on how they are applied. Article 28 of the GATT states that countries should be allowed "to maintain sufficient flexibility in their tariff structure to be able to grant the tariff protection required for the establishment of a particular industry."

Other trade issues relate to whether governments are subsidizing their domestic timber industries; the long-standing dispute between the United States and Canada is an example. The WTO Agreement on Subsidies and Countervailing Measures (SCM) addresses the legitimacy of subsidies and countervailing duties. To the extent that legislators address price supports, tax rates, or concession or stumpage fees in legislation, their efforts should be consistent with the WTO SCM so that they do not create domestic trade preferences that would be considered unfair practices.

While there is a continuing debate about the impact of timber trade restrictions, there is a growing consensus that, at least as they pertain to export limits, they provide only limited economic and environmental benefits. According to a World Bank study of several countries, "[t]he economic consequences of imposing log-export restrictions have been negative, from the perspective of both the forestry sector and the country as a whole."[246] The study indicates that restrictions can potentially cause major distortions of international trade in wood products.

There are also environmental arguments against log export bans. Some studies argue that log export bans encourage overcapacity and keep the wood processing industry inefficient. For example, Ghana's log export restrictions created 27 percent more capacity in wood processing than the estimated timber yield

---

[245] *See, for example,* WT/CTE/W/164 (Intergovernmental Panel on Forests) and WT/CTE/W/169 (ITTO).

[246] R. Crossley, *The Economic and Environmental Consequences of Log Export Bans: A Review of Evidence* (World Bank 1994).

would support, posing the danger of pressures to overharvest.[247] Log export bans have often discouraged adoption of sustainable practices in timber harvesting and reduced incentives to implement modern technology that would increase recovery ratios for environmentally preferable wood.[248] On the other hand, if removal of log export bans were coupled with application of regulations for sustainable management, it should not cause excessive pressures for deforestation.

Another issue here is the use of "eco-labeling." Eco-labeling is placing authorized markings on timber before it enters the market; it can be a market-based condition for commercial use. Generally, eco-labeling arrangements do not require that a law be enacted, although some laws require that the labeling take place under government oversight. Recently in Bosnia, legislation set up a national eco-labeling scheme operated through the national forest agency. It is hoped that this will prove to be a market-based incentive for better protection of forests and natural resources if it is combined with adequate product certification schemes.

Eco-labeling can also support sustainable forestry. Thus, for example, the European Commission has issued regulations establishing criteria for the eco-labeling of toilet paper[249] and paper towels.[250] As this type of eco-labeling tends to address the life cycle of a timber-based product, it can ensure that the harvesting and production of the tree was sustainable.

Some concern has been expressed, especially in developing countries, about trade obstacles arising from the use of eco-labels. The WTO Agreement on Technical Barriers to Trade (TBT Agreement) states that government-sponsored technical regulations and standards must not discriminate between domestic and foreign products that are alike (national treatment) and must not discriminate between like products from different WTO members (most-favored nation).[251] Some in the environmental community have argued that most eco-labeling schemes are voluntary and private sector–driven and therefore do not come under the oversight of the intergovernmental WTO regime. Not all governments and producers agree with this. In any case, such schemes are growing and eco-labeling

---

[247] *See* J. Vincent & C. Binkley, *Forest-Based Industrialization: A Dynamic Perspective, in Managing the World's Forests* 99, 112 (N. Sharma, ed., Kendall/Hunt Pub. Co. 1992).

[248] *See* N. Kishor, M. Mani & L. Constantino, *Economic and Environmental Benefits of Eliminating Log Export Bans: The Case of Costa Rica,* 27 World Econ. 609, 612 (2004).

[249] Reg. 94/924/EC: Commission Decision of 14 November 1994 establishing ecological criteria for the award of the Community eco-label to toilet paper, OJ L 364, 31/12/1994, pp. 0024–0031.

[250] Reg. 94/925/EC: Commission Decision of 14 November 1994 establishing the ecological criteria for the award of the Community eco-label to kitchen rolls, OJ L 364, 31/12/1994, pp. 0032–0041.

[251] Agreement on Technical Barriers to Trade, Apr. 15, 1994, WTO Agreement, Annex IA, Legal Instruments: Results of the Uruguay Round (1994).

participants contend that they are seeking to comply with the TBT Code of Good Practice for the Preparation, Adoption and Application of Standards.[252] Concern has also been expressed about the possible impact of phytosanitary measures based on the WTO Agreement on Sanitary and Phytosanitary Measures (SPS). For example, some countries may restrict imports of forest products, particularly timber that is not debarked, due to often legitimate concerns over the spread of pests and diseases. Such measures can raise operating costs for producers that must clean or sterilize their consignments.

Many eco-labeling advocates recall a dispute over Austria's Mandate Labeling Law (1992)[253] that demonstrates the potential trade-related effects of forest law. The government of Malaysia, on behalf of states that are members of ASEAN, raised the following issue before the Council of the GATT: Although the law required that all tropical timber and products sold in Austria carry a label identifying them, it did not require mandatory labeling of other types of wood and wood products, whether imported into Austria or produced domestically. ASEAN charged that the Austria law violated both the MFN and national treatment provisions of GATT and was a discriminatory and unjustifiable obstacle to trade. Recognizing that it was likely to lose the case, Austria amended its law to make the labeling requirement voluntary and to apply it to all kinds of timber and timber products.[254]

The dispute between Austria and Malaysia should not detract from the interest many countries have today in addressing bilateral timber trade. As long as such arrangements are not discriminatory, they may be consistent with WTO rules and even supportive of them. Trade in forest products is also increasingly influenced by laws and policies pertaining to procurement of goods. There is a growing movement to make procurement more environmentally and socially responsible.

---

[252] The TBT Agreement categorized standards into either (A) "Technical regulations," referring to mandatory standards or (B) "Standards," referring to voluntary standards, the principles of which are regulated to prevent them from becoming unnecessary trade barriers. The following applies to Standards adopted by non-governmental bodies:

(1) Standardizing bodies of the governments of member nations (regardless of whether they are central government bodies, local government or non-governmental bodies) shall maintain strict adherence to the TBT Annex III "Code of Good Practice for the Preparation, Adoption and Application of Standards."

(2) Conformity assessment procedures [TBT Agreement arts. 5, 6 (excluding the provision pertaining to the obligation to render conformity assessment procedure notification)] by non-governmental bodies.

[253] *See supra*, n. 72, "Law on the Creation of a Certification Label for Timber and Timberproducts from Sustainable Forestry" (1992); *see* Bundesgesetz zur Schaffung eines Gütezeichens für Holz und Holzprodukte aus nachhaltiger Nutzung, BGBl. Nr. 309/1992, idF: BGBl. Nr. 228/1993 und BGBl. I Nr. 59/2002.

[254] C. Di Leva, *The Conservation of Nature and Natural Resources Through Legal and Market-Based and Mechanisms,* 11 RECIEL 84, 94 (2002).

Hence, there are a number of environmental and social considerations that can affect the purchase of goods based on the 2004 European Union Directive "coordinating the procurement procedures of entities operating in the water, energy, transport and postal services sectors."[255] Many other public and private actors are formulating practices, binding or voluntary, relating to "green procurement" or "responsible procurement."

The EU Directive allows contracting entities to define environmental requirements for the technical specifications of a given contract; they may set forth environmental characteristics, including a "given production method, and/or specific environmental effects of products groups or services." EU contracting entities "may use, but are not obligated to use, appropriate specifications that are defined in eco-labels . . . drawn up and adopted on the basis of scientific information."[256] Contracting parties can also take into account whether the supplier is using an environmental management system or whether it has violated national law.[257]

EU-supported Forest Law Enforcement, Governance and Trade (FLEGT) Voluntary Partnership Agreements seek to arrange for voluntary agreements between the EU and timber-exporting countries under which only licensed timber can be imported into the EU. The timber would have to be legally harvested under the laws of the exporting nation and identified by an EU license issued to the harvester.[258]

For countries that are already party to it, the WTO Agreement on Government Procurement could also affect trade in forest products, particularly timber for construction, and government-led rural electrification programs in developing countries. The agreement has both MFN and national treatment provisions. It also covers a potentially large range of products.

10.3   Domestic Trade

Regulation of timber trade, especially transport, is commonly used to help control illegal logging and timber theft. Permits for removal[259] and transport[260] of timber reinforce the requirements of official marking of timber to allow its origins to be traced.

---

[255] Directive 2004/17/EC of the European Parliament and of the Council of 31 March 2004 coordinating the procurement procedures of entities operating in the water, energy, transport, and postal services sectors. OJ L 134, 30.4.2004, pp. 1–113.

[256] *See id.* ¶ 42.

[257] *See id.* ¶¶ 53 and 54.

[258] EU Action Plan for Forest Law Enforcement, Governance and Trade (FLEGT), http://europa.eu.int/comm/development/body/theme/forest/initiative/index_en.htm.

[259] Sabah Forest Rules (1969), forms IV, V, and VI.

[260] Kosovo Forest Law (2003), § 25; Sabah Forest Rules (1969), form VII.

In principle, if there are no counterfeit or reused transport certificates in circulation, this should be effective, but it is not a substitute for direct surveillance of logging activities. Attempts to plug holes in the system include licensing of specific vehicles; licensing of timber dealers, processors, and exporters; record-keeping requirements; and multiple inspections.[261] The use of modern information technology for real-time tracing of logs promises to considerably increase the effectiveness of this form of control. Though the costs of secure systems are still high for routine use, they seem likely to drop and they can reduce not only the inefficiency but also the aggravation of obtaining, keeping, presenting, and re-presenting the multiple pieces of paper of which current systems are composed.[262] To obtain reliable results from a paper-based system requires tight cross-checking of logger, dealer, and processor records and tabulation of forest inspection and permitting, road checks, final inspections, and surrendered documents. Only a very effective traditional bureaucracy can do this.

Aside from the efficiency problems, transport documentation has a serious adverse effect on private forest owners, though they are not normally the target of the system. To sort out public from private timber, documentation has to be the same for all. This gives rise to one of the most common complaints of forest owners, that to cut their own logs legally they are forced to seek multiple permits and certificates, which, they say, discourages legal logging on private lands. At the very least it would have a discouraging effect on private investment in forestry. To help reduce the need for transport certification of private timber, the lawmaker might consider (1) where there is a significant difference in species grown on private and public land, not requiring permits for transit of the typical private land species; or (2) if public land occurs primarily in certain districts of the country, restricting the permit system to those districts; or (3) if illegal transport happens primarily at night, replacing or augmenting the permit system with a ban on transport by night.

Where transport has to be documented, the forest law obviously must at least prohibit transport of timber without the required documentation. In drafting the law it is well to prohibit "possession" to avoid quibbles over the meaning of "transport."

---

[261] Niger, Ordonnance No 92-037 (1992) portant organisation de la commercialisation et du transport de bois dans les grandes agglomérations, et la fiscalité qui lui est applicable; Décret no. 96-390/PRN/MH/E (1996); Tanzania, Registration of Forest Produce Dealers and Traders Order (1995).

[262] Technologies for Wood Tracking (2003); SGS, Log Tracking Systems, http://www.sgs.com/forestry-monitoring-programme; H. Thiel, *El Inicio de una Reforma Política, Institucional y Normativa en el Sector Forestal Ecuatoriano y el Sistema Nacional Tercerizado de Control Forestal del Ecuador,* FAO, 2004.

Unless the system is very thorough, it is usually unprocessed timber that has to be documented; what constitutes processing may vary according to local circumstances. Some countries include all wood products,[263] but this promotes either law-breaking or unnecessary bureaucracy when applied to the transport of furniture and other finished products. A more refined approach may cover some processed products, especially charcoal, which is usually made in the forest, while excluding some raw material, such as Christmas trees and maple syrup in New Brunswick, Canada.[264]

It is essential that the transport document be linked to a source, normally a forest officer who has ascertained the origins, kind, and amount of the timber. Where private forestry is significant and the problem of passing off public timber as private is not severe, the private forest owner may also issue transport documents.[265]

If it is to have any purpose, there must be a requirement that the transport document be shown on proper request, and officers must be given the power to request it and to inspect the timber for conformity with it. There also need to be provisions, which are usually already in general legislation, against falsifying documentation.

A complementary measure is the marking of individual logs. The traditional form is hammer-marking, with a distinctive sign registered for each logging licensee. Official hammers may be used to indicate that the log has been scaled and may be moved.[266] Other methods of marking individual logs (paint, bar-code labels, and computer chips) are in use or being tested, but for all the legal issues are similar: the type of mark and the authority to apply it must be specified, and there must be an obligation for timber in transport to bear the relevant marks and for the transporter to make them available for inspection. Fraudulent use of the marks must be prohibited.

Transport or movement of forest produce is often controlled for phytosanitary reasons. Sometimes this is regulated under a general plant protection act, sometimes in forest-sector legislation.[267] Both must be consulted to ensure that they do not conflict or overlap.

---

[263] El Salvador, Decreto No. 53 of 2004, Reglamento de la Ley Forestal, art. 21.

[264] Transportation of Primary Forest Products Act, October 18, 2004, cap. T-11.02, sec. 1; Forest Products Act, June 30, 2004., cap. F-21, § 1. New Brunswick also exempts fuel wood less than 1.22 meters long from the requirements of a transportation permit (cap. T-11.02, § 2).

[265] Colombia's Resolución no. 619 (2002), art. 7.

[266] Cambodia's Law on Forestry, August 31, 2002, arts. 65–67.

[267] New South Wales, Timber Marketing Act (1977), §§ 4A–11.

There are also trade regulations designed to ensure the quality of timber, either directly[268] or by providing for timber and lumber grading. The most common standard that forest law sets directly has to do with planting material.[269] Grading standards are more commonly found in general standards legislation[270] and, for construction timber, national and local building codes.[271] These standards may be promulgated by trade associations, specialized grading bureaus, or general standards organizations.

Trade in forest products has been controlled for a number of other economic and social reasons as well. In some cases general legislation controlling trade in agricultural products applies to forest as well as other products. Some of these laws date from colonial times, some are relics of socialism, but there are some very recent examples.[272] Whether these laws are useful in promoting trade and ensuring a supply of food and other necessities is beyond the scope of this guide. What is clear in the case of forest produce, however, is that licensing and other requirements for local trading often tend to discourage both private forestry and compliance with forest law.

As economic policy generally is liberalized, control of timber processing is an important instrument for forest management. It has been seen repeatedly (for example, in Cambodia and Indonesia) that establishing processing capacity creates intense pressure for raw material. Forest administrators do not stand up well to such pressure, which is reinforced by appeals to support national industry. If forests are well managed and timber trade is free, overcapacity may be considered a private matter, but these conditions do not obtain everywhere. In this context, processing capacity and location can be controlled either by a license or other approval under the forest law or by a particular kind of approval under a general industrial licensing law. In the latter case it is important that the forest authorities approve the processing of licenses, or at least be consulted.

---

[268] Ecuador, Acuerdo No. 04-071 sobre la derterminación de propiedades físicas e mecánicas del bambú (2004); Queensland's Timber Utilization and Marketing Act (1987), §§. 33–35; Vietnam, Decision No. 121/2002/QD-BNN (2002) promulgating branch standards in the field of forestry industry.

[269] *See* France's Arrêté of 2003 relatif à certaines normes qualitatives applicables à la production sur le territoire national de matériels forestiers de reproduction; Panama's Resolución no. 774—Criterios técnicos para árboles semilleros, 29 December 2004.

[270] China's Regulations on the implementation of the Standardization Law (1990); Ukraine's Law No. 2408-III (2001) on standardization.

[271] Canada's National Housing Act (1962).

[272] Venezuela, Ley de Mercadeo Agricola (2002).

PART FIVE

Financial and Enforcement Measures

CHAPTER 11

Financing and Taxation

Public finance in the field of forestry is complicated by the different ownership regimes and by the use of terminology that sometimes confuses conceptually distinct kinds of payment. For instance, "forest taxes" may refer to taxes on private forestry or to fees for logging in public forests. The matter is further confused by the complexity of taxation systems generally and the prevalence of forestry rebates and subsidies. Some of the tax issues related to private forestry were discussed in Chapter 5. This section focuses on fees, by whatever name, for the exploitation of public forests and on the financial management they entail.

11.1   Prices/Stumpage

There are a number of ways in which fees for the exploitation of forests can be calculated and collected. The traditional method is stumpage, in which the value of standing timber is estimated by establishing the value of logs and the cost of felling, extraction, and transport to market. There may also be land rent, reforestation fees, export fees, and a variety of other levies and payments.

The DRC manages to impose almost all these fees, among them surface (rent), felling, export, deforestation, and reforestation fees.[273] Papua New Guinea imposes a stumpage fee ("royalty")[274] and authorizes a series of special charges ("levies") to be imposed "in respect of, but not limited to, all or any of the following: (a) follow-up development; (b) provincial development; (c) forest management and development; (d) Papua New Guinea Forest Authority."[275] While there may be policy reasons for each of the charges authorized, it is doubtful that the different charges can be calibrated to maximize revenues and minimize distorting effects on forest activities.

Even with a single royalty payment based on stumpage value, there are considerable practical problems in setting and maintaining the proper value of payments. The obvious one is that it is difficult to keep up with the fluctuations in timber prices, although indexing can be used to provide an automatic adjustment.

---

[273] Democratic Republic of the Congo, Code forestier, art. 121.

[274] Papua New Guinea, Forest Act (1991), § 120.

[275] *Id.*, § 121.

Over the longer term, it is also difficult for a public administration to keep pace with developments in logging and extraction costs, or, more to the point, with what should be developments based on improved techniques. The stumpage fee itself does not offer any incentive for innovation, and any standard fee deprives the administration (or any resource owner) of the benefits of competition with potential licensees.

Some stumpage problems can be avoided by careful drafting. It is essential to avoid fixing fees in a law or other instrument that is hard to change, but unfortunately this is all too common.[276] As with other elements of forest law, it is also very useful to require that the process and formulas for setting forest fees be disclosed to the public to reduce collusion between licensees and administrators.

Fees calculated as a percentage of market or free on board value in exporting countries have the advantage of being easier to calculate and more transparent, but they, too, require that market values be monitored to avoid under-declaration.[277] Even simpler are fees per cubic meter[278] at a fixed rate for each species or group of species.[279]

Partly because of dissatisfaction with the results of fixed fees, recent forest legislation tends to favor auctions or competitive tenders for assigning cutting rights. This coincides with increasing reliance on long-term concessions, although those are usually adopted for management rather than revenue reasons.[280]

In principle, auctions or tenders offer the best chance of obtaining a good price or other benefits for timber, but realizing this objective depends on conditions that may not be present. In the first place, there need to be enough bidders for the process to be competitive. Then the bidders have to actually compete—collusion between regular bidders is a common flaw in auctions and tenders in all fields, not just forestry. The administration of the process then needs to be alert and honest: where there is much corruption, auction procedures are not likely to escape the taint. Tenders in particular also require real skill to identify the requisites of a good offer and negotiate final terms.

Even where auctions work well and major concessions are negotiated, standard fees have their uses. They are essential for small licenses where the transaction cost of auctions and negotiations would not only exceed any gain in revenue

---

[276] *See* Cirelli, *et al., supra* n. 51, at 133–34.

[277] Republic of Congo's Arrêté no. 637 du 31 décembre 2002 fixant le taux de la taxe d'abattage des bois des forêts naturelles (fee of 3 percent FOB).

[278] Or per tree: Senegal's Décret no 96-572 fixant les taxes et redevances en matière d'exploitation forestière.

[279] Peru's Resolución Ministerial no. 0245-2000-AG.

[280] *See* Cirelli, *et al., supra* n. 51, at 127–28.

but also exacerbate a process many forest users already see as too bureaucratic. Stumpage values also give a baseline for auctions and for negotiated fees. Forest laws can provide that fees be applied universally, and that concessions be awarded on the basis of additional payments.[281] Cameroon, for instance, does not require additional payments but judges applications for concessions in part on the amount the applicant promises to invest.[282]

As important as setting fees is collecting them. Licensees can be required to deposit estimated fees or post a bond before starting operations. This would seem mere prudence on the part of a forest owner, but the approach may not be feasible for small operators in some countries. A less satisfactory substitute is to provide in the forest law that unpaid fees create a lien on the timber and provide for enforcement through seizure.[283]

11.2   Reforestation Fees

Reforestation fees serve several different functions in a forest revenue system. They are often a substitute for the reforestation that would otherwise be required.[284] They may also be used to guarantee reforestation, being refunded if the task is properly executed. They may simply be another fee, the value of which has no necessary relation to the costs of reforestation. Or they may allow the forest administration to keep some of its revenue away from the general accounts.

As a means of ensuring reforestation, fees have distinct advantages over requiring trees to be planted. Logging companies are not necessarily the best candidates for reforestation operations. They may of course contract with specialized firms to carry it out, but this has the disadvantage of placing the logging company in the way of direct supervision by the forest administration. Reforestation may also be more desirable in a location other than the logged area, so the fee allows more flexibility for arrangements with other operators and perhaps other landowners.[285] Finally, if the forest administration is the reforester of last resort,

---

[281] Bolivia, Ley Forestal 1996.

[282] Cameroon, Décret no. 95/531/PM fixant les modalités d'application du régime des forêts, art. 64; Arrêté no. 0315/MINEF fixant les critères de présélection et les procédures de choix des soumissionnaires des titres d'exploitation forestière.

[283] New Brunswick's Crown Lands and Forest Act of May 17, 2005, cap. C-38.1, §§ 61–64.

[284] Guatemala Forest Act of December 2, 1996, arts. 46 and 47.

[285] *See id.*: if forest land is cleared, an equal area must be reforested or the equivalent sum paid; *see* Texier *supra* n. 53, at 90–91.

it may need an earmarked fee it can use for that purpose without impinging on its regular budget and without the delays often encountered in funding through the regular budgetary cycle.

11.3 Forest Funds

Forest funds are commonly found in legislation, although they are not always stocked with money. Rosenbaum and Lindsay give a thorough discussion of the legislation providing for forest funds.[286] Though recognizing that they vary in many respects, the authors set out the essential characteristics of a forest fund as:

- setting aside some part of national revenue for forestry;
- extending over more than one budgetary cycle; and
- having specified sources of revenue, such as forest fees and fines from forest offenses.

The purposes for which forest funds can be used are usually specified. Often payment of normal salaries or operating expenses is excluded. The funds may be limited to particular objects, such as reforestation, but often the list of permissible activities is so long that it does not appear to be designed to limit activities.

Besides earmarked forest revenues, forest funds may also receive appropriations in the general budget. Among the more inventive revenue sources are the proceeds of a hydrocarbon tax and a fuelwood tax in Costa Rica. Some funds can take out loans as well. This may be dangerous if fund managers can borrow without Ministry of Finance control.

Forest funds range from simple accounting devices to institutions with legal personality and independent decision-making power. It is quite common, and certainly in the interests of accountability, that decisions about expenses are referred to a management or advisory committee or similar body.

Forestry departments advocate for forest funds as a way of keeping revenues in the forestry sector and avoiding delays in disbursement of regular budget funds. The latter is particularly important when operations must be carried out at a particular time of year. Ministries of Finance, on the other hand, often oppose forest funds in the interest of general budget management. Though the arguments pro and con do not raise important legal issues, they do require broad political agreement.

---

[286] K. Rosenbaum & J. Lindsay, *An Overview of National Forest Funds: Current Approaches and Future Opportunities.* FAO Legal Paper Online No. 15 (FAO 2001).

Box 11–1: Forest Funds under the Cameroon Law

Cameroon Décret no. 96/237/PM of 1996 fixant les modalités de fonctionnement des Fonds Spéciaux, art. 8:

Article 8: Les dépenses supportées par le Fonds Spécial comprennent:

—les frais d'aménagement des réserves forestières non concédées en
exploitation;

—les frais de régénération et de reboisement;

—les frais d'inventaire forestier;

—les opérations de matérialisation des limites et de création des infrastructures;

—les équipements requis pour la réalisation des travaux d'inventaire et
d'aménagement forestier;

—les frais de contrôle technique et de suivi des aménagements forestiers
réalisés dans les concessions;

—les frais de vulgarisation des techniques et des résultats des recherches
sur les ressources forestières;

—le coût des études sectorielles dans le domaine forestier, notamment sur
la conservation durable de la biodiversité;

—les frais de fonctionnement du Comité de programmes prévu par le
présent décret, du comité technique des agréments et de la commission
interministérielle d'attribution des titres d'exploitation forestière;

—les frais d'appui aux activités de l'agent comptable tels qu'approuvés par
le Ministre chargé des forêts après avis du Ministre chargé des finances;

—les frais d'audit du Fonds Spécial;

—les fonds de contrepartie aux projets lorsque de tels fonds sont fournis
par l'Etat;

—les contributions de l'Etat aux organismes internationaux. Toutefois, ces
contributions ne peuvent être imputées ni sur le produit des recettes
énumérées à l'article 5, ni sur les frais de participation du concession-
naire aux travaux d'aménagement;

—les remises aux agents de l'administration chargée des forêts et de toute
autre administration ayant participé aux activités de répression et de
recouvrement, dans la limite du produit disponible à cet effet.

*The assets of the fund are not part of the general revenues of the treasury,
but they are often subject to normal public finance rules. If they are not,
alternative rules to ensure they are properly managed and used, often under
Ministry of Finance supervision, are provided.*

CHAPTER 12

Offenses and Penalties

Law enforcement has an essential role, but because of the complex nature of the forest itself it is really the last resort for obtaining compliance with the law. Where illegal logging, for example, is tied up with conflicting views of forest tenure (see Chapter 3), using the criminal law to resolve land disputes has obvious limitations.

Even when rights are clearly understood, the remoteness of forested areas creates enormous enforcement challenges. These expanses are more like those of open sea-fishing than other terrestrial resource uses. Almost by definition, forests are far from centers of population and even by rural standards are barely populated. Roads are rare, the forest itself is an impediment to movement, and the canopy hinders direct observation.

As a result, illegal loggers are hard to spot. Forest operators within the system of legal logging are much easier to keep track of because they are already identified. They also usually supply some information on where they are operating, which gives a good indication of where they may be conducting any unauthorized activities. They should in any case have an interest in maintaining their legal status and an incentive to reduce the competition of illegal products.

Christy treats the question of inducing loggers to enter the legal logging system at some length.[287] Here it is sufficient to say that the costs of legal logging have to be lower and the benefits higher than the costs and benefits of illegal logging. Once they are in the legal system, loggers have to comply with essential requirements.

Enforcement based on voluntary compliance does not assume that everyone will comply—even the volunteers need some encouragement. Even if the forest is remote, the forest administration must establish a presence if it is not to give the impression that the forest is abandoned. And though constant surveillance is not usually possible, monitoring based on information from forest users should usually be attainable.

Timely information on operations can be a basis for on-the-ground inspection.[288] This has to be based on legal requirements that operators supply information

---

[287] L. Christy, *Designing Forestry Legislation to Improve Compliance* (FAO 2004).

[288] A. Casson, A. Setyarso & M. Boccucci, *Illegal Logging and Law Enforcement in Indonesia,* 38 (World Bank/WWF Alliance 2004).

according to a standard and schedule; that they supply complementary information on request; and that officers have the power to inspect all sites relevant to the operation. Reporting is more often a requirement of licenses than a provision of forest law; either method is effective—if it is used.[289]

Reporting may also be required of timber dealers and processors, but to be effective this has to be tied into a comprehensive monitoring system. Simply compiling a list of transactions is not helpful; it must be done in concordance with a register of licensees and accurate reporting of logging operations. With the increased availability of computer networks, different data series can be correlated in real time—a powerful tool for both prevention and detection of forest crime.

12.1 Powers of Forest Officers

There is a general need for forest officers to inspect forest activities, at least those subject to license, but intrusive searches of houses and even shops are likely to be counterproductive. Every society has a certain sense of the limits of public powers. It is necessary to compare general criminal procedure law, police law, tax procedures, and health and safety legislation, for instance, with the actual use of powers and the training of that staff that exercise them. In general there will always be some tension between effective law enforcement and other social interests. Simple distinctions like that between public and private property break down when people are living in forest that is classed as state property.

There are at least three degrees of inspection powers that need to be considered in drafting a forest law. The first is routine inspections, which need to take place regardless of whether a crime is suspected and which cannot reasonably require a warrant. The next two are both undertaken when a crime is suspected and relate to those situations where a warrant should be required and those where it should not. How this is resolved depends on the general legal system, but considerations include the urgency of inspection (a moving vehicle), the difficulty of getting a warrant (when the site is deep in the forest), and the privacy normally accorded the site (a dwelling).

Normally all sites in a licensed area and all the transport, storage, and processing facilities adjunct to it should be subject to routine inspection. Otherwise inspection is useless for verifying the reliability of self-reporting. The Tanzania inspection power requires 48 hours notice, which is too long for real-time monitoring.[290] Compare the authority in Malawi,[291] pursuant to which an officer may

---

[289] DRC, Code forestier (2002), arts. 49–51, 130–33, 136–37, and 145–46; Malawi's Forest Act (1997), §§ 6(b) and 86(f); Tanzania's Forest Act (2002), § 104.

[290] Tanzania, Forest Act (2002), § 103.

[291] Malawi, Forest Act (1997), § 6(b).

(b) without a warrant—

    (i) stop and inspect any carrier or vehicle which the officer reasonably suspects is carrying any forest produce which has been obtained in contravention of this Act or for which a transportation document is required under this Act;

    (ii) enter any premises in a forest reserve, any land or premises in which any activity licensed under this Act is conducted or any village forest area or protected forest area and inspect such premises or land;

    (iii) enter upon any land, building, tent, carriage, motor vehicle, trailer, aircraft, boat or locomotive for ensuring that the provisions of this Act are being complied with, or for the purposes of detecting any offense against this Act; and

    (iv) enter any land or premises and inspect silvicultural, forest harvesting, and forest produce processing activities and wherever necessary provide advice on proper methods for carrying out such activities.

The Republic of Congo authorizes free access to facilities and vehicles but not to houses and domestic enclosures except in the case of a crime and in the presence of a police officer. Enforcement officers are not authorized to enter houses between 7:00 pm and 5:00 am.[292] Tanzania does not allow searches of dwellings except when a crime is suspected.[293]

Where a crime is suspected, powers must extend to the seizure of any evidence the disappearance of which could make further action futile. Seizure of tools and vehicles is also used in practice to prevent further offenses. This is often a punishment as well: even if seized items are eventually returned, being deprived of them for a time may represent a substantial loss from legitimate uses.

Custody and disposal of seized items must be handled carefully. Where quantities of timber are large, it is obviously impractical to carry it away. It may also be impractical to keep it for very long because of the risk that it will deteriorate. The forest administration therefore needs the power to sell or dispose of items at risk of deterioration, including discarding or destroying them if there is no buyer. The Tanzania Forest Act (2002) is typical[294]:

(1) Any article or forest produce seized . . . shall be brought to the nearest police station or if it is not feasible to deliver it to a police station it shall be delivered into the custody of the nearest reserve manager and a report of such

---

[292] Republic of Congo, Loi no. 16-2000 portant code forestier, art. 113.

[293] Tanzania, Forest Act (2002), §§ 93 and 103.

[294] § 94.

seizure shall be made forthwith to the senior police officer having jurisdiction within the area.

(2) Any article or forest [produce] held in custody by the police or a forest reserve manager shall be retained until the offense in connection with which it has been seized has been prosecuted or compounded or a decision has been taken not to prosecute.

(3) Where any seized article or forest produce is perishable, a forest reserve manager may order that the said article or forest produce be sold or destroyed and where it has been sold, the proceeds of the sale shall be retained and the provisions of subsection (2) shall apply to any such proceeds.

(4) Where the owner or a person in control of seized property fails to appear or absconds and abandons his property for a period of thirty days, the Director or and authorized officer may dispose of such property.

Cameroon also provides explicitly for the sale of perishable seized produce but does not explicitly deal with the destruction of items in a condition that prevents sale.[295]

The power of arrest also has to be specified if it is not already allowed by general police or criminal procedure acts. As with searches, there are both general and forest-specific considerations related to when arrest should be authorized and whether a warrant should be required. Some laws simply allow arrest for all forest offenses,[296] but this seems unnecessarily broad and risks subjecting authorized operators to harassment. Probably the most common requirement is that a suspected offender identify himself, or be subject to arrest if he refuses to do so credibly.[297] Arrest is also permitted if the suspect seems likely to flee. In many civil law jurisdictions arrest without a warrant is permitted where a suspect is caught in the act or cannot be identified[298]; otherwise a warrant is generally required.

Other powers are also needed to stop illegal activities. One that is very useful is the power to order an authorized forest user to stop some or all activities, but to avoid abuse the rank of officer that may order it and the circumstances in which it may be ordered should be specified. It is surely justified where continued operations threaten irreparable harm to the forest, but there is such a large middle ground where the threat is less that it is practically impossible to specify the degree of harm in legislation.

---

[295] Cameroon, Loi portant régime des forêts, de la faune et de la pêche (1994), art. 144.

[296] Namibia, Forest Act (1968) (repealed), § 17(2).

[297] Dominica, Forests Act (1991), § 14(f).

[298] DRC, Code forestier, art. 131.

Related to the power to stop operations is the power to suspend a license. This is extremely useful in preventing harmful operations while giving the operator an opportunity to correct faults. A particularly well-articulated structure of notifications and orders leading in the last resort to cancellation of licenses is found in the Vanuatu Forestry Act (2001).[299] Suspension may also be authorized without regard to prevention as a punishment for minor offenses,[300] but this seems wasteful unless there is no provision for fines in such circumstances.

Any power to stop operations has to be granted and exercised with care to avoid undermining the balance of incentives for compliance. In particular, licenses or concessions should be protected against arbitrary termination; disruptions in operations should be limited to cases where they are necessary to prevent serious damage; where there are violations, reasonable opportunity should be given to remedy them; and where operations are interrupted, they should be resumed as soon as the risk of damage has diminished (it will never entirely cease).

12.2 Offenses and Penalties

To correctly frame the gradation of offenses and penalties, offenses must be clearly defined; a provision like "any violation of this law is an offense punishable by 20 years imprisonment" is clearly unsuitable by this standard. It is also unsuitable for the practical purpose of stating clearly to both forest users and enforcement officers what actions are prohibited. The consequences of this failure are a loss of focus in enforcement and an invitation to corrupt officials to interpret the law according to their own interests.

It is also unsatisfactory to simply cite the section of the law that is violated without clearly defining the act that is considered to be a violation. For example, a provision stating that all operations shall be carried out in accordance with an approved management plan does not clearly distinguish between lack of a plan, defects in a plan, and failure to follow a plan.

Clarity is required not only in defining prohibited acts but also in attributing responsibility for the acts of employees and contractors. It is fairly straightforward to make a licensee responsible for the acts of employees and contractors because forest officials can easily see the relationship. It is usual but not universal to relieve the licensee of liability if the act was committed by a trespasser

---

[299] §§ 37–38.
[300] Cambodia, Law on Forestry (2002), § 79.

where licensee, employees, and contractors took all reasonable precautions to prevent the illegal act.

Where there is a corporate licensee, it is also possible to hold directors and officers responsible, although there may be good reason to excuse those who did not know about the offense or who did what a reasonable person might have done to prevent it. This is much less obvious in the case of an illegal logger, where even though connivance between the fellers and an eventual buyer may be suspected, it is difficult to prove. It is hard to identify a corporate defendant if there is no liability as licensee.

There is good reason for careful gradation of penalties, at least for offenses committed by authorized forest users, so as not to discourage licensed logging. There is also good reason for penalties that the community, especially forest users, and judges will consider reasonable. There is ample experience that, where judicial independence is respected, judges will not impose what they regard as draconian penalties. At the same time, the penalty must represent a real cost to the offender; otherwise it will be cheaper to log illegally. Because a reasonable penalty in one country might be highly unreasonable in another, no absolute level can be specified.

One problem that has arisen in many countries is how to preserve the real value of monetary penalties against devaluation. One solution is to authorize the responsible minister to increase fines, though in many jurisdictions this collides with the prerogatives of the legislature. Another solution is to index the fines to some unit, such as the minimum wage[301] or even a foreign currency, that is expected to have a reasonably constant value. Some countries simply revise all fines at regular intervals by a law or a Ministry of Justice regulation under specific legislative authority. Any of these can work, depending on local usage. What is necessary in high-inflation countries is to anticipate the way fines will be adjusted and, if no method is already in use, to incorporate one into the forest law.

An extremely useful complementary penalty is compensation for the amount of harm an illegal act has caused.[302] Laws can set compensation in various ways: in terms of the market value of the thing taken or damaged (useful for large trees); in terms of loss of future income from the land (useful for young trees with little present market value); in terms of the benefit to the wrongdoer (including profit made and government fees avoided); and in terms of the cost of repairing the damage.[303] The last is particularly useful for forests: when it includes the cost of

---

[301] Mexico, Ley General de Desarrollo Forestal Sustentable (2003), art. 165.

[302] Tanzania, Forest Act (2002), §§ 97(1)(b)–(d).

[303] *See* Kosovo, Forest Law (2003), § 28.2.

repairing damage to water bodies, soils, and habitat, restoration can recapture some of the environmental costs of illegal activity.

Collecting compensatory damages allows for some proportion between the size of the offense and the size of the penalty. Otherwise there would be the risk that illegally cutting one tree would be punished exactly the same as illegally cutting a thousand. This is also very useful in cases like fires, where the damage that negligent or willful acts may cause is enormous.

Another approach is to make each tree cut or damaged or each hectare burned a separate offense, raising the theoretical possibility of thousands of fines and prison sentences. The problem is that this leaves the judge with an enormous range of punishments and no real guidance on which to impose. The value of trees damaged, on the other hand, is relatively precise. Yet another approach to the problem is a fine per tree or, as in the DRC, per cubic meter of tree illegally cut.[304]

Another very common penalty is forfeiture of articles used to commit the offense, such as equipment and vehicles, and of the fruits of the crime, mainly timber. Forfeiture may also be ordered in civil proceedings in some jurisdictions; this gives the prosecution at least two advantages: a lower standard of proof and the ability to resolve the matter if the accused is not present. The disadvantage of forfeiture is the lack of proportion that may exist between the articles forfeited and the harm done in minor cases. For that reason, items subject to forfeiture might be limited to the fruits of the crime except in the most serious cases, which would include unlicensed logging but not violations of license conditions.

The loss of a forest license and disqualification from future licenses might be a criminal sanction, although there are also reasons to make cancellation of licenses a purely administrative measure.

12.3   Administrative Sanctions and Compounding

There are several alternatives to criminal proceedings that may carry the same kind of sanctions (except imprisonment). One is the administrative sanction in civil law, which is imposed directly by the executive branch without judicial involvement, although judicial appeals are allowed. In the United States there is a civil penalty for some natural resource offenses. Though it is imposed by the court, the standard of proof is civil rather than criminal. Considering that the essence of illegal logging is damage to property, this may be the most suitable way to proceed.

A related procedure is "compounding": the executive is empowered to accept a fine instead of bringing criminal proceedings, on condition that the offender accepts this procedure rather than insist on exercising the right to be tried. Compounding is clearly useful where the alternative is proceedings that may take

---

[304] DRC, Code forestier, art. 147.

place far from the home or workplace of the defendant and that in any case will cause expenses to both sides. The objection to compounding and to administrative fines levied on the spot is that they allow field staff to harass citizens, especially in the rural areas, with ill-founded requests for money. To some extent this can be countered by requiring that action be taken by an officer of a certain rank, which gives some assurance that the officer is familiar with the law and the policy of the administration.

A typical provision is found in Tanzania's Forest Act (2002), which authorizes the Director of Forestry or any officer specifically authorized by him or her to compound offenses. The amount payable may reach five times the maximum fine for the offense, in addition to fees, expenses, and damages. Compounding is a defense to prosecution for the same offense.[305] The DRC has issued an order setting out the procedure for compounding. It authorizes different levels of authority to compound for different amounts, ending with the minister where the amount exceeds 500,000 "constant" Congolese francs. The amount to be paid can be worked off as well as paid in cash.[306]

12.4 Evidence

There are at least three approaches to overcoming the difficulties of proving offenses that have taken place in remote locations. One is to focus enforcement on more visible acts, such as transport. Another, common in civil law, is to make the official report of a sworn official admissible as evidence in further proceedings. This effectively shifts the burden of proof to the defendant.[307] A third device is the use of evidentiary presumptions, which similarly shifts the burden of proof to the defendant.

Possession of logging and sawing equipment is easier to detect than the illegal act itself; allowing that in obviates the need to find evidence of actual illegal logging. As with many such provisions, this may be effective if the owner has little legitimate use for the equipment, but otherwise it can be a disproportionate (and thoroughly unpopular) burden on ordinary farm operations. If the restriction is limited to certain areas, such as classified forests, it may be more effective and less unpopular.[308] A similar consideration applies to evidentiary presumptions.

---

[305] Tanzania, Forest Act (2002), § 95.

[306] Arrêté ministerial n. CAB/MIN/AF.F-E.T/259/2002 fixant la procédure des transactions en matière forestière.

[307] DRC, Code forestier, arts. 116–19.

[308] Jamaica Forest Act (1996), §§ 31(1)(g) and 31(3).

A more nuanced aid to detection is to focus on those acts or elements that are most easily detected and proved. This is especially important in establishing the basis for forest fees. If scaling is a foreseeable problem, consideration can be given to payments based on surface area, which is difficult to hide. Contreras cites the example of Bolivia, which replaced an elaborate concession-fee system with a single fee of $1 per hectare.[309] A competitive market for forest licenses or concessions through auctions or competitive tenders with area-based bids can maximize revenue. It also allows the public to know how much revenue can be expected, so that shortfalls are more evident. The disadvantage is that area-based fees may create perverse incentives, but these can accompany stumpage systems as well.

Something similar would apply to control of charcoal-making, where it is easier to charge a fee for the finished product in the urban market than to try to supervise activities in the forest. If collecting the fees is difficult, forest supervision is even harder. A similar consideration would apply to large timber operations where, if there is the political will to do so, particular transport, collecting, processing, and export points are more effectively controlled than logging sites.

A method often used to monitor extraction is the transport permit. This is required almost everywhere but seems to be much less effective than it should be.[310] If the logs transported can be linked electronically with other information from the forest and destination points, transport monitoring could be very useful.[311]

Evidentiary presumptions may be factually reasonable, such as that any person found with forest produce in a forest has taken it from that forest. In other cases, the defendant is in the best position to prove a matter, such as having paid royalties or having a license.[312] In still other cases, however, the presumption seems unreasonable, as that any person with logging equipment in a forest intends to take forest produce there.[313] Some laws go further by presuming the essential elements of the crime, as in New South Wales, Australia, where the allegation that a sign was altered without authority is to be accepted unless the defendant proves the contrary.[314] Several countries require the defendant to prove that any forest produce in his or her possession was not acquired illegally.[315]

---

[309] *See* Contreras-Hermosilla, *supra* n. 45, at 19.

[310] *See* Casson, *et al., supra* n. 130.

[311] W. Magrath & R. Grandalski, *Forest Law Enforcement: Policies, Strategies and Technologies* (World Bank 2004).

[312] Namibia's Forest Act (1968) (repealed), § 22(2).

[313] Sabah's Forest Act (1968), § 38(9)(d).

[314] Forestry Act (1916), § 45B.

[315] Ghana's Forest Protection Decree (1974), § 7.

Some of the best evidence of forest activities comes from aerial surveillance and satellite detection, but its evidentiary value may be uncertain. Expertise is required to interpret remote sensing data, and courts may not be willing to admit expert testimony if they are not familiar with the subject matter. Getting new kinds of evidence, such as remote sensing data, accepted may require a law, a decision of the judicial council, or a court ruling. It will also probably require work with the judiciary to explain the relevant techniques and qualifications.

Another aid to detection of forest offenses may be to encourage informers. General law often provides for rewards to persons who help in the conviction of offenders, and in some countries, like the DRC, even forest officials, whose job it is to enforce the law, are entitled to rewards.[316] While rewards for conviction may have their place, they are not likely to be paid out very often. Where officials are allowed to share the reward, nonofficial collaborators are likely to have difficulty collecting. In fact, the DRC example allows for citizen informers in the law but not in the order setting out the division of rewards. Even when officials are excluded, the requirement of a conviction means that most helpful information will not be eligible for a reward. Giving a share of rewards to officials, especially combined with the ability to levy fines on the spot (see below), may also encourage petty harassments to gain rewards at the expense of more laborious investigation of major offenses. It has even been suggested[317] that such rewards give officials a stake in the continuation of illegal logging.

What is more likely to produce useful information is allowing for rewards to be paid without conviction and protection from vengeful defendants. These may well be employers, in the case of corporate misdeeds, or neighbors or others able to inflict real harm on an informer. In the common case of official corruption, the best informers may be civil servants, who would need protection from their own departments and the normal civil service duty not to divulge official information. However, the problem of how to treat informers seems to be a general problem of law enforcement, so if new legislation is needed it should be part of the general criminal law.

Several commentators have argued that money-laundering laws can be used effectively against large-scale illegal logging.[318] Where there is a determined anticorruption program, tracing the proceeds of illegal activities is highly likely

---

[316] DRC, Code forestier (2002), art. 172 and Arrêté n. 6385; *cf.* Namibia Forest Act (1968), § 25.

[317] *See* Casson, *et al., supra* n. 130, at 33.

[318] *See id.* at 47, and L. Tacconi, M. Boscolo, & D. Brack, *National and International Policies to Control Illegal Forest Activities,* 27 (CIFOR 2003).

to be a way both of detecting crimes and of recovering the proceeds, but in the typical circumstances of massive illegal logging it seems unlikely to be used effectively.[319]

12.5   Training

A forest law is not self-enforcing. To make good use of its administrative and criminal provisions, forest officers, police, prosecutors, and judges need to be familiar with them and understand the reasons for them. Sectoral administrators for all of the natural resources complain of their frustration when prosecutions fail or inappropriate sanctions are imposed because prosecutors and judges do not understand the law.

One solution is fairly straightforward: authorize forest officers to prosecute cases. This is quite common in both civil and common law forest legislation.[320] Tanzania has an interesting variation: the Director of Forestry and any officer authorized by the Director of Public Prosecutions may prosecute forestry offenses.[321]

No matter who prosecutes forestry offenses, personnel must be well trained. Training forest personnel in the law should be a matter of course, but it is surprising how unfamiliar forest officers are with forestry law, especially newer provisions. Forest officers also require specialized training in law enforcement, especially evidentiary matters, if they are to play an essential role in prosecuting forestry offenses. If they actually prosecute cases, they also need training in case preparation and court procedures.

In many countries stakeholders are active in reporting on illegal logging.[322] It has been suggested that many of them would benefit from training in the use of modern detection techniques, such as photography, log tracking, and remote sensing. The effects of this training would depend in part on the admissibility of the evidence they produced.

For police, prosecutors, and judges, workshops and written explanations of the law should be sufficient to begin to familiarize them with it. Longer term, including forestry in environmental law courses and law enforcement training is needed.

---

[319] *See* Casson, *et al., supra* n. 130, at 47.

[320] DRC, Code forestier (2002), art. 127; Dominica, Forests Act (1991), § 19; Gabon, Code forestier (2001), art. 268.

[321] Tanzania's Forests Act (2002), § 96.

[322] *See* Global Witness, *supra* n. 18.

It is also important for forestry law to follow the style and procedure of the general criminal law. Where forest offenses are already provided for in criminal law, it is essential to amend the latter if new offenses are created or penalties modified. Otherwise judges are likely to continue to apply the law they know and ignore the new one.[323] Issues like warrants, administrative procedures, and criminal penalties need to be considered in terms not only of forestry but also of the general legal system and its officers if prosecutors, judges, and other nonforesters are to understand and apply the forestry law.

---

[323] *See* Casson, *et al., supra* n. 130, at 50.

CHAPTER 13

Conclusion

The purpose of this study is to give the reader a systematic guide to the basic features of modern forestry legislation and to issues that must be confronted as countries seek to improve the legal framework for sustainable forest management. It has examined how forest laws deal—sometimes well, sometimes poorly—with a wide range of issues, from forest demarcation, management planning, and inventories to community and private management, institutional and financial arrangements, and enforcement measures. It has also tried to locate forestry law within a wider legal context, emphasizing its complex interactions with land, environment, trade, criminal, and other areas of domestic law and the influence of international treaties and norms.

The emphasis here has been on analyzing and improving the texts of laws. The basic premise is that getting the law right is an essential part of creating an enduring foundation for sustainable forest management. In closing, however, it is important to stand back for a moment and acknowledge some limitations.

In many countries the contrast between what forestry law prescribes and what actually happens on the ground is both stark and obvious. Even where the law is strong, illegal behavior by both public and private actors often thrives. The explanations put forward for this phenomenon are familiar: forest departments lack the financial and human resources to monitor and control forest activities, which often take place in very remote areas; government officials entrusted with enforcing the law may be under immense pressure to condone violations, or engage in violations themselves; court systems are backlogged or bankrupt; the difficulties of daily life for the rural poor may overwhelm any likely risks associated with violating the law; etc.

These explanations underscore the point that while good forestry legislation is necessary, it is obviously not sufficient. The laws in many countries lie unused or underused for reasons like failure of political will, weak institutions, or even general disregard for the rule of law.

Aside from reinforcing the truism that good law is not in and of itself enough, however, the disconnect between the law on the books and the law in action offers very important lessons for the drafters of forestry legislation. These lessons relate both to the process by which laws are drafted and disseminated and to their content.

With respect to process, the drafting of sound and workable legislation requires that all categories of stakeholders be genuinely involved—government and nongovernmental institutions, central and local institutions, communities and local forest-dependent people, and private sector organizations. This recommendation flows not only from a belief that people should have the right to be involved but more practically from the fact that unless they are involved, there is little hope of passing laws that reflect reality and will be honored.

Governments often fail to engage civil society in the design of important laws and to educate people about their content once they have been passed. They therefore fail to build up support for the law among the people most directly affected. The result is that many may resist implementation of the law or may be ignorant of how to comply with it or take advantage of the opportunities it offers. Similarly, too often drafting of a forest law is not sufficiently grounded in the technical knowledge of practicing foresters who are best placed to know the constraints faced in the field and what remedial options are practical.

On the other hand, the drafting of a forest law may be too much dominated by the perspectives of the forestry sector or the legal profession. As this study has demonstrated, the concerns of modern forestry law are increasingly intertwined with numerous other areas of law and policy. Failure to take these linkages into account during drafting, in terms both of substance and of engaging collaboration from other sectors and disciplines, can lead to laws that are inconsistent with other national laws and that are poorly understood or resented by important actors. Yet legal drafting is often seen as a technical exercise that only lawyers can understand, with the result that the process often does not benefit from insights from other disciplines, such as sociology—insights that are particularly important as we learn more about the interrelationships between social systems and forest practices.

In recent years there has been a growing effort to identify and implement best practices to address these concerns. In an increasing number of cases formulation of forestry laws has been accompanied by extensive consultation and outreach at all levels, supported by social and economic research. There has also been a new emphasis on educating a wide range of people, from forest communities and local forest officers to judges and administrators, about laws once they have been passed. Yet in most cases, much deeper and more sustained attention to these dimensions is still needed.

There is no doubt that extralegal factors, such as corruption or fragile institutions, can often undermine the effectiveness of well-drafted laws. But this concern should not obscure the fact that how forestry laws are drafted can have a powerful influence on their success. If a law is to create a realistic foundation for its own implementation, it needs to provide scope for meaningful participation in forest decision-making; to increase the stake that people have in sustainable management; to improve the transparency and accountability of forest institutions; and to set forth rules that are coherent, comprehensible, and realistic.

APPENDICES

APPENDIX **1**

The World Bank Forests Policy

The World Bank Operational Manual (OP) 4.36— Operational Policies

These policies were prepared for use by World Bank staff and are not necessarily a complete treatment of the subject.

November 2002

Forests

This Operational Policy statement was revised in August 2004 to reflect the term "development policy lending" (formerly adjustment lending), in accordance with OP/BP 8.60, issued in August 2004.

Note: OP and BP 4.36, *Forests,* replace OP and GP 4.36, *Forestry,* dated September 1993, and are based on *A Revised Forests Strategy for the World Bank Group,* endorsed by the Board of Executive Directors on October 31, 2002. Other related Bank policies include OP 4.01, *Environmental Assessment,* OP 4.04, *Natural Habitats,* OP 4.10, *Indigenous Peoples,* OP 4.11, *Physical Cultural Resources,* and OP 4.12, *Involuntary Resettlement.* These OP and BP apply to all projects for which a Project Concept Review takes place after January 1, 2003. Questions may be addressed to the Director, Rural Development Department, or the Director, Environment Department, ESSD.

Policy Objectives

1. The management, conservation, and sustainable development of forest ecosystems and their associated resources are essential for lasting poverty reduction and sustainable development, whether located in countries with abundant forests or in those with depleted or naturally limited forest resources. The objective of this policy is to assist borrowers[1] to harness the potential of

---

[1] "Bank" includes IBRD and IDA. "Borrower" includes the member country guarantor of a loan made to a nonmember and, for guarantee operations, a private or public project sponsor receiving from another financial institution a loan guaranteed by the Bank. "Project" covers all operations financed under Bank loans, credits or guarantees and IDA

159

forests[2] to reduce poverty in a sustainable manner, integrate forests effectively into sustainable economic development, and protect the vital local and global environmental services and values of forests.

2. Where forest restoration and plantation development are necessary to meet these objectives, the Bank assists borrowers with forest restoration activities that maintain or enhance biodiversity and ecosystem functionality. The Bank also assists borrowers with the establishment and sustainable management of environmentally appropriate, socially beneficial, and economically viable forest plantations to help meet growing demands for forest goods and services.

Scope of Policy

3. This policy applies to the following types of Bank-financed investment projects:

(a) projects that have or may have impacts on the health and quality of forests;

(b) projects that affect the rights and welfare[3] of people and their level of dependence upon or interaction with forests; and

(c) projects that aim to bring about changes in the management, protection, or utilization of natural forests or plantations, whether they are publicly, privately, or communally owned.

Country Assistance Programs

4. The Bank uses environmental assessments, poverty assessments, social analyses, Public Expenditure Reviews, and other economic and sector work to identify the economic, environmental, and social significance of forests in its borrowing countries. When the Bank identifies the potential for its Country Assistance Strategy (CAS) to have a significant impact on forests, it integrates strategies for addressing that impact into the CAS.

---

grants, but excludes development policy lending (for which the environmental provisions are set out in OP/BP 8.60, *Development Policy Lending*) and debt and debt service operations. "Project" also includes projects and components funded under the Global Environment Facility, but excludes such projects executed by organizations identified by the GEF Council as eligible to work with the GEF through expanded opportunities for project preparation and implementation (such organizations include, inter alia, regional development banks and UN agencies such as FAO and UNIDO).

[2] Definitions are provided in Annex A.

[3] The rights and welfare of people affected by projects should be assessed in relation to the requirements and procedures of OP 4.10, *Indigenous Peoples,* OP 4.11, *Physical Cultural Resources,* and OP 4.12, *Involuntary Resettlement.*

Bank Financing

5. The Bank does not finance projects that, in its opinion, would involve significant conversion or degradation[4] of critical forest areas[5] or related critical natural habitats.[6] If a project involves the significant conversion or degradation of natural forests or related natural habitats that the Bank determines are not critical, and the Bank determines that there are no feasible alternatives to the project and its siting, and comprehensive analysis demonstrates that overall benefits from the project substantially outweigh the environmental costs, the Bank may finance the project provided that it incorporates appropriate mitigation measures.[7]

6. The Bank does not finance projects that contravene applicable international environmental agreements.[8]

Plantations

7. The Bank does not finance plantations that involve any conversion or degradation of critical natural habitats, including adjacent or downstream critical natural habitats. When the Bank finances plantations, it gives preference to siting such projects on unforested sites or lands already converted (excluding any lands that have been converted in anticipation of the project). In view of the potential for plantation projects to introduce invasive species and threaten biodiversity, such projects must be designed to prevent and mitigate these potential threats to natural habitats.

Commercial harvesting

8. The Bank may finance commercial harvesting operations[9] only when the Bank has determined, on the basis of the applicable environmental assessment or

---

[4] *See* OP 4.04, *Natural Habitats,* Annex A, *Definitions*. (In determining the significance of any conversion or degradation, the Bank applies a precautionary approach; *see* OP 4.04, paragraph 1.)

[5] *See* Definitions, item c.

[6] *See* OP 4.04, *Natural Habitats,* Annex A, *Definitions*, item b.

[7] For provisions on designing and implementing mitigation measures for projects that may have an impact upon forests and natural habitats, *see* OP 4.01, *Environmental Assessment,* and OP 4.04, *Natural Habitats.*

[8] *See* OP 4.01, paragraph 3.

[9] Commercial harvesting operations are conducted by entities other than those described in items d and e in the Definitions.

other relevant information, that the areas affected by the harvesting are not critical forests or related critical natural habitats.[10]

9. To be eligible for Bank financing, industrial-scale commercial harvesting operations must also

(a) be certified under an independent forest certification system acceptable to the Bank[11] as meeting standards of responsible forest management and use; or

(b) where a pre-assessment under such an independent forest certification system determines that the operation does not yet meet the requirements of subparagraph 9(a), adhere to a time-bound phased action plan acceptable to the Bank[12] for achieving certification to such standards.

10. To be acceptable to the Bank, a forest certification system must require:

(a) compliance with relevant laws;

(b) recognition of and respect for any legally documented or customary land tenure and use rights as well as the rights of indigenous peoples and workers;

(c) measures to maintain or enhance sound and effective community relations;

(d) conservation of biological diversity and ecological functions;

(e) measures to maintain or enhance environmentally sound multiple benefits accruing from the forest;

(f) prevention or minimization of the adverse environmental impacts from forest use;

(g) effective forest management planning;

(h) active monitoring and assessment of relevant forest management areas; and

(i) the maintenance of critical forest areas and other critical natural habitats affected by the operation.

---

[10] However, the Bank may finance community-based harvesting activities that take place within Category VI Protected Areas, Managed Resource Protected Areas that are established and managed mainly for the sustainable use of natural ecosystems (*see* Definitions footnote 2). In these areas, Bank financial support is restricted to situations where such activities are permitted under the legislation governing the establishment of the area and where the activities form an integral part of the management plan for the area. Any such financial support must comply with paragraph 12 of this OP.

[11] A forest certification system puts in place a process where a forest area is inspected by an independent certification body to determine whether its management meets clearly defined criteria and performance standards. The requirements for a certification system to be acceptable to the Bank are outlined in paragraphs 10 and 11 of this OP.

[12] *See* BP 4.36, paragraph 5.

11. In addition to the requirements in paragraph 10, a forest certification system must be independent, cost-effective, and based on objective and measurable performance standards that are defined at the national level and are compatible with internationally accepted principles and criteria of sustainable forest management. The system must require independent, third-party assessment of forest management performance. In addition, the system's standards must be developed with the meaningful participation of local people and communities; indigenous peoples; non-governmental organizations representing consumer, producer, and conservation interests; and other members of civil society, including the private sector. The decision-making procedures of the certification system must be fair, transparent, independent, and designed to avoid conflicts of interest.

12. The Bank may finance harvesting operations conducted by small-scale landholders,[13] by local communities under community forest management, or by such entities under joint forest management arrangements, if these operations:

(a) have achieved a standard of forest management developed with the meaningful participation of locally affected communities, consistent with the principles and criteria of responsible forest management outlined in paragraph 10; or

(b) adhere to a time-bound phased action plan[14] to achieve such a standard. The action plan must be developed with the meaningful participation of locally-affected communities and be acceptable to the Bank.

The borrower monitors all such operations with the meaningful participation of locally affected communities.

Project Design

13. In accordance with OP/BP 4.01, *Environmental Assessment*, the environmental assessment (EA) for an investment project addresses the potential impact of the project on forests and/or the rights and welfare of local communities.[15]

14. For projects involving the management of forests proposed for Bank financing, the borrower furnishes the Bank with relevant information on the forest sector concerning the borrower's overall policy framework, national legislation, institutional capabilities, and the poverty, social, economic, or environmental

---

[13] "Small-scale" is determined by the national context of a given country and is generally relative to the average size of household forest landholdings. In some situations, small-scale landholders may control less than a hectare of forests; in others they may control 50 hectares or more.

[14] *See* BP 4.36, paragraph 5.

[15] *See* Definitions, item d.

issues related to forests. This information should include information on the country's national forest programs or other relevant country-driven processes. On the basis of this information and the project's EA,[16] the borrower, as appropriate, incorporates measures in the project to strengthen the fiscal, legal, and institutional framework to meet the project's economic, environmental, and social objectives. These measures address, among other issues, the respective roles and legal rights of the government, the private sector, and local people. Preference is given to small-scale, community-level management approaches where they best harness the potential of forests to reduce poverty in a sustainable manner.[17]

15. As appropriate, the design of projects that use forest resources or provide environmental services includes an evaluation of the prospects for the development of new markets and marketing arrangements for non-timber forest products and related forest goods and services, taking into account the full range of goods and environmental services from well-managed forests.

---

[16] *See* BP 4.36, paragraph 3, for guidance on the assignment of EA categories for forest projects.

[17] *See* BP 4.36, paragraph 4.

A Summary of the Forest Policies of the African and Asian Development Banks

A. Forestry Policy of the African Development Bank (2003)

The Forestry Policy of the African Development Bank is elaborated in the framework of the "Integrated Environmental and Social Impact Assessment Guidelines."[1] It defines the factors that must be taken into account in developing forest projects or projects that might have potential impacts on forests.

The Integrated Environmental and Social Impact Assessment Guidelines aim to assist in developing forestry projects that can address the Bank's priority crosscutting themes. They highlight major issues and potential impacts that should be taken into account during project preparation and impact assessment. The appropriate enhancement and mitigation measures should be integrated as early as possible, preferably in the project design.

The Guidelines focus on the activities inducing the most significant environmental and social impacts, particularly commercial harvesting. Appendix 3 of the Guidelines covers agroforestry, tree planting, and natural forest management that are generally components of rural development projects.

The major issues related to forestry projects are as follows:

Poverty

Ensuring that projects help to reduce poverty requires considering the status of social and economic components influencing poverty. Key components that are considered under poverty are (i) economic activity, employment, and incomes; (ii) access to benefits, particularly for the poor and other vulnerable groups; (iii) skills, knowledge, and attitude toward forest management; (iv) availability of and access to infrastructures and services; and (v) access and ownership of forest products.

---

[1] African Development Bank, Integrated Environmental and Social Impact Assessment Guidelines, October 2003.

Environment

Key components are (i) protection of soils; (ii) water management; (iii) wildlife habitat and biodiversity; (iv) tree species selection; (v) forest products management; (vi) vegetation coverage, diversity, and climate change; and (vii) waste management.

Gender

Integrating a gender perspective into the environmental and social assessment process implies taking into account gender differences in roles, rights, priorities, opportunities, and constraints. Key issues are (i) control over the land and land proceeds; (ii) income-generating activities for women; (iii) access of women to new facilities and services; (iv) women's specific demands; and (v) involvement of women in decision-making processes.

Public Participation

Participation refers to the goal of actively involving project stakeholders, particularly those who stand to gain or to lose from a project, into the development, implementation, and evaluation of Bank activities. This goal implies sharing information and control over social, political, and development initiatives, decisions, and resources. Key issues are (i) participation of affected groups in consultations; (ii) creation of community-based organizations in forestry management; and (ii) expansion of civil society organization networks working on environmental protection.

B. Forestry Policy of the Asian Development Bank (1995)

Basic Principles

The Asian Development Bank issued its Policy on Forestry in February 1995. The Policy is founded on three imperative:

(i) *Protection:* The protective functions of forests with respect to soil, water, and biodiversity are vital for the welfare of present and future generations; hence sustainability of forest ecosystems is an essential component of environmental conservation.

(ii) *Production:* Forests provide renewable resources for the production of goods and services increasingly in demand; sustainable harvesting is a legitimate objective of the management of natural forests and forest plantations.

(iii) *Participation:* The involvement of people, where appropriate with the help of NGOs, in policy formulation and implementation is both an objective and a means of development. The participation of all stakeholders can ensure a rational balance between its ecological and economic roles.

The policy stresses the need to strengthen national regulatory and management frameworks for the conservation, management, and development of forest resources. Since government resources and capacities are typically limited, it is necessary to devise approaches to delegating responsibilities to the private sector, NGOs, and forest-dependent communities. Governments need to devise tenure policies and instruments and timber pricing regimes that act as incentives for the long-term sustainable management of forests; and to introduce supportive legislation, long-term planning, and responsive research and enforcement mechanisms, as well as strengthen local institutions and impact assessment systems.

Key Policy and Regulatory Elements

Forest zoning and regulation

The Bank supports natural resource inventories not restricted to forestlands alone and helps countries to zone lands based on appropriate use. The Bank also helps countries develop and strengthen mechanisms by which the use of forest lands will be regulated to ensure that adequate areas remain under tree cover and that a balance is achieved between protected and production forests.

Macroeconomic and intersectoral policies

In the agriculture sector, the Bank promotes a policy framework that will encourage intensive production on existing lowlands; agroforestry in upland areas already under cultivation; reforestation; plantation forest development; and soil conservation technology on degraded forest lands.

Land tenure policies

The Bank encourages and helps countries to establish proper land use policies and rationalize user rights to publicly owned forest areas. The Bank will, before financing any forestry project, carry out social assessments and necessary social design studies in accordance with standard Bank procedures to examine the degree to which customary land rights and land tenure of relevant forest dwelling and forest-dependent communities are satisfactory. It will also design and agree upon, with borrowers, necessary steps to rectify significant shortcomings in these areas.

Terms of access to timber resources

The Bank encourages policy changes in the terms of timber concessions and access to forest resources that will require lessees to bear the full cost of timber production, including the environmental costs to the extent these can be identified and quantified, and will ensure that the lessees themselves shoulder the cost of and responsibility for maintaining the asset. The Bank encourages the imposition of a performance deposit sufficient to provide a financial incentive for concessionaires to undertake sustainable forestry practices.

Promoting public consultation in forestry development

The Bank actively promotes the involvement of people from a wide cross-section of society in forestry policy formulation and implementation. The Bank together with country governments will, before financing any forestry project, carry out social assessments and necessary social design studies in accordance with standard Bank procedures, including assessing the role of women in total resource utilization and production to identify constraints facing women so as to ensure appropriate levels of beneficiary consultation/participation at all stages of project identification, preparation, and implementation; and to design and agree upon, with borrowers, necessary activities in this regard. The Bank will also help countries to develop and strengthen mechanisms by which public consultation on forestry issues can be facilitated and forest-dwelling and forest-dependent communities can be involved in land-use decisions related to forest lands.

APPENDIX 3

Concessions

1. Cambodia[a]

Law on Forestry (2002); Chapter 5: Forest Concession Management (articles 13–19).

Since 1998 the forest administration has adopted regulations and guidelines to control and safeguard forest management practice in those forest areas under concession. The three most important documents are the Forest Law, the Subdecree on Forest Concession Management (especially Chapter 3), and the Forest Concession Management Planning Manual.

Article 18 of the Forestry Law states that concessionaires shall prepare a concession management plan and implement it in compliance with guidance provided in the Planning Manual, the Cambodian Code of Practice for Forest Harvesting, and the terms stated in the Concession Agreement. Each concessionaire shall prepare:

—Long-term management plan for the entire concession;
—Annual operational plans for each coupe; and
—Block management plans for each annual harvest.

The Subdecree sets out the following overall objectives related to planning:

—To develop a forest concession planning, implementation, and control system that will lead to balanced, sustainable, and technically competent management of production forests;
—To ensure that concession forest management regimes conserve and protect natural biodiversity, ecosystem function, and important forest services such as soil conservation and watershed regulation;
—To protect and maintain rights of access to those forest resources occurring on concession areas that are of economic, subsistence, and spiritual value to local communities;
—To ensure regular consultation with, and participation by, local communities and other stakeholders in the development of concession management plans and the monitoring of operational activities over the life of the concession; and
—To establish a competent forest management planning and control system that will provide a context for and encouragement to applications by the Cambodian Timber Industry for International Forest Management Certification.

The concession forest management planning system is based on the three-stage planning process described in the Planning Manual. The task of drawing up the management plan is given to the concessionaire, while the forest administration has responsibility to approve and control each planning step.

The Planning Manual is understood as a beginning step in forest concession planning reform, and it is foreseen that difficulties that will be encountered during the implementation of this manual may lead to its continuous review and improvement. The concessionaires were available for consultation during preparation of later versions of the management plans, and the Strategic Forest Management Plans (SFMPs) and Environmental and Social Impact Assessments (ESIAs) reflect all relevant regulations.

The primary purposes of the SFMPs as defined in the Planning Manual are to:

—Demonstrate the technical and administrative capacity of the concessionaire to manage the plan area;
—Describe and evaluate the commercial potential of the forest resources in the plan area;
—Protect fragile land on steep slopes, conserve water resources, and protect wildlife and biodiversity;
—Obtain community support for, and participation in, forest management;
—Optimize social, environmental, and economic benefits from the plan area;
—Sustain the supply of timber and other forest products and services;
—Support research that will lead to improved management practices; and
—Serve as the primary document for both the forest management approval process and the environmental impact assessment process.

The spirit of the Planning Manual is to promote an open, transparent planning process. A commitment to the harmonization of the interests of different stakeholders is envisaged from the outset. The Manual states that "each plan will be guided by terms-of-reference prepared prior to the beginning of plan preparation in consultation with all stakeholders, relevant national and provincial government agencies and local communities."

A prospective forest concession requires an environmental impact assessment (EIA) as part of its approval process. The Ministry of Environment, as the lead agency for environmental protection, has formulated two principal Subdecrees and one Declaration governing EIA and the preparation of reports. With forest concessions, however, there has been considerable confusion regarding whether the Ministry of Environment or the Ministry of Agriculture, Forestry, and Fisheries has the authority to review, approve, and control the environmental work. According to the legislation, the Ministry of Environment has the authority for all EIA processes but under concession management guidelines, social impact assessment was incorporated with the EIA, creating the Environmental and Social Impact Assessment (ESIA), and the authority for this was then considered to rest with the Ministry of Agriculture, Forestry, and Fisheries. To address this confusion, it was agreed that the Ministry of Environment will approve the Terms of Reference (TOR) and work plan for the proposed ESIA.

a. Adapted from A. Hinrichs & C. McKenzie, *Results of the Independent Review of Strategic Forest Management PlansPprepared by Concession Companies Operating in Cambodia* (GFA 2004).

2. Cameroon[b]

The allocation of forest concessions by auction is one of the elements of forestry policy changes in Cameroon that began with a new forestry law, Law No 94/01 of January 20, 1994. Others include restrictions on log exports, fiscal incentives for local wood processing, the creation of community and communal forests, fiscal decentralization, and measures to improve the amount and quality of information made public. It was expected that the timber auctions would provide several benefits compared to the so-called *de gré à gré* (mutual agreement) system, such as greater transparency in concession allocation decisions and less corruption; an increased flow of revenue to the government; and an economically more efficient forest sector.

Timber auctions are organized under Decree No 95/531 of August 23, 1995 (articles 63–78) that established four categories of timber-harvesting permits. The two relevant to the auction system are *ventes de coupe* (VC) and *unités forestières d'aménagement* (UFA). VCs are short-term logging permits; UFAs are long-term forest management permits. UFA permit holders are required to prepare forest management plans that must be approved by the Ministry of Environment and Forest (MINEF) before full-scale logging can begin. Regulation of logging in UFAs is based on area control, with a 30-year cutting cycle: 1/30th of the concession area may be logged each year. The 30-year cutting cycle is the reason the contract length for a UFA is 30 years. UFAs are in the permanent forest estate (PFE); VCs are outside it, often in forests that have been previously logged. The other two new types of permits, *autorisations de récupération* and *permis d'exploitation*, are short-term permits for harvesting small volumes of timber (30 and 500 cubic meters, respectively) in forests outside the PFE. They are reserved for Cameroon nationals.

Basic auction procedures are similar for VCs and UFAs. The Ministry of Environment and Forest announces the list of tracts that have been placed on the auction block several months before bids are due to allow prospective bidders time to collect information. Bids are submitted in writing and are sealed. Bids consist of more than financial offers because allocations take into consideration bidders' technical capabilities. Bidders submit documents that enable the Ministry to construct a technical profile for each bidder. Bidders earn points for various criteria, such as the company's experience in Cameroon, its wood-processing facilities, and is past compliance with forest laws and regulations. The technical criteria are similar for VCs and UFAs. The Ministry constructs an overall score for each bidder by weighting the bidder's financial offer 70 percent and its technical score 30 percent. Based on these scores recommended allocations are submitted for approval to the Prime Minister. For UFAs, the recommendations are made by an interministerial commission, not the MINEF alone. The Prime Minister is allowed to overrule the recommendations if national interests are threatened. Allocations are typically announced several months after bids have been submitted. Several more months elapse before the contract for a VC or UFA is signed.

After timber auctions began, the World Bank proposed the appointment of an independent observer to enhance the transparency of the allocation process. The government did not do so until 1999, when it appointed a Cameroonian law firm as the Independent Observer of Forest Concession Allocation. The Independent Observer participates in meetings of the interministerial commission, reviews bidding documents, observes the process whereby award recommendations are made, and submits a report to the Minister of Environment and Forests and the Prime Minister.

The auction system was a more competitive and transparent mechanism for the allocation of logging permits than the former administrative system. Although government revenue from the forest sector declined after the system was put in place, that was due to the government's decision to restrict log exports. With the assistance of the World Bank, the government has responded to problems with the auction system in innovative ways, in particular by appointing independent observers for the auctions and forest law enforcement and by putting in place an interministerial program that has improved forest revenue collection.

b. Adapted from the following texts: J. Vincent, M. Boscolo & C. Gibson, draft, *Cameroon Timber Auctions: An Economic and Political Analysis;* Global Witness, *Forest Law Enforcement in Cameroon,* 1st Summary Report of the Independent Observer, May–November 2001 (Global Witness 2002); Global Witness, *Forest Law Enforcement in Cameroon,* 2nd Summary Report of the Independent Observer (Global Witness 2003); J. Collomb, & H. Bikié, *1999–2000 Allocation of Logging Permits in Cameroon: Fine-Tuning Central Africa's First Auction System,* (Global Forest Watch, World Resources Institute 2001).

APPENDIX 4

Forest Taxation System

1. Cameroon[c]

The 1994 Forest Law (Chapter IV: articles 66–70) established a taxation system for the forestry sector. The main taxes and charges are

—The Annual Royalty for the Forest Area (RFA), charged to all licenses allocated through a bidding process (Concessions and Sales of Standing Volume Permits) and linked to the area covered by the license;
—The Felling Tax (FT), which is intended to combat wastage at the point of felling and to help monitor the real level of logging in the forest;
—An exit duty on logs;
—Factory taxes, divided into exit duty on sawn products and entry taxes on logs taken into factories.

Of the taxes collected 45 percent of both the RFA and FT is intended for a special national forestry fund, set up to defray the costs of forest management. The assessment and collection of forestry taxes (RFA, FT, various licenses and surtaxes) have long been the responsibility of the Ministry of Forest and Environment. In 1999 a forestry tax revenue securement program was set up to centralize declarations and payments linked to the RFA and the FT. This is an interinstitutional program, coordinated by the Ministry of Finance tax department. The SGS company has been mandated by the Customs Department to assess timber export taxes; taxes linked to factory exports are the responsibility of the Customs Department.

The decentralized forestry taxation system has two main instruments: the share of the RFA and the FCFA 1000 tax.

—The first tool of the decentralized taxation system is the share of the RFA that is reserved for the communities. The 1994 Forest Law (article 68) states that this share should render sustainable and develop the economic, ecological, and social functions of forests within the framework of an integrated management ensuring sustainable conservation and use of the resources and of various ecosystems. The part reserved for the communities is determined by the Finance Law and is currently 50 percent for the State and 50 percent for local councils, of which 10 percent is for communities neighboring the forest.
—The FCFA 1000 tax was introduced by a circular at the end of the 1996/1997 fiscal year and went into effect in the following fiscal year. It represents a contribution by logging companies to social projects (such as schools, roads,

173

and clinics) and its terms are included in logging contracts. It is charged on sales of standing volume (SSV) permits at FCFA 1000/m³ of timber logged.

The decentralized forestry taxation system, the third major component of the new forest policy, has led to some innovative strategies for allocating part of forestry revenue to local communities. Before 1994 village communities benefited only from the construction of social and economic infrastructure, which was included in logging contracts. The new system for the redistribution of forestry income, established since 1994, is based on two fundamental principles: (i) payment of forestry fees by a company logging a given concession to local communities (10 percent of the total amount); the rural local government (40 percent); and the State (50 percent); (ii) and the allocation of a village tax, in fact an eco-tax, to village communities neighboring forest concessions of up to 2,500 hectares. Amounts are calculated on the basis of US$1.50 per cubic meter of wood felled. The decentralized forestry taxation system regularly transfers financial sums to local communities. For example, in 2001/2002 thirteen logging companies paid a total of US$1,000,000 to the Yokadouma (East province) rural local government and US$145,000 to villages in that area.[1]

Between 1994 and 1998 the 10 percent allocated to each local government was indeed transferred to the village communities concerned. Originally intended to promote local development, these royalties, like the village tax, were to a large extent allocated to consumables. To avoid misuse of the 10 percent, on April 29, 1998, the Ministry of Economy and Finance and the Ministry of Territorial Administration published a joint legal order on the use of revenue from logging. This order states that the 10 percent previously transferred directly to villages communities would be managed by local government, at the regional level. At the village level, the order requested that management committees be created as local branches of a regional committee composed of the mayor, representatives of the government, and other civil servants.

The regional committee is responsible for ensuring that the funding is used for micro-projects identified and planned jointly by the authorities, government authorities, and representatives of the village forestry fees management committee. When funding is allocated to socioeconomic projects, the beneficiary communities are subject to strict control by members of the regional committee.

c. Adapted from: *Reforming Forest Fiscal Systems: An Overview of Country Approaches and Experiences; Chapter 2: Cameroon Background Paper*, Proceedings of the International Workshop on Reforming Forest Fiscal Systems to Promote Poverty Reduction, and Sustainable Forest Management (World Bank, Washington, DC, Oct. 19–21, 2003); T. Fomété, *The Forestry Taxation System and the Involvement of Local Communities in Forest Management in Cameroon*, Paper 25b (Rural Development Forestry Network 2001).

---

[1] *See Cameroon Tribune* Oct. 13, 2002.

2. Indonesia[d]

Based on Indonesian regulation No 34 of 2002, paragraph 3, section 48, the government attaches three basic fees to the operation of forest concessions:

—Forest Utilization Business Permit Fees. This fee is based on the area of forest allocated in the permit. It is paid when the concession is granted and typically costs US$3 to US$10 per hectare. The Ministry of Forestry collects the FUBPF and sends 80 percent of it back to the region (16 percent to the province and 64 percent to the producing district) and 20 percent to the central government.

—Reforestation Funds. This fee per cubic meter of wood harvested varies by region and species group. The rate since 1999 has been US$16 per m³ for higher-priced species harvested in Kalimantan, collectively grouped under the name *meranti*. These funds are allocated 40 percent to the provinces and 60 percent to the central government.

—Forest Resource Tax. This is a royalty on logs charged on the basis of volume and collected by the Ministry of Forestry. The FRT varies by region and species and is calculated by multiplying the check price (local market price for the lowest quality log, established twice a year by decree of the Ministry of Trade and Industry) by the rent capture factor, set by the Ministry of Forestry at 10 percent. These revenues are allocated 80 percent to the region (16 percent to the province, 32 percent to the producing *kabupaten*, and 32 percent to other *kabupatens*), and 20 percent to the central government.

Decentralization has caused some problems with the forest fiscal system. Although Law 25 of 1999, dealing with fiscal balance between the central government and the regions, does not authorize the region to levy new charges and taxes, some regions appear to have interpreted the spirit of Law 22 of 1999, dealing with regional governance, as a mandate to manage natural resources, including forests and the function of revenue capture.

These special levies are collected and spent locally. With more than 400 districts in the country, half of which are still forested, these levies vary greatly and there is little information on actual figures. It is difficult to know the legal status of this situation or the exact amounts of these levies because most district leaders do not communicate with central government.

Timber concessions and mills are also thought to pay a corporate income tax of 35 percent on all profits. When reporting to tax authorities, however, timber concessionaires are believed to be underestimating how much the mills paid for their timber and timber mills tend to exaggerate the amount they paid the concessionaires. Meanwhile, the tax authorities do not seem to be particularly diligent about cross-checking these two conflicting figures. As a result, national tax authorities collect little in corporate income taxes from concessionaires and mills. The taxes levied on the export of some types of processed timber are not considered particularly significant.

d. Adapted from *Reforming Forest Fiscal Systems: An Overview of Country Approaches and Experiences; Chapter 4: Indonesia Background Paper.* Proceedings of the International Workshop Reforming Forest Fiscal Systems to Promote Poverty Reduction, and Sustainable Forest Management (World Bank, Washington, DC, Oct. 19–21, 2003); D. Brown, *Addicted to Rent: Corporate 2nd Spatial Distribution of Forest Resources in Indonesia; Implications for Forest Sustainability and Government Policy*, Report No. PFM/EC/99/06 (DFID/Indonesia–UK Tropical Forest Management Program 1999); URS Forestry, *Review of Formal and Informal Costs and Revenues Related to Timber Harvesting, Transporting and Trading in Indonesia* (World Bank 2002).

APPENDIX 5
Forest Comanagement

Ghana and Cameroon[e]

The principle of comanagement is embodied in the concepts of participatory, collaborative, and joint forest management. It is a collaborative partnership between stakeholders in the management of forest resources.

1. In Ghana, the strategy of forest sector reform has focused on changes in revenue policy and institutional reform of the main sector institution, the Forest Department. This was intended to become the Ghana Forest Service, a self-funding, service-oriented agency, freed to a large extent from the constraints of public sector management. A new long-term area-based concession arrangement, the Timber Utilization Contract, has been introduced to cover exploitation of natural timber both on-reserve and off. There has been no single legislative or tenure change to fuel the process of community involvement in forest management. Rather, a range of measures has been adopted to increase the flow of benefits to traditional authorities and local populations.

In the area of comanagement relevant measures have included:

—*Social responsibility agreements*, in which a maximum of 5 percent of the annual royalty accruing from the operations of logging companies is to be used to provide social amenities to the populations of the contract area.
—*Interim measures*, felling procedures introduced in 1995 that require the participation of both forestry authorities and affected local populations in pre- and post-felling operations off-reserve, as well as the payment of compensation to affected farmers for the destruction to property and farm crops.
—*Pilot activities* in areas such as harvesting of nontimber forest products (NTFP), including changes to the permit system to lower transaction costs for the rural poor and domestic users; NTFP domestication; and community participation in boundary maintenance.

The 1992 Ghana Constitution governs the allocation of royalties from forest concessions, both on- and off-reserve. Article 272(6) states:

10% of the revenues accruing from the stool lands shall be paid to the office of the Administrator of Stool Lands to cover administrative expenses; and the remaining revenue shall be disbursed in the following proportions:

(a) 25% to the stool through the traditional authority for the maintenance of the stool in keeping with its status;
(b) 20% to the traditional authority;
(c) 55% to the District Assembly, within the area of authority of which the stool land is situated.

2. Cameroon presents a contrast with Ghana because it has radically revised the legislative framework as a means of both increasing the efficiency of the industry and promoting community participation in forest management. The main instrument for changes in forest management practice in Cameroon is provided by the 1994 Forest Law.

In Cameroon, all land that have not been sold into freehold is the property of the State. This reflects Cameroon's civil law inheritance. While traditionally conversion of forest grants a person the status of landowner, this is not recognized in national law, particularly with regard to standing timber.

Enactment of the new law in 1994 was followed by changes in the procedures for allocating logging concessions and in forest tax rates. These changes were strongly promoted by the World Bank and IMF as part of the process of dialogue on the forest sector relating to discussions about Cameroon's enhanced structural adjustment facility. These included

—allocation of concessions by competitive bidding (auction) rather than administrative allocation;
—progressive changes to the tax regime to simplify the system, use free on board (FOB) prices as the taxable base, and increase the importance of area-based taxation.

The changes in the tax system were supported by improvements in the mechanisms for independent surveillance and inspection, involving forest management companies such as SGS Forestry.

The table on the next page presents the policy and legislative elements of comanagement in Ghana and Cameroon.

	Ghana	Cameroon
Strategy of sector reform	—Reform of the Forest Department to make it a self-funding agency. —Increase in timber revenues based on use of FOB lumber price —Administrative allocation retained, timber utilization contract (TUC) added on reserve, licensing off-reserve —Absolute increase in revenues to rural populations through increased taxes and improved efficiency	—Major legislative change (1994 Forest Law) promoted community forestry —Increase in timber revenues —Auction to replace administrative allocation of concessions for *Unité forestière d'aménagement* (UFA) in permanent forest estate (PFE), *ventes de coupe*/community forests in the nonpermanent forest estate (NPFE) —Log export ban (1999)
Rationale for reform	Economic, livelihood and conservation benefits. Sustainable management to be promoted by: —Increased resource flows to traditional owners —More responsive extension agency —More efficient timber industry —Increased timber prices.	Economic, livelihood and conservation benefits. Sustainable management to be promoted by: —More rational management of industry —Involvement of rural communities in forest management through community forests and increased revenues —Increased timber prices.
Centrality of comanagement to process of change	Active comanagement a limited component, change led by institutional reform of the Forest Department.	Community forestry a central component of 1994 Law, strongly supported by donors.

	Ghana	Cameroon
Ownership of change process	National constituency for change, supported by range of bilateral and multilateral donors.	Limited national constituency for change, change forced through by donors, particularly World Bank.
Landowners (public lands)	Traditional landowners through the agency of the stool (chieftaincies).	The State.
Tree tenure	Ownership of natural trees vested in the President in trust for traditional landowners.	Natural trees owned by the State.
Timber industry	—In decline —Oversupplied —Powerful processing industry.	—Growing —Under-developed processing industry.
Rural communities	—Long history of rural migration —Universally complex: high labor migration, share-cropping, and tenancy arrangements.	Rural migration more localized, though it has increased in extent.
Land pressures	—High in most rural areas —Almost all rural land effectively owned.	—Low in most forest areas, particularly in the south —Forest land still in surplus (though perhaps subject to ownership claims).
Forest reserves	Extensive, generally secured.	Extensive, unsecured.

e. Adapted from D. Brown, *Principles and Practice of Forest Co-Management: Evidence from West-Central Africa* (Overseas Development Institute/European Commission 1999); S. Egbe, *Forest Tenure and Access to Forest Resources in Cameroon: an Overview*, Forest Participation Series No. 6 (IIED 1998).

APPENDIX 6
Forest Code of Practice

1. South Africa[f]

The South African Harvesting Code of Practice provides guidelines for the planning, management, and control of efficient harvesting operations to ensure long-term site productivity. It also sets criteria for a safe and healthy working environment and cost-effective forest products. In the Code harvesting refers to all activities required to convert a standing tree to the required product delivered to the timber-processing sector or end user. The values reflected in the Code are those society and the forestry industry rate as important and to be safeguarded for the future. Environment and commercial values of natural renewable timber resources should be balanced to ensure optimum utilization and a sustained yield of quality timber.

The chapter on forest roads and extraction routes provides guidelines for opening up access. It presents general principles, potential effects, and tactics to reduce negative impacts during the planning and construction of the network of forests roads, depots, extraction routes, and landings. Operational guidelines for harvesting and transport activities are presented in the chapter on timber harvesting, which refers to the processes required to transform the standing tree into a grade corresponding to a state of conversion as required by the market and to deliver it to the conversion site.

Environmental audits are intended to be a management tool comprising a systematic, documented, periodic, and objective evaluation of the performance of the organization and its management systems and processes. They are designed to protect the environment by facilitating management control of practices that may have an impact on the environment, and assessing compliance with company environmental practices.

For such an objective evaluation to be of any use it is necessary for a company to have an environmental management system in operation. It is also necessary that company standards and the regulations according to which performance can be measured are documented.

Formulating and implementing an environmental management system requires top management commitment and an awareness campaign that reaches everybody involved with the company. The harvesting audit is a means to obtain the information necessary to identify the need for and types of corrective action. Specifically this means using the audit:

—as part of an internal system of monitoring company activities to help improve the quality of management decisions by providing accurate, unbiased, and current information;

—internally to reveal potential problems before they are identified by an external audit;

—as verification of compliance with the Harvesting Code of Practice and company policies, thus assuring management that harvesting activities are managed in an uniform, efficient, responsible, and legal manner.

It is important that audits are conducted by competent trained auditors. According to international standard ISO 10011 an auditor needs formal training not only in auditing but also in management systems, environmental processes and effects, relevant legislation, and risk assessment. Auditors must also gain a certain amount of practical experience under a lead auditor. A company should establish a pool of trained auditors that are specialists in their field of operation (e.g., roads, harvesting, silviculture, or conservation).

f. FAO, *Forest Codes of practice*, FAO Forestry Paper 133 (FAO 1996); FAO, *South Africa Forestry Facts–July 1994*, Forest Owners Association (FOA) (FAO 1994).

2. New Zealand[g]

The New Zealand Forest Code of Practice, published in 1990, was revised in 1993. The aim of the code is "to plan, manage and carry out forestry operations in a sustainable manner" as required by the Resource Management Act adopted in 1991. The code is intended to be a practical document for both environmental planning of forestry operations and an information base on forestry operations.

The code starts with a description of the beneficial aspects of the relationship between forestry, the environment, and the community. The objectives of the code relate to the protection of ten common production forestry values: soil and water, scenery, cultural, recreation, science and ecology, forest health, site productivity, off-site impacts, safety, and commercial viability.

Environmental Planning

Thorough environmental planning is considered to be key to achieving the best possible environmental outcome. Minimizing the adverse effects of operations starts in the planning phase with clear and systematic identification of values. These common values are not always all present, but by consultation with a wide range of local interest groups, important site-specific values can be specified.

Impact of Operations

Considering how operations might impact on the values identified can be achieved using a systematic matrix checklist such as the one provided in the code. The checklist is designed for use in the field; it can highlight operations that may have high impact at an early stage. It is not intended to substitute for a comprehensive environmental plan for the whole forest but to provide site-specific information.

Selecting Cost-Effective Law-Impact Techniques

Mitigation methods must be specified by forest managers and supervisors and carried out by individual operators. The Code Operations Database contains detailed information that helps identify the risks associated with certain operations. It lists considerations for the stages of forest development: access, land preparation, establishment, tending, protection, and harvesting. For each stage it lists the range of methods for undertaking the operation, potential adverse impacts, and methods for reducing those impacts.

Obtaining Approvals and Monitoring Performance

Operations that may have a significant impact on the environment can require consent from the district or regional council. It is important to ensure the correct approvals have been obtained before commencing operations. Performance monitoring is expected to be the last step that is essential for achieving the best possible outcome. Postoperational monitoring will help ensure that adverse effects on identified values have been minimized. Implemented along with a regular maintenance program, monitoring can continue to protect the site values and prevent problems. A common example of inadequate postharvest management is poor maintenance of road, track, and landing. Failure to check up on a regular basis is often the reason for erosion and water quality problems.

For forestry to meet its entire requirement for sustainable management as set out in the Resource Management Act, it must "avoid, remedy and mitigate" any adverse environmental impacts. People managing, planning, or carrying out forestry operations must have access to information on how to do this. Presenting this information in the form of nonprescriptive guidelines places the emphasis on correct implementation of protection measures to protect the values at that site.

g. Adapted from FAO, *Forest Codes of Practice*, FAO Forestry Paper 133 (FAO 1996); L. Vaughan, R. Visser & M. Smith, *New Zealand Forest Code of Practice* (2d ed., Logging Industry Research Organization 1993).

Forest Function Zoning

Cambodia—Synopsis of Forest Function Zoning and Relationship with Concession Management[h]

Forest function zoning is one of the most important tasks set for concession planning. It is through the process of zoning that the principle of multiple use concession management is realized. By establishing areas for community use, biodiversity conservation, and environmental protection, and by identifying and excluding forest types and stands unsuitable for harvesting, it makes clear the fact that concessions are not reserved exclusively for commercial timber production. The process is also vital for commercial planning because it is the basis for determining the net operable area from which timber may be harvested. The operable area—what is left after this process of elimination—is the foundation of the commercial operation: designing the forest inventory, assessing total commercial volume available, calculating the estimated allowable yield, and allocating compartments.

The process of forest function zoning is in principle relatively simple. It begins with a baseline forest and vegetation analysis and then, through a series of investigations, allocates different areas to different uses. Despite the fundamental importance of the activity, there is very little practical guidance on how to do it, and the multiplicity of sources complicates and confuses rather than clarifies the task, with predictable results. Problems with zoning begin with the numerous terms for technical areas used in guidelines and planning manuals without clear and consistent definition. The following terms and their approximate meanings are used:

—*Zone:* a subdivision of a forest concession area that has specific ecological characteristics or resource values that dictate a management regime different from that of adjacent zones.

—*Production zone or production area:* an area within a concession containing productive areas where there are no restrictions on harvesting from topography, non-forest features, or designation for protection or community use.

—*Protection zone:* an area with special importance for protecting the watershed or conserving flora and fauna.

—*Community zone:* an area reserved for local uses, including community forests, buffer zones around settlements, and hunting preserves; harvesting is feasible, if done in cooperation with the community.

—*Nonoperable area:* an area within the production zone that cannot be harvested, such as the biodiversity conservation network, fragile areas, critical degraded areas requiring rehabilitation, and designated community forest areas.

—*Net operable area:* the area within the production zone where timber can be harvested at appropriate times; sometimes also called the wood production zone.

Concessions are divided on the one hand into operable and nonoperable areas, and on the other into production, protection, and community zones. Although it would seem that operable area should be the same as production zone and protection and community zones together the same as the nonoperable area, these categories do not perfectly overlap.

The planning manual does not provide sufficient guidance on how to delineate the logged forest. The definition of logged areas is based on company logging records rather than actual logging even, though the standing volume of timber will be affected. However the new *Handbook for the Review of Forest Management Plans* give more advice; it indicates that besides visible earlier logging companies should place a 1,500 m buffer area on both sides of each main road and consider this as logged forest.

Although the sources of guidance do not set out a full process for forest function zoning, the main tasks and steps should be:

1. forest and vegetation typing, to distinguish forest from nonforest areas
2. identification and mapping of sustainable management areas (SMAs) of national importance for existing livelihoods, excluding soils, riparian strips, biodiversity conservation, and community uses from the production zone
3. identification of net operable area from what is left after step 2
4. proposal of forest and land use as forest function zones.

Several of the guidelines make it clear that the final zoning process should be participatory, bringing in multiple stakeholders. It would be useful for operators if detailed guidance could be given for these negotiations, indicating which stakeholders should participate, what information should be brought to the table, the particular tasks that need to be conducted, and the outputs that should be produced.

h. Adapted from A. Hinrichs & C. McKenzie, *Results of the Independent Review of Strategic Forest Management Plans Prepared by Concession Companies Operating in Cambodia* (GFA 2004).

APPENDIX 8

Report of the United Nations Conference on Environment and Development

(Rio de Janeiro, June 3–14, 1992)

Annex III

Non-Legally Binding Authoritative Statement of Principles for a Global Consensus on the Management, Conservation and Sustainable Development of all Types of Forests.

Preamble

(a) The subject of forests is related to the entire range of environmental and development issues and opportunities, including the right to socio-economic development on a sustainable basis.

(b) The guiding objective of these principles is to contribute to the management, conservation and sustainable development of forests and to provide for their multiple and complementary functions and uses.

(c) Forestry issues and opportunities should be examined in a holistic and balanced manner within the overall context of environment and development, taking into consideration the multiple functions and uses of forests, including traditional uses, and the likely economic and social stress when these uses are constrained or restricted, as well as the potential for development that sustainable forest management can offer.

(d) These principles reflect a first global consensus on forests. In committing themselves to the prompt implementation of these principles, countries also decide to keep them under assessment for their adequacy with regard to further international cooperation on forest issues.

(e) These principles should apply to all types of forests, both natural and planted, in all geographical regions and climatic zones, including austral, boreal, subtemperate, temperate, subtropical and tropical.

(f) All types of forests embody complex and unique ecological processes which are the basis for their present and potential capacity to provide resources to satisfy human needs as well as environmental values, and as such their sound management and conservation is of concern to the Governments of the countries to which they belong and are of value to local communities and to the environment as a whole.

(g) Forests are essential to economic development and the maintenance of all forms of life.

(h) Recognizing that the responsibility for forest management, conservation and sustainable development is in many States allocated among federal/national, state/provincial and local levels of government, each State, in accordance with its constitution and/or national legislation, should pursue these principles at the appropriate level of government.

Principles/Elements

1. (a) States have, in accordance with the Charter of the United Nations and the principles of international law, the sovereign right to exploit their own resources pursuant to their own environmental policies and have the responsibility to ensure that activities within their jurisdiction or control do not cause damage to the environment of other States or of areas beyond the limits of national jurisdiction.

(b) The agreed full incremental cost of achieving benefits associated with forest conservation and sustainable development requires increased international cooperation and should be equitably shared by the international community.

2. (a) States have the sovereign and inalienable right to utilize, manage and develop their forests in accordance with their development needs and level of socio-economic development and on the basis of national policies consistent with sustainable development and legislation, including the conversion of such areas for other uses within the overall socio-economic development plan and based on rational land-use policies.

(b) Forest resources and forest lands should be sustainably managed to meet the social, economic, ecological, cultural and spiritual needs of present and future generations. These needs are for forest products and services, such as wood and wood products, water, food, fodder, medicine, fuel, shelter, employment, recreation, habitats for wildlife, landscape diversity, carbon sinks and reservoirs, and for other forest products. Appropriate measures should be taken to protect forests against harmful effects of pollution, including air-borne pollution, fires, pests and diseases, in order to maintain their full multiple value.

(c) The provision of timely, reliable and accurate information on forests and forest ecosystems is essential for public understanding and informed decision-making and should be ensured.

(d) Governments should promote and provide opportunities for the participation of interested parties, including local communities and indigenous people, industries, labour, non-governmental organizations and individuals, forest dwellers and women, in the development, implementation and planning of national forest policies.

3. (a) National policies and strategies should provide a framework for increased efforts, including the development and strengthening of institutions and programmes for the management, conservation and sustainable development of forests and forest lands.

(b) International institutional arrangements, building on those organizations and mechanisms already in existence, as appropriate, should facilitate international cooperation in the field of forests.

(c) All aspects of environmental protection and social and economic development as they relate to forests and forest lands should be integrated and comprehensive.

4. The vital role of all types of forests in maintaining the ecological processes and balance at the local, national, regional and global levels through, inter alia, their role in protecting fragile ecosystems, watersheds and freshwater resources and as rich storehouses of biodiversity and biological resources and sources of genetic material for biotechnology products, as well as photosynthesis, should be recognized.

5. (a) National forest policies should recognize and duly support the identity, culture and the rights of indigenous people, their communities and other communities and forest dwellers. Appropriate conditions should be promoted for these groups to enable them to have an economic stake in forest use, perform economic activities, and achieve and maintain cultural identity and social organization, as well as adequate levels of livelihood and well-being, through, inter alia, those land tenure arrangements which serve as incentives for the sustainable management of forests.

(b) The full participation of women in all aspects of the management, conservation and sustainable development of forests should be actively promoted.

6. (a) All types of forests play an important role in meeting energy requirements through the provision of a renewable source of bio-energy, particularly in developing countries, and the demands for fuelwood for household and industrial needs should be met through sustainable forest management, afforestation and reforestation. To this end, the potential contribution of plantations of both indigenous and introduced species for the provision of both fuel and industrial wood should be recognized.

(b) National policies and programmes should take into account the relationship, where it exists, between the conservation, management and sustainable development of forests and all aspects related to the production, consumption, recycling and/or final disposal of forest products.

(c) Decisions taken on the management, conservation and sustainable development of forest resources should benefit, to the extent practicable, from a comprehensive assessment of economic and non-economic values of forest goods and services and of the environmental costs and benefits. The development and improvement of methodologies for such evaluations should be promoted.

(d) The role of planted forests and permanent agricultural crops as sustainable and environmentally sound sources of renewable energy and industrial raw material should be recognized, enhanced and promoted. Their contribution to the maintenance of ecological processes, to offsetting pressure on primary/old-growth forest and to providing regional employment and development with the adequate involvement of local inhabitants should be recognized and enhanced.

(e) Natural forests also constitute a source of goods and services, and their conservation, sustainable management and use should be promoted.

7. (a) Efforts should be made to promote a supportive international economic climate conducive to sustained and environmentally sound development of forests in all countries, which include, inter alia, the promotion of sustainable patterns of production and consumption, the eradication of poverty and the promotion of food security.

(b) Specific financial resources should be provided to developing countries with significant forest areas which establish programmes for the conservation of forests including protected natural forest areas. These resources should be directed notably to economic sectors which would stimulate economic and social substitution activities.

8. (a) Efforts should be undertaken towards the greening of the world. All countries, notably developed countries, should take positive and transparent action towards reforestation, afforestation and forest conservation, as appropriate.

(b) Efforts to maintain and increase forest cover and forest productivity should be undertaken in ecologically, economically and socially sound ways through the rehabilitation, reforestation and re-establishment of trees and forests on unproductive, degraded and deforested lands, as well as through the management of existing forest resources.

(c) The implementation of national policies and programmes aimed at forest management, conservation and sustainable development, particularly in developing countries, should be supported by international financial and technical cooperation, including through the private sector, where appropriate.

(d) Sustainable forest management and use should be carried out in accordance with national development policies and priorities and on the basis of environmentally sound national guidelines. In the formulation of such guidelines, account should be taken, as appropriate and if applicable, of relevant internationally agreed methodologies and criteria.

(e) Forest management should be integrated with management of adjacent areas so as to maintain ecological balance and sustainable productivity.

(f) National policies and/or legislation aimed at management, conservation and sustainable development of forests should include the protection of ecologically viable representative or unique examples of forests, including primary/old-growth forests, cultural, spiritual, historical, religious and other unique and valued forests of national importance.

(g) Access to biological resources, including genetic material, shall be with due regard to the sovereign rights of the countries where the forests are located and to the sharing on mutually agreed terms of technology and profits from biotechnology products that are derived from these resources.

(h) National policies should ensure that environmental impact assessments should be carried out where actions are likely to have significant adverse impacts on important forest resources, and where such actions are subject to a decision of a competent national authority.

9. (a) The efforts of developing countries to strengthen the management, conservation and sustainable development of their forest resources should be supported by the international community, taking into account the importance of redressing external indebtedness, particularly where aggravated by the net transfer of resources to developed countries, as well as the problem of achieving at least the replacement value of forests through improved market access for forest products, especially processed products. In this respect, special attention should also be given to the countries undergoing the process of transition to market economies.

(b) The problems that hinder efforts to attain the conservation and sustainable use of forest resources and that stem from the lack of alternative options available to local communities, in particular the urban poor and poor rural populations who are economically and socially dependent on forests and forest resources, should be addressed by Governments and the international community.

(c) National policy formulation with respect to all types of forests should take account of the pressures and demands imposed on forest ecosystems and resources from influencing factors outside the forest sector, and intersectoral means of dealing with these pressures and demands should be sought.

10. New and additional financial resources should be provided to developing countries to enable them to sustainably manage, conserve and develop their forest resources, including through afforestation, reforestation and combating deforestation and forest and land degradation.

11. In order to enable, in particular, developing countries to enhance their endogenous capacity and to better manage, conserve and develop their forest resources, the access to and transfer of environmentally sound technologies and corresponding know-how on favourable terms, including on concessional and preferential terms, as mutually agreed, in accordance with the relevant provisions of Agenda 21, should be promoted, facilitated and financed, as appropriate.

12. (a) Scientific research, forest inventories and assessments carried out by national institutions which take into account, where relevant, biological, physical, social and economic variables, as well as technological development and its application in the field of sustainable forest management, conservation and development, should be strengthened through effective modalities, including international cooperation. In this context, attention should also be given to research and development of sustainably harvested non-wood products.

(b) National and, where appropriate, regional and international institutional capabilities in education, training, science, technology, economics, anthropology and social aspects of forests and forest management are essential to the conservation and sustainable development of forests and should be strengthened.

(c) International exchange of information on the results of forest and forest management research and development should be enhanced and broadened, as appropriate, making full use of education and training institutions, including those in the private sector.

(d) Appropriate indigenous capacity and local knowledge regarding the conservation and sustainable development of forests should, through institutional and financial support and in collaboration with the people in the local communities concerned, be recognized, respected, recorded, developed and, as appropriate, introduced in the implementation of programmes. Benefits arising from the utilization of indigenous knowledge should therefore be equitably shared with such people.

13. (a) Trade in forest products should be based on non-discriminatory and multilaterally agreed rules and procedures consistent with international trade law and practices. In this context, open and free international trade in forest products should be facilitated.

(b) Reduction or removal of tariff barriers and impediments to the provision of better market access and better prices for higher value-added forest products and their local processing should be encouraged to enable producer countries to better conserve and manage their renewable forest resources.

(c) Incorporation of environmental costs and benefits into market forces and mechanisms, in order to achieve forest conservation and sustainable development, should be encouraged both domestically and internationally.

(d) Forest conservation and sustainable development policies should be integrated with economic, trade and other relevant policies.

(e) Fiscal, trade, industrial, transportation and other policies and practices that may lead to forest degradation should be avoided. Adequate policies, aimed at management, conservation and sustainable development of forests, including, where appropriate, incentives, should be encouraged.

14. Unilateral measures, incompatible with international obligations or agreements, to restrict and/or ban international trade in timber or other forest products should be removed or avoided, in order to attain long-term sustainable forest management.

15. Pollutants, particularly air-borne pollutants, including those responsible for acidic deposition, that are harmful to the health of forest ecosystems at the local, national, regional and global levels should be controlled.

APPENDIX 9

The Forest Law Enforcement and Governance Ministerial Process

The approach of the Forest Law Enforcement and Governance (FLEG) Ministerial Processes, supported by the World Bank since 2001, has been to convene a regional preparatory conference followed by a high-level ministerial conference. This approach has allowed for:

- a multi-stakeholder technical meeting where experiences with FLEG issues are shared;
- intergovernmental negotiations for the drafting of a declaration and/or action plan for commitments to improve governance, combat illegal logging, corruption and associated trade; and
- other stakeholder discussions and development of statements for consideration by the intergovernmental negotiators.

National-level actions with multistakeholder participation have helped prepare input to the conferences and draft follow-up action plans. The processes aim to create the political space at national and regional levels to address these complex and politically sensitive issues, in partnership with major stakeholders from civil society and the private sector.

(i) Southeast Asia: *Although only 5 percent of the world's forests are located in Southeast Asia, the region accounts for nearly 25 percent of the global forest loss over the past decade, with illegal logging a major force driving the deforestation.* In September 2001 the East Asia Ministerial Conference on Forest Law Enforcement and Governance (FLEG) took place in Bali, Indonesia. The Conference adopted the Bali Declaration, in which participating countries committed themselves to, inter alia, intensify national efforts and strengthen bilateral, regional, and multilateral collaboration to address forest crime and violations of forest law. A regional FLEG task force was created to advance the declaration's objectives; it held meetings in May 2002 and January 2003. The Bali Declaration and the discussions it spawned have led to agreements on specific national and regional efforts needed to address forest threats. A memorandum of understanding (MOU) between the United Kingdom and Indonesia to improve FLEG and combat illegal logging and international trade in illegally logged timber, and an MOU between Japan and Indonesia with similar objectives are noteworthy.

(ii) Africa: *Initial estimates for annual revenue losses due to illegal logging and ineffective forest taxation systems in seven African countries (Benin, Cameroon, Central African Republic, Democratic Republic of the Congo, Gabon, Ghana, and the Republic of the Congo) total US$ 63 million—equivalent to 4 percent of official development aid these countries.* The Africa Forest Law Enforcement and Governance (AFLEG) Ministerial Conference took place October 13–16, 2003, in Yaoundé, Cameroon; it produced the AFLEG Declaration and Action Plan. In the Declaration, governments expressed their intention to, inter alia, mobilize financial resources for FLEG; promote cooperation between law enforcement agencies within and among countries; involve stakeholders in decision making; and explore means of demonstrating the legality and sustainability of forest products. An AFLEG Support Group of active producer, consumer, and donor governments was established in May 2004 to maintain momentum for action to implement the Declaration. Efforts are being made to integrate AFLEG-related objectives and actions into existing initiatives, such as the National Economic Plan for African Development (NEPAD) and other regional bodies (e.g., Central Africa Forests Commission (COMIFAC), Economic Commission of West African States (ECOWAS), and Southern African Development Community (SADC).

(iii) Europe and North Asia: *In Russia it is estimated that more than 20 percent of the timber logged may be in violation of the law. Preliminary estimates in Albania and Georgia indicate that illegal harvests could be several times larger than official removals.* Concerned about these circumstances, in May 2004 the Russian Federation announced its interest in initiating a similar FLEG process for Europe and Northern Asia in collaboration with regional partners. An international steering committee has been established to advise on the process. A FLEG preparatory conference was held in June 2005 and the Ministerial Conference is scheduled for November 2005. A draft Ministerial Declaration and Indicative Action Plan is being prepared to allow governmental delegations to begin mapping out issues that may serve as the foundation for intergovernmental negotiations. A follow-up program of national, bilateral, and multilateral actions to implement the ministerial agreements and action plans will be essential to the process.

These initiatives have been successful in creating partnerships between donors and development agencies that share a common concern with improving forest governance. They have fostered a spirit of collaboration among governments, the private sector, and stakeholders and have also promoted a sense of joint responsibility between producer and consumer countries for tackling the problem. However, important questions and challenges remain: How to encourage producer countries to take a more proactive role in the process? Can the political space and mandate be utilized more effectively to implement concrete action programs at the regional and country levels? How to ensure continuing cooperation among donors and various stakeholder groups? What additional efforts are being financed by donor partners and how can they be linked to the FLEG programs? Where is the low-hanging fruit and where are the real success-stories amenable to replication and scaling up? These are only some of the questions that need to be addressed.

Selected Bibliography

Note on availability of national legal texts: Forestry laws and other laws related to natural resource management from most countries are accessible through FAOLEX, the online legislative database maintained by the FAO Legal Office (http://faolex.fao.org/ faolex/index.htm), and through ECOLEX (http://www.ecolex.org/index.php), a gateway to environmental law jointly operated by FAO, International Union for Conservation of Nature (IUCN), and United Nations Environment Programme (UNEP).

Abrudan, I., F. Schmithüsen, & P. Herbst, eds., *Legal Aspects of European Forest Sustainable Development*, Proceedings of the 6th International IUFRO RG 6.13.00 Forest Law and Environmental Legislation Symposium, Brasov, Romania (2005).

Alden Wily, L., & S. Mbaya, *Land, People and Forests in Eastern and Southern Africa at the Beginning of the 21st Century* (IUCN 2001).

———— *Forest Law in Eastern and Southern Africa: Moving Towards a Community-Based Forest Future?* 51 UNASYLVA, No. 203 (2000).

Arnold, J., *Managing Forests as Common Property* (FAO 1998).

Assessing the International Forest Regime, IUCN Environmental Law Paper 37 (R. Tarasofsky, ed., IUCN 1999).

Bass, Susan, *Legal Aspects of Forest Management in Mexico* (Environmental Law Institute [ELI] 1998).

Best Practices for Improving Law Compliance in the Forestry Sector, FAO Forestry Paper 145 (A. Contreras and E. Peter, eds., FAO 2005).

Brack, D., K. Gray, & G. Hayman, *Controlling the International Trade in Illegally Logged Timber and Wood Products* (Royal Institute of International Affairs 2002).

Brack, D., & G. Hayman, *Intergovernmental Actions on Illegal Logging: Options for Intergovernmental Action to Help Combat Illegal Logging and Illegal Trade in Timber and Forest Products* (Royal Institute of International Affairs 2001).

Brown, D., *Addicted to Rent: Corporate and Spatial Distribution of Forest Resources in Indonesia; Implications for Forest Sustainability and Government Policy*, DFID/Indonesia-UK Tropical Forest Management Program, Report No. PFM/EC/99/06 (DFID 1999).

————, *Principles and Practice of Forest Co-Management: Evidence from West-Central Africa* (Overseas Development Institute/European Commission 1999).

Bruce, J., *Legal Bases for the Management of Forest Resources as Common Property*, Community Forestry Paper 14 (FAO 1999).

Casson, A., A. Setyarso, & M. Boccucci, *Illegal Logging and Law Enforcement in Indonesia*, 38 (World Bank/WWF Alliance 2004).

Christy, L., *Designing Forestry Legislation to Improve Compliance* (FAO 2004).

Cirelli, M., *Forestry Legislation Revision and the Role of International Assistance*, 44 UNASYLVA (1993).

Cirelli, M., F. Schmithüsen, J. Texier, & T. Young, *Trends in Forestry Law in Europe and Africa*, Legislative Study No. 72, 45 (FAO, 2001).

Collomb, J. & H. Bikié, *1999–2000 Allocation of Logging Permits in Cameroon: Fine-Tuning Central Africa's First Auction System* (Global Forest Watch, World Resources Institute 2001).

Contreras-Hermosilla, A., background paper, *Policy Alternatives to Improve Law Compliance in the Forest Sector* (FAO meeting of experts, Rome, January 2002).

Cornu, M., & J. Fromageau, *Le droit de la forêt au XXIe siècle—Aspects internationaux* (Harmattan 2004).

————, *Le droit de la forêt au XXIe siècle—Enjeux politiques et juridiques* (Harmattan 2004).

Cousins, T. & D. Hornby, *Leaping the Fissures: Bridging the Gap Between Paper and Real Practice in Setting Up Common Property Institutions in Land Reform in South Africa* (CASS/PLAAS 2000).

Crossley, R., *The Economic and Environmental Consequences of Log Export Bans: A Review of Evidence* (World Bank 1994).

de la Rochefordière, A., *Excluding Illegal Timber: Border Controls and Procurement—Making the System Work* (Royal Institute of International Affairs 2003).

Daes, E., *Indigenous Peoples and Their Relationship to Land*, U.N. Doc. E/CN.4/Sub.2/2001/21.

Di Leva, C., *The Conservation of Nature and Natural Resources Through Legal and Market-Based and Mechanisms*, 11 RECIEL 84, 94 (2002).

Egbe, S., *Forest Tenure and Access to Forest Resources in Cameroon: an Overview*, Forest Participation Series No. 6 (IIED 1998).

FAO, *Forest Codes of Practice*, FAO Forestry Paper 133, (FAO 1996).

————, *Forests out of Bounds: Impacts and Effectiveness of Logging Bans in Natural Forests in Asia-Pacific* (FAO 2001).

————, *Governance Principles for Concessions and Contracts in Public Forests*, Forestry Paper 139 (FAO 2001).

————, *Law and Sustainable Development Since Rio: Legal Trends in Agriculture and Natural Resource Management* (FAO 2002).

————, *Legal Trends in Wildlife Management* (FAO 2002).

————, *South Africa Forestry Facts—July 1994*, Forest Owners Association (FOA), Rivonia (1994).

FAO & ITTO, *Best Practices for Improving Law Compliance in the Forestry Sector*, FAO Forestry Paper 145 (FAO 2005).

Fingleton, J., *Resolving Conflicts Between Custom and Official Forestry Law in the Southwestern Pacific* 44 UNASYLVA 175 (1993).

————, *Legal Recognition of Indigenous Groups*, FAO Legal Paper Online No. 1. (FAO 1998).

————, *Regional Study on Pacific Islands Forestry Legislation*, FAO Legal Paper Online No. 30 (FAO 2002).

Fomété, T., *The Forestry Taxation System and the Involvement of Local Communities in Forest Management in Cameroon*, Paper 25b (Rural Development Forestry Network 2001).

Forêts tropicales et mondialisation—Les mutations des politiques forestières en Afrique francophone et à Madagascar (Harmattan 2005).

Gallardo Gallardo, E. & F. Schmithüsen, eds*., La Contribución del Derecho Forestal—Ambiental al Desarrollo Sustentable en América Latina*, IUFRO World Series Vol. 16 IUFRO 2005).

Global Witness, *Forest Law Enforcement in Cameroon*, 1st Summary Report of the Independent Observer, May—November 2001 (Global Witness 2002).

————, *Forest Law Enforcement in Cameroon*, 2nd Summary Report of the Independent Observer (Global Witness 2003).

Gray, J., *Forest Concession Policies and Sustainable Forest Management of Tropical Forests* (World Bank 2000).

Hinrichs, A. & C. McKenzie, *Results of the Independent Review of Strategic Forest Management Plans Prepared by Concession Companies Operating in Cambodia* (GFA 2004).

IUCN, *Landscape Conservation Law—Present Trends and Perspectives in International and Comparative Law* (IUCN 2000).

Jacobs, H. & B. Hirsch, *Indigenous Land Tenure and Land Use in Alaska: Community Impacts of the Alaska Native Claims Settlement Act* (Land Tenure Center, U. Wisc.-Madison 1998).

Kaimowitz, D., *Forest Law Enforcement and Rural Livelihoods*, 5 International Forestry Review 199–210 (2003).

Kishor, N., M. Mani, & L. Constantino, *Economic and Environmental Benefits of Eliminating Log Export Bans: The Case of Costa Rica*, 27 World Economy 609, 612 (2004).

Lindsay, J., A. Mekouar, & L. Christy, *Why Law Matters: Design Principles for Strengthening the Role of Forestry Legislation in Reducing Illegal Activities and Corrupt Practices*, 11, FAO Legal Papers Online No 27 (FAO 2002).

Lindsay, J., *Creating Legal Space for Community-Based Management: Principles and Dilemmas*, in *Decentralization and Devolution of Forest Management in Asia and the Pacific*, (T. Enters, B. Patrick, P. Durst, & M. Victor, eds., FAO and RECOFTC 2000).

Lynch, O., *Promoting Legal Recognition of Community-based Property Rights: Rethinking Basic Concepts*, 57(2) Common Property Resource Digest (2001).

Lynch, O., & K. Talbott, *Balancing Acts: Community-Based Forest Management and National Law in Asia and the Pacific* (World Resources Institute 1995).

Magrath, W. & R. Grandalski, *Forest Law Enforcement: Policies, Strategies and Technologies* (World Bank 2004).

Manguiat, M., R. Verheyen, J. Mackensen, & G. Scholz, *Legal Aspects in the Implementation of CDM Forestry Projects* (IUCN 2005).

Pachego, P. & D. Pachego, paper, *Decentralization and Community Forestry: Main Approaches and Their Implications in the Lowlands of Bolivia*, Tenth Biennial Conference of the International Association for the Study of Common Property, Oaxaca, Mexico, August 9–13, 2004.

Patlis, J., *A Rough Guide to Developing Laws for Regional Forest Management* (CIFOR 2004).

Pope, J., *Confronting Corruption: The Elements of a National Integrity System* (Transparency International Source Book 2000).

Reforming Forest Fiscal Systems: An Overview of Country Approaches and Experiences; Chapter 2: Cameroon Background Paper, Proceedings of the International Workshop on Reforming Forest Fiscal Systems to Promote Poverty Reduction and Sustainable Forest Management (World Bank, Washington, DC, October 19–21, 2003).

Ribot, J., paper, *Decentralization Without Representation: Rural Authority and Popular Participation in Sahelian Forestry*, FAO Technical Consultation on Decentralization, (Rome, December 16–18, 1997).

———, *Democratic Decentralization of Natural Resources: Institutionalizing Popular Participation* (World Resources Institute 2002).

Rosenbaum, K., D. Schoene, & A. Mekouar, *Climate Change and the Forest Sector*, FAO Forestry Paper 144 (FAO 2004).

Rosenbaum, K., & J. Lindsay, *An Overview of National Forest Funds: Current Approaches and Future Opportunities*, FAO Legal Paper Online No. 15 (FAO 2001).

Rosenbaum, K., *Tools for Civil Society Action to Reduce Forest Corruption: Drawing Lessons from Transparency International* (World Bank 2005).

Sarin, M., N. Singh, N. Sundar, & R. Bhogal, *Devolution as a Threat to Democratic Decision-making in Forestry? Findings from Three States in India* (ODI 2003).

Schmithüsen, F., G. Iselin, P. Herbst & D. Le Master, eds., *Experiences with New Forest and Environmental Laws in European Countries with Economics in Transition*, Proceedings of the 4th International Symposium (Jaunmokas, Latvia, August 2002).

——, *El papel de la legislación forestal y ambiental en países de América Latina para la conservación y gestión de los recursos naturales renovables*, FAO Legislative Studies Online # 49 (FAO 2005).

Shine, C., N. Williams, & L. Gündling, *A Guide to Designing Legal and Institutional Frameworks on Alien Invasive Species* (IUCN 2000).

Silva-Repetto, R., *Latin America*, in *Trends in Forest Law in America and Asia* (E. Kern, K. Rosenbaum, R. Silva Repetto, & T. Young, eds.), FAO Legislative Studies # 66, 26 (FAO 1998).

Tacconi, L., M. Boscolo, & D. Brack, *National and International Policies to Control Illegal Forest Activities*, 27 (CIFOR 2003).

Talla, P., *Contribution du droit à la lutte contre la délinquance et la corruption dans le secteur forestier: Approches conceptuelles*, FAO Legal Paper Online # 34 (FAO 2003).

Tanaka, H., *Forest Management Plans for Collective Forest Managers in Developing Countries: a Review of Constraints and Promising Experience* (FAO 2002).

Texier, J. & B. Kante, *Tendances du droit forestier en Afrique Francophone, Hispanophone et Lusophone*, FAO Legal Paper Online # 47 (FAO 2005).

Upton, C. & S. Bass, *The Forest Certification Handbook* 42 (St. Lucie Press 1996).

URS Forestry, *Review of Formal and Informal Costs and Revenues Related to Timber Harvesting, Transporting and Trading in Indonesia* (World Bank 2002).

Vaughan, L., R. Visser, & M. Smith, *New Zealand Forest Code of Practice* (2d ed., Logging Industry Research Organization 1993).

Vincent, J. & C. Binkley, *Forest-Based Industrialization: A Dynamic Perspective*, in *Managing the World's Forests* 99, 112 (N. Sharma, ed., Kendall/Hunt Publishing Company 1992).

Vincent, J., M. Boscolo, & C. Gibson, draft, *Cameroon Timber Auctions: An Economic and Political Analysis*.

Volker, K. & F. Schmithüsen, *Comparative Analysis of Forest Laws in Twelve Sub-Saharan African Countries*, FAO Legal Paper Online # 37 (FAO 2004).

World Bank, *Sustaining Forests: A Development Strategy* (World Bank 2004).

World Commission on Dams, *Dams and Development: A New Framework for Decision-Making*, 112, 281 (Earthscan 2000).

Index